The Politics of Housing
in Older Urban Areas

edited by
Robert E. Mendelson
Michael A. Quinn

The Praeger Special Studies program—
utilizing the most modern and efficient book
production techniques and a selective
worldwide distribution network—makes
available to the academic, government, and
business communities significant, timely
research in U.S. and international economic, social, and political development.

The Politics of Housing in Older Urban Areas

PRAEGER SPECIAL STUDIES IN U.S. ECONOMIC, SOCIAL, AND POLITICAL ISSUES

Praeger Publishers   New York   Washington   London

02779l

Library of Congress Cataloging in Publication Data
Main entry under title:

The Politics of housing in older urban areas.

   (Praeger special studies in U.S. economic, social,
and political issues)
   Includes bibliographies and index.
   1. Housing—United States—Addresses, essays,
lectures.   2. Housing policy—United States—Addresses,
essays, lectures.   I. Mendelson, Robert Eugene.
II. Quinn, Michael A.
HD7293.P56   301.5'4'0973   75-23984
ISBN 0-275-56120-8

PRAEGER PUBLISHERS
111 Fourth Avenue, New York, N.Y. 10003, U.S.A.

Published in the United States of America in 1976
by Praeger Publishers, Inc.

Printed in the United States of America

TO MARGARET AND SUE

ACKNOWLEDGMENTS

Thanks are owed a number of people whose assistance made this work possible. We are deeply grateful for the material support and moral encouragement provided by Leo Cohen and Jane Altes, the two persons responsible for direction of work at the Center for Urban and Environmental Research and Services, Southern Illinois University at Edwardsville, during the two years that this project was under way. The editing of these essays, and the seminar that occasioned their preparation were undertaken with CUERS support as part of the center's continuing commitment to public service and applied research.

We also acknowledge the indispensable role played by six of our colleagues who skillfully moderated the seminar sessions held at the Edwardsville campus on June 6 and 7, 1974. They are Francis X. Fallon, Jr., then assistant director of the Illinois Housing Development Authority; William G. Grigsby, professor of city and regional planning at the University of Pennsylvania; Jerome J. Hollenhorst, professor of economics at Southern Illinois University at Edwardsville; Hugh O. Nourse, professor of economics at the University of Missouri at St. Louis; and Jerry D. Sternstein, then chief of the Office of Housing and Buildings with the Illinois Department of Local Government Affairs. The sixth panel moderator was CUERS assistant director Jane Altes, whom we owe a special debt of thanks for her handling of the discussion that followed Brian D. Boyer's presentation.

We also are indebted to others at the center for their help during various stages of the project. Sally Ferguson and Jeff Thoman helped with the mechanics of the seminar presentations. Rose Modene handled ably the bulk of the typing chores with assistance from Gloria Harner, Debbie Barr, and Connie Riecan. Ms. Riecan also helped with the notes and reference work, as did Jim Cox. Special thanks are due to Eleanor Ellis for her expert assistance in every phase of the project, from preliminary planning through the handling of seminar registrations and proofreading of the manuscript.

Finally, we would like to express our sincere appreciation for the interest of the 125 people who attended and participated actively in the seminar sessions. Coming from diverse backgrounds and many places throughout Illinois and the St. Louis metropolitan area, all shared an intense concern with the problems of urban housing. We hope that they will be able to act more effectively in the housing game as a result of what they gathered from the seminar.

Robert E. Mendelson
Michael A. Quinn
September 1975

CONTENTS

The ten original chapters that form the core of this book deal with various aspects of the politics of housing in older urban regions of the United States. Collectively, the essays are designed to provide a highly readable, nontechnical introduction to a complex subject that has long been of interest to Americans. As such, the volume should be particularly useful for college courses in city planning, urban politics, and public policy analysis, as well as for government officials and groups of citizens concerned with housing. Although approached from different perspectives, each of the contributors focuses on a central, essentially political question: who gets what, when, and how in urban housing markets?[1] This concern with the distribution of costs and benefits—and the role of public policies in creating, sustaining, and modifying current allocations—provides a unifying theme for the entire collection.

The authors' arguments are based primarily on the experience of older urban regions in the East and the Midwest. Much of the material deals specifically with housing conditions in the St. Louis area, but Chicago, Detroit, Washington, D.C., and numerous other cities also are discussed. The number of illustrations drawn from the St. Louis case can be explained by describing some of the background that led to preparation of the manuscript.

The chapters contained in this book are revised versions of essays originally prepared for delivery at a seminar on "The Politics of Housing in Older Urban Areas" that was held in June 1974 on the campus of Southern Illinois University at Edwardsville, which is located in the eastern portion of the St. Louis metropolitan area. Under the sponsorship of the Center for Urban and Environmental Research and Services at SIU-E, the seminar was designed to bring together academic specialists and practitioners to consider a number of important issues applicable to housing in St. Louis and other older urban regions. Some of the major questions raised were:

- Does our production-oriented housing delivery system primarily benefit upper-income groups and middlemen at the expense of minorities and the poor?
- Are investors, developers, mortgage bankers, and other intermediaries earning profits out of proportion to their contribution to the production of decent housing?
- Are scapegoating and rhetoric essential aspects of housing politics? Do they obscure important issues and undermine solutions?

- Will future directions in housing policy like leased public housing
  and cash allowances provide benefits to those in need and result
  in greater conservation of existing structures?

The seminar was held during the moratorium on federal housing subsidies, an opportune time to stimulate discussion of the consequences of public policy choices in housing. By providing a forum for reexamining the performance of urban housing markets and public policies with respect to them, the seminar brought out several themes of lasting value.

CENTRAL THEMES

One important fact about the urban housing system is that it results in a very uneven distribution of costs and benefits to groups and individuals living in older metropolitan areas. Upper-income groups enjoy a large share of the advantages although they fail to bear the full costs associated with their exercise of choice in the housing market. Rather than conserve existing housing and neighborhoods, the more affluent families seek out new units constructed on the suburban fringe. The areas they leave behind are given over to occupancy by a slightly lower-income group that, in turn, frees its old housing for use by still lower-income groups.

At the bottom end of this hand-me-down, filtering process are the older core neighborhoods that are characterized by decreases in population and tax base, drastically increased public service needs, premature abandonment of still useful structures, and underutilization of many public facilities, like schools. Meanwhile, the outward migration of the upper-income families necessitates costly extension of highways, public services, and utilities in the newly developed areas. A disproportionate share of the costs generated by this wasteful, production-oriented system are borne by the people left behind, especially the poor, the elderly, and racial minorities.

This is not to say that most Americans are not served reasonably well by urban housing markets. Despite complaints about the increasing burden of housing costs and the arguments of critics like Jane Jacobs and Ada Louise Huxtable, who claim that urban neighborhoods no longer possess the rewarding sense of community and diversity that they once did,[2] the vast majority of people currently residing in U.S. metropolitan areas have managed to obtain standard housing. Indeed, in a physical sense, the quality of housing available to Americans probably is better than it has ever been.

Since World War II, the proportion of physically substandard units in the housing stock has declined significantly.[3] In 1950, the Bureau of the Census reported that approximately 35 percent of all U.S. housing was substandard. By 1960, that figure had fallen to 19 percent. Ten years later, an estimated 8 percent of all units were classified substandard. The overall conclusion does not change drastically if, in addition to physically substandard conditions, overcrowding and excessive expense are included as criteria for inadequate housing. Using the figures presented by David M. Gordon, a radical critic of urban housing conditions, ". . . a minimum of 11 million families, or one-sixth of all households in the country, could not find adequate housing in 1970 by one or more of these criteria."[4]

It is noteworthy that the ability to afford housing only recently has joined physical condition and overcrowding in discussions of housing quality. With the marked overall improvement in physical condition and densities experienced during the past 30 years, public attitudes also have changed. Americans, rich and poor, now believe that they should have to pay no more than 20 or 25 percent of their incomes for reasonably spacious, standard housing. Like Alice in Wonderland, the housing system has had to run very hard just to keep in the same place and, until recently, it did a pretty fair job for the majority of American families, even when scrutinized against the statistician's existing financial measures. Of particular note, housing costs for homeowners and renters declined relative to incomes throughout the 1960s.[5] Then, something went wrong.

The Joint Economic Committee of the U.S. Congress reported recently that, nationwide, the average monthly cost of new and existing single-family housing sold between 1973 and 1974 had increased by roughly 25 percent, from $397 to $486 for new homes and from $348 to $441 for existing ones.[6] If this shocking trend continues, housing is likely to become "too expensive" for more and more people, and many will find themselves unable to afford the single-family detached dwelling that has long been a part of the American Dream.

In view of the present situation, and assuming that affordability is accepted as one of the measures of housing quality, it would perhaps be prudent to raise somewhat Gordon's estimate of inadequate housing. However, even allowing a more liberal estimate of the phenomenon— for example, one out of every four or five households in the country— the fact remains that the poorly housed are clearly a minority.

To be outnumbered in the housing arena is a serious problem for those still living in bad housing. With the substantial reduction in substandard dwellings that has taken place in the years since World War II, the number of those poorly housed dwindled, producing an obvious difficulty for the minority that has yet to benefit from this long term trend. Of course, there would be no problem if the people in question had purchasing power sufficient to obtain decent housing in the marketplace without substantial public assistance, but they do not. Most of the ill-housed in U.S. metropolitan areas today are comprised of the poor, the elderly, and racial minorities, especially blacks.

Ironically, those who are poor in economic resources are the same people who lack the political influence necessary to get an adequate response to their housing needs in the public policy arena. Whether competing for subsidies to improve housing within the older core areas or to build affordable units in the newer suburbs, low-income groups and minorities have had little success. It is a well-known fact, for example, that the urban renewal program, ostensibly intended to provide "a decent home and a suitable living environment for every American family, worked to the advantage of luxury housing tenants and powerful economic interests at the expense of less fortunate area residents who were displaced by redevelopment efforts.[7]

In a similar vein, indirect subsidies that provide tax advantages for homeowners, and disproportionately benefit upper-income families, are about three to four times the size of the direct federal housing assistance provided to low- and moderate-income families.[8]

Moreover, once a comfortable home is attained with the help of tax credits and other indirect government subsidies like mortgage insurance and grants for highway construction, the relatively well-to-do suburbanite uses zoning ordinances and building codes to keep out publicly assisted projects designed to serve lower income groups.[9] The overall pattern suggests that the poor, racial minorities, and many of the elderly have not been able to generate an effective demand for shelter in either the economic or the political marketplace.

This leads to another important point that emerged during the seminar—public intervention in urban housing has not contradicted or substituted for the logic of the private market. Rather, public policies for the most part have been designed consciously to stimulate and work through basic market mechanisms.[10] This pattern was apparent, for example, when the federal government first entered the housing subsidy business significantly during the Depression. The Federal Housing Administration was established in 1934 to assist homeowners by insuring substantial numbers of home mortgages. With the full faith and credit of the U.S. government standing behind these insured mortgages, commercial lenders became more willing to make residential loans because the risk could be transferred to the government in case of foreclosure.

Government support of the mortgage market is even more apparent in the operations of "Fannie Mae," the Federal National Mortgage Association, another federally sponsored undertaking that started during the Depression.[11] Fannie Mae's primary job has been to enhance the liquidity of government-insured mortgages by engaging in secondary market operations. As with the government's mortgage insurance programs, Fannie Mae activities are intended to benefit the homeowner indirectly by providing assistance to lending institutions operating in the marketplace. Since 1970, Fannie Mae has extended its support to the conventional market, thereby including mortgages written without the benefit of government insurance.

Other federal housing programs also have worked through the marketplace. These include programs intended to assist low- and moderate-income families, which traditionally have been unable to cope with the market on their own. Through the 1960s, most of the federally assisted programs intended for these groups—especially the below-market interest rate programs like 221(d)(3), 235, and 236— were characterized by the belief that help for the poor could best be provided through incentives to private developers, builders, and lenders. Even conventional public housing programs were modified to encourage private participation in construction and project management. Most recently, this pattern has been manifest in the new Section 8 program that enables public housing clients to lease units from private developers and landlords.

The experimental cash allowance concept, which would put subsidy dollars directly into the low-income consumer's pocket, also makes several assumptions about the response of the market. For example, it is assumed that tenants will use their allowances to bargain with landlords for improved conditions. However, there is the danger that the bottom end of the market will experience an inflation of rents without materially improving the quantity or quality of services provided to tenants.

This commitment to work through the marketplace, which is apparent in all of these programs, has several implications. First, acceptance of market mechanisms entails a substantial commitment to an uneven allocation of costs and benefits in housing. The logic of the marketplace is similar to that of the poker game in various ways. It is impossible to get into the game or the market without a stake; and the larger the stake, the greater the staying power and the more likely that the odds will eventually turn in one's favor. In both the market-place and the poker game, the fact that there are going to be losers as well as winners is accepted implicitly.

In the context of the market, government intervenes at the margins. The overall allocation of costs and benefits is not altered radically. Those who would have done well in the unassisted market-place continue to receive the bulk of the advantages distributed by public policymakers and those who would have fared poorly without public subsidy remain toward the bottom on the scale of housing benefits. At best, government assistance to lower-income families prevents some of them from having to occupy the very worst housing or from having no housing at all.

Commitment to market mechanisms has another important consequence. It insures a continuing flow of business for producers and
various private intermediaries in the housing delivery system.
Builders, labor and craft unions, developers, lenders, mortgage
bankers, speculators, and title companies are among those who gain
from government support of the housing market.

One of the major criticisms of federal housing programs is that
the intended beneficiaries of government action do not benefit as much
as the middlemen in the delivery system. The housing opportunities of
low- and moderate-income families are expanded little while middlemen
reap substantial profits from their involvement in government programs. [12] Although there is some evidence to support this line of
reasoning, it overlooks some basic facts. Public programs in housing
are designed to provide multiple payoffs. Housing producers and
intermediaries do not necessarily gain at the expense of the intended
beneficiaries. In most instances, both the middlemen and the clients
receive some measure of advantage from the operation of federal
programs. If this fact is acknowledged, the key issue concerning the
intermediaries in the delivery system becomes the relative question
of asking how much they ought to benefit in comparison with the
intended clients, not whether they should gain any advantages at all.

The fact of the matter is that a modern society with a highly
complex division of labor cannot build, rehabilitate, or conserve
housing without middlemen. Whether reliance is placed on private
entrepreneurs or public bureaucrats, on private construction or direct
government delivery, there are costs associated with performing the
middleman function, and someone is going to collect. It would be nice,
of course, if the system could function in a straightforward manner
without the complexity that makes intermediaries essential. Unfortunately, such simplicity is unattainable outside the realm of fantasy.

In reality, housing delivery in urban areas is a highly disjointed
process in which the major decisions are made by thousands of individuals acting in their own interests. [13] New housing is built for the
comparatively well-to-do and older units trickle down to the less
advantaged. At the bottom end, there is considerable substandard
housing and abandonment, as the poor often cannot afford to buy or
rent housing that is habitable.

From the perspective of the poor and racial minorities, the overall process may look like a conspiracy of affluent homeowners,
producers, and middlemen. This highly charged viewpoint accounts
for much of the emotion and rhetoric that frequently characterize discussion of housing policies. In their well-intentioned, but frequently
misdirected, search for individual villains to bear the blame, those
who subscribe to the conspiracy theory are likely to miss an important
point. While it may be comforting to assume that evil intentions and

conspiracy lie at the heart of urban housing problems, this is not the basic problem. Although there are dishonest speculators who profit from the plight of some disadvantaged residents, in a larger sense the undesirable results of urban housing market operations are not intentional. By and large, the outcomes follow from the impersonal logic of the marketplace and the trickle-down process. If this assumption is correct, then removing the villains would not bring about a millenium in urban housing. There are no simple, easy solutions to the problems of the poorly housed.

Given the commitment to work through the disjointed forces of the marketplace, government intervention at best only results in slow, incremental improvement of housing conditions at the bottom end. In fact, public policies sometimes may change nothing or make things worse than they were to begin with, as happened during the late 1960s with the ill-fated venture of the Federal Housing Administration into the high-risk mortgage insurance market. In that particular case, the racial disturbances of the 1960s, and the heated rhetoric that accompanied them in cities like Cleveland, Detroit, Newark, and Los Angeles, pressured the FHA into using its mortgage insurance to promote homeownership in blighted center-city neighborhoods. Many low-income people were put into housing in neighborhoods that were declining rapidly at great expense to the taxpayers, while speculators and mortgage companies reaped substantial windfall profits. Eventually, the government was left to pick up the tab for thousands of foreclosed and abandoned dwellings. [14]

THE URBAN HOUSING GAME

The incremental, disjointed nature of the housing process can be understood with the aid of an appropriate metaphor—the urban housing market as "an ecology of games." [15] In applying Norton Long's well-known analogy to the housing system, it should be emphasized that adult "games" are not trivial diversions. Rather, ". . . man is both a game-playing and a game-creating animal, . . . his capacity to create and play games and take them deadly seriously is of the essence, . . . [and] it is through games or activities analogous to game-playing that he achieves a satisfactory sense of significance and a meaningful role." [16] Once this point is understood, it is possible to look earnestly for similarities between the metaphor and games acted out in real-life situations.

In many respects, what happens in the urban housing market is similar to the activities that characterize gaming situations. In games and in the housing market there are players competing for scarce rewards or prizes. Each player has some resources, as well as a more or less conscious strategy and tactices, that he employs to pursue his objectives. Urban housing activity is also similar to games in that play is structured by a well-understood set of rules that may result in penalties for players found to have violated them. The existence of these rules and their effectiveness in practice is demonstrated by the fact that players and spectators alike know the score and they can readily identify both the winners and the losers.

In the urban housing market, there is no single game that sets common objectives for the players. Rather, the housing market encompasses a series of discrete, loosely interrelated games. There is a developer's game, a lending game, a labor union game, a speculator's game, a consumer game, and numerous others. Players in the various contests attempt to make use of one another in pursuit of their own particular ends. Often, cooperation is undertaken willingly when players envision mutual benefits. For example, both lenders and housing developers seek out profitable uses for their dollars in the development of land and structures when they perceive a healthy and enduring demand in the marketplace.

In other cases, as in the troubled relationship between the "slumlord" and the poor family dependent on public aid, players make unwilling use of one another. Individuals may play in more than one game simultaneously, but, in the regular course of events, players devote the bulk of their energies to a single competition. Of course, movement of players back and forth between games both in the short term and in the long run is one important way that the different games are tied together in the marketplace.

The essence of this ecology of games related to housing is that no single authority controls it. The games are not coordinated consciously; they "intermesh." Players maneuver for personal advantage and almost no one takes the longer view concerned with the overall rationality of the system. The few exceptions to this rule—for example, area-wide newspapers, federal planners, and college professors—lack the power necessary to transform this loose assemblage of games into a purposeful, aesthetically pleasing whole. Lacking the power to effect significant change, these participants focus on their own short-run games. Newspapers sell copy with lurid exposes, planners promote themselves by devising "demonstration" programs, and professors get security by publishing their books and articles.

In the absence of shared objectives or a benevolent dictator capable of bringing order to the entire system, the give and take of the political process provides the only ground rule that permits adjustment of players' conflicting aims without a serious breakdown in the game. The result of this bargaining process is largely unplanned, a consequence of thousands of practical accommodations made by individuals acting in their own short-term interests. The final product has many imperfections, and the challenge facing potential reformers is to develop new strategies that can be used to improve both the quantity and quality of payoffs produced in the housing game.

Improvement in urban housing conditions is not likely to occur overnight. The heated arguments advanced by the impatient and the inflexible make the case for radical change in the short run. While rhetoric underscores the need for change, practical considerations largely determine the outcomes of innovative efforts. Established relationships in the urban housing market are highly resistant to change, and innovative ideas, no matter how compelling they may seem to reformers, must be weighed against the maintenance needs of the many different actors who play a role in the housing arena. As a consequence, change comes about slowly, in piecemeal fashion, or not at all.

ORGANIZATION OF THE WORK

This collection of articles is divided into five major sections, each of which is preceded by an introduction designed to summarize and comment on the main points of the individual essays and to locate them with respect to the overall scheme. The elements of the gaming metaphor developed earlier provide a useful framework for organizing the essays of the ten contributing authors.

In part I, Robert E. Mendelson and S. Jerome Pratter provide an overview of the housing markets that operate in older urban areas, with particular attention to the payoffs received by various groups and interests in the population. Both writers conclude that the new construction game has produced losers as well as winners, and they urge that more consideration should be given by public policymakers to housing conservation strategies.

The essays in part II by Michael A. Quinn and Brian D. Boyer illustrate the kind of heated verbal debate associated so frequently with the urban housing game. Though disagreeing on most points, both articles suggest that the use of rhetoric in the housing policy arena has important consequences. Boyer's piece expresses an implicit faith in the positive power of words, while Quinn remains skeptical, observing that rhetoric has a perverse way of eroding the stated objectives put forward by those who use it. The contrast of perspectives apparent in this section is striking.

Parts III and IV describe and analyze various players with stakes in the urban housing game. In the third section, Charles B. Liebert and James E. Murray use their firsthand experience to discuss the roles played by intermediaries in the housing delivery system. Contrary to standard views on the subject, both writers bring out some of the positive functions performed by middlemen in the housing arena. If middlemen profit from their involvement in housing, both contributors argue that housing is not a zero-sum game. In other words, the benefits of the housing game are distributed widely, and the activities of the intermediaries produce payoffs for consumers as well. The section concludes with an editors' note on the politics of the secondary mortgage market that undertakes a preliminary assessment of this particular argument.

The views expressed by the middlemen contrast sharply with those presented in part IV, where Phillip Thigpen and Ira F. Ehrlich describe the urban housing game from the perspective of two client groups that have not done particularly well in the marketplace or at the hands of public policy—blacks and the elderly. Both writers reaffirm one of the central themes to emerge from the essays—urban housing markets are biased in favor of young, affluent whites. Blacks and the elderly are two consumer groups that bear a disproportionate share of the costs generated by "urban sprawl," and their minority group status has prevented them from turning the situation around through political activity. Dissension within and between these two groups and the greater political resources of adversaries have seriously handicapped them in competition for the benefits allocated by the urban housing market.

Part V concludes the collection with three contributions that analyze the nature and significance of two relatively new strategies in the housing policy game. They are leased public housing and cash allowances. The main essays by Charles L. Edson and James P. Zais detail recent developments involving the two strategies. The editors close with some reflections on the politics of these new policy directions. While the new directions might improve on the past performance of urban housing markets, neither one is likely to provide a panacea for the problems of low- and moderate-income families. Constraints imposed by limited public resources and the maintenance needs of established interests will inevitably affect the future of both strategies. At best, only gradual modification of past patterns is likely. In all probability, the new strategies will come to occupy a limited place alongside the old.

NOTES

1. See Harold Lasswell, Politics: Who Gets What, When, and How (New York: McGraw-Hill Book Co., Inc., 1936).

2. See Jane Jacobs, The Death and Life of Great American Cities (New York: Vintage Books, 1961) and Ada Louise Huxtable, Will They Ever Finish Bruckner Boulevard? (New York: Macmillan Co., 1970). For data on the increasing burden of housing costs in selected metropolitan areas, see Arthur P. Solomon, Housing the Urban Poor: A Critical Evaluation of Federal Housing Policy (Cambridge, Mass.: MIT Press, 1974), p. 12.

3. "Substandard" is not an official Bureau of the Census classification. The Department of Housing and Urban Development defines substandard to include all units rated "dilapidated" in the census (that is, not providing safe and adequate shelter) in addition to those without piped hot water, or flush toilet, or bathing facilities for the exclusive use of the household. For details on the procedures used currently to estimate the number of substandard units, see Bureau of the Census, U.S. Department of Commerce, "Proposed Procedure for Estimating Substandard Housing in 1970" (Washington, D.C., February 1972).

4. David M. Gordon, ed., Problems in Political Economy: An Urban Perspective (Lexington, Mass.: D. C. Heath and Company, 1971), p. 356. Housing normally is considered overcrowded if it provides less than one room per person for its occupants; it is too expensive if families must spend more than 25 percent of their income for it.

5. See Council on Municipal Performance, "City Housing," Municipal Performance Report 1, No. 2 (November 1973), 3.

6. U.S. Congress, Joint Economic Committee, "$23,000 Income Required to Buy Average New Home in the U.S.," Notes from the Joint Economic Committee 1, no. 11 (May 5, 1975), 2-3.

7. See Martin Anderson, The Federal Bulldozer: A Critical Analysis of Urban Renewal, 1949-1962 (Cambridge, Mass.: MIT Press, 1964).

8. See Anthony Downs, Federal Housing Subsidies: How Are They Working? (Chicago: Real Estate Research Corporation, October 1972), p. 11; or William C. Baer, "On the Making of Perfect and Beautiful Social Programs," The Public Interest, no. 39 (Spring 1975), p. 83.

9. For a detailed treatment of the problems involved here, see Anthony Downs, Opening Up the Suburbs: An Urban Strategy for America (New Haven, Conn.: Yale University Press, 1973).

10. For an overview of federal housing policies, see Henry J. Aaron, Shelter and Subsidies: Who Benefits from Federal Housing

Policies? (Washington, D.C.: The Brookings Institution, 1972).

11. In 1968, Fannie Mae was transferred wholly to private ownership and a new public entity, the Government National Mortgage Association ("Ginnie Mae"), was established to take over certain special assistance functions formerly performed by Fannie Mae. The development of these agencies which operate in the secondary mortgage market is traced in detail in James Murray's paper in this collection.

12. This thesis is made, for example, by Brian D. Boyer, one of the contributors to this volume, in his Cities Destroyed for Cash: The FHA Scandal at HUD (Chicago: Follett Publishing Company, 1973). A similar case is made by Leonard Downie, Jr. in his Mortgage on America (New York: Praeger Publishers, 1974).

13. See Nathan Glazer, "Housing Problems and Housing Policies," The Public Interest, no. 7 (Spring 1967), pp. 21-51.

14. This scandal is treated in detail in Boyer, op. cit.

15. See Norton E. Long, "The Local Community as an Ecology of Games," American Journal of Sociology 64, no. 3 (November 1958), 251-261. The basic concepts of the gaming metaphor also are dealt with at length in Wallace S. Sayre and Herbert Kaufman, Governing New York City (New York: Russell Sage Foundation, 1960), pp. 39-91.

16. Ibid., p. 252.

PART

I

THE POLITICS

Forty years ago, a well-known social scientist offered a succinct definition of political activity that remains as useful and provocative today as it was then. According to Harold Lasswell, politics focuses on who gets what, when, and how in any given society. Implicit in this simple definition is the notion that politics results in an uneven distribution of costs and benefits to various groups and individuals. It is precisely this expectation of differential outcomes that supplies the incentive for active participation in the political arena. Players in the political game want to be counted as winners rather than losers in the competition for scarce societal resources.

The fact that there are winners and losers at politics is especially evident when one considers the way in which housing is distributed in the United States. In the first essay, Robert E. Mendelson describes the operation of urban housing markets. He notes that the continuing emphasis on new construction in areas experiencing stable or declining rates of population and economic growth has resulted in widespread, premature abandonment of dwelling units. This is particularly true of many of the older cities and suburbs in the East and Midwest. While upper-income groups have benefited from this tandem of new production and concurrent abandonment, the poor, and members of racial minority groups, are left behind to suffer the consequences.

Mendelson describes how the wealthy reap the largest payoffs from the urban housing game, while not bearing the full costs produced as a result of their pursuit of newness and fashion in housing. The hidden costs of a declining center-city tax base, underutilized public facilities, and the extension of public services to new suburban areas are borne by those least able to afford them. Instead of underwriting this state of affairs, public policies should be changed so as not to encourage early abandonment of residential structures and neighborhoods that might well remain useful for years to come. Throughout his presentation, Mendelson argues that we should move away from the wasteful emphasis on new construction toward a policy of conservation and rehabilitation, not only of housing, but of neighborhoods and entire communities too.

This sentiment in favor of conserving housing resources is shared by S. Jerome Pratter, a St. Louis housing and planning consultant whose experiences are recorded in the second essay in this section. In the first part of his essay, Pratter recounts the

"melancholy tales" of federally-assisted housing efforts in the St.
Louis area. He finds that unrealistic planning, bureaucratic insensitivity, and citizen hostility to subsidized housing characterize the
process. Given the immense difficulties associated with locating
subsidized projects outside the blighted urban core, the author suggests that much more attention be given to devising policies to save
and revitalize existing neighborhoods.

In the second half of his essay, Pratter sketches a provocative
strategy for public action in the inner city. While some neighborhoods
clearly merit conserving, others should be abandoned and a public
land bank established in these areas until private market response
indicates that redevelopment is feasible. Paraphrasing Pratter,
planners cannot decree redevelopment with a wave of the magic
market. Unless and until market conditions are ripe for renewal,
public funds should not be squandered on fantasies about the rebirth
of dying neighborhoods. For the time being, relocation and land
banking subsidies are the only programs that can be justified in these
badly blighted areas, which he calls "depletion sectors."

In the short term, Pratter's suggestion that decay be allowed to
run its course in the "depletion sectors" means cutting back on
municipal services in those neighborhoods where the very poor and
racial minorities are concentrated. This process of public disinvestment seems to have been implemented in many older urban areas,
official disclaimers notwithstanding. Still, one can hardly blame
groups that would be affected for being upset over proposals to give
formal approval to disinvestment. This occurred recently in the city
of St. Louis.

Team Four, Inc., Pratter's planning firm, conducted a study
that recommended that the city reduce its services in blighted neighborhoods lacking potential for redevelopment so that scarce public
resources could be concentrated in those areas that might be saved.
The report containing this piece of advice was presented to the city's
Community Development Agency for consideration, but when word of
the report was leaked to the press, city officials were visibly
embarrassed. At first, they tried to disavow knowledge of the document. Later, they simply refused to release it to the press, arguing
that the report was preliminary and, therefore, not a public record
subject to disclosure laws. The public was not to be denied. A copy
of the controversial document was obtained from the Department of
Housing and Urban Development—the federal agency that had financed
the study and had received the report as a matter of course. It was
perhaps predictable that in the uproar over the local nondisclosure
decision, most observers would neglect the overall positive emphasis
on conservation and redevelopment that characterized the Team Four
recommendations.

The two essays presented in this section raise important questions concerning the conservation strategies that they propose. They discuss the inequitable distribution of housing resources under the present production-oriented housing system. Presumably, there would also be costs as well as benefits under the rehabilitation alternatives that they advocate. What is needed, then, is a supplementary analysis of probable winners and losers under a conservation approach.

Unhappily, the limited experience that we have had to date with alternatives to new construction suggests that those with low and moderate incomes will not fare appreciably better at the hands of the conservationists. As Mendelson notes in his concluding remarks, "unslumming" may price those with restricted incomes out of the inner city market.

The moderator of the leadoff panel at the seminar, Francis X. Fallon, Jr., then assistant director of the Illinois Housing Development Authority, cited Chicago as an example of privately sponsored neighborhood rehabilitation. Developers came into areas occupied by low-income minority groups, acquired properties at relatively low prices, and remodeled them. When the dwelling units came back onto the market, rents were 50 to 100 percent higher than they had been. The old structures were sufficiently sound to support new investment, but the people who benefited were not those who lived there before the housing was improved. Uniformly, when private redevelopment or restoration has occurred, the old residents have been pushed out. Furthermore, rehabilitation requires the participation of many of the same individuals involved in the production of new units. Mortgage lenders, attorneys, title companies, developers, and contractors, among others, all take a piece of the action. In short, it is doubtful whether rehabilitation would produce a distribution of costs and benefits markedly different from that which has characterized the emphasis on new construction.

One final point should be raised concerning the presentations by Mendelson and Pratter. The problems of realigning interests to secure a political consensus favorable to conservation and reuse are formidable. Neither essay has any "answers" for this difficulty, although both suggest conditions under which a reorientation of the present system might become possible. A severe recession and energy shortages might make conservation mandatory where the best efforts of housing planners and public officials have failed. In the absence of such pressures for change, both authors would probably agree that a significant alteration in the rules of the urban housing game is unlikely, because the beneficiaries will not voluntarily trade their present rewards for a new, relatively untried approach.

THE MORE WE BUILD, THE MORE WE WASTE: HOUSING IN OLDER URBAN REGIONS
Robert E. Mendelson

This chapter examines housing patterns in older industrial areas of the eastern and midwestern United States. It also advocates change from a production-oriented system of providing shelter to one in which conservation of existing housing and neighborhoods is emphasized. The time for change seems appropriate because the housing industry is in its worst slump in 30 years, and declining birth rates and new life-styles have diminished the number of units that will be required in the future.

In regions like St. Louis, Cleveland, Detroit, Philadelphia, and Baltimore new housing has been and is being built on the suburban fringes, usually near high-speed beltways, while in the core, the central cities and older suburbs, there is widespread elimination of housing units through fires, vandalism, demolition, and abandonment. This tandem of new production and concurrent abandonment would make sense if the units being abandoned were of sufficiently poor original construction or design that they could not be rehabilitated into desirable living environments. Often, this is not the case. The units demolished are far from jerry-built. Many of them are eliminated from the housing inventory for reasons that have little, if anything, to do with their physical characteristics. In relation to the housing in most of the world's urban communities, the buildings disposed of in U.S. cities are worth saving.

Neighborhoods that were once functional are no longer attractive to buyers and renters. They have filtered downward so far that only a residue of unwanted structures remains. Consumers of housing have exhibited such an overwhelming preference for the new and the fashionable that units serving groups at the bottom of the socioeconomic ladder are systematically discarded. After the poor and dependent live in housing, it is rarely used again. This abandonment process prevails in many regions of the East and Midwest. Because the populations and economies of these areas have stabilized and, in some instances, are declining, new housing construction accelerates the elimination of older units.

In the midst of recession, the advocates of production call for continuation of this wasteful process. They want more and cheaper financing, extension of road and sewer systems, and government subsidies to build more units. Their interests are to continue present practices and policies, because they have benefited from them.

In many instances, physical shortage of dwellings has not been the reason for new construction. Rather, there has been a decline in willingness to use available units in extensive and spreading portions of metropolitan areas. This process has persisted not only because it catered to consumers' desires for the current and stylish, but also because it provided an escape route for those who wanted to leave the central city. It was not a nefarious plot foisted upon unwilling and unsuspecting victims. Much of the movement outward was by choice, either in search of certain advantages or to avoid situations that were considered unsatisfactory. Upper- and middle-income whites and, in recent years, blacks participated in the exodus from the central city. As a result, they created a strong market for new suburban housing and concomitantly, a weaker one in the core. Public actions and policies facilitated operation of the system and discouraged longer occupancy of existing residential, industrial, and commercial structures.

However, the costs of maintaining this system have been high and often rested upon those who are least able to carry the burden. Producing sizeable amounts of new housing while abandoning comparable quantities has been wasteful but it also injured, in a social and financial sense, those forced to remain in or near neighborhoods of abandonment.

To effectively conserve urban resources would require a major change in the way the system works. Rewards for saving and for adapting structures would have to be established along with penalties for squandering land and for unnecessary utility and road extensions. This change seems particularly logical in nongrowth areas, however, where the reasons for new construction are not directly the result of population and employment expansion. Difficult economic conditions also make conservation appear to be an alternative at the present time.

A TIME FOR ANALYSIS

Changing Conditions

For those with stakes in housing production, the current situation
seems like a depression. Unemployment in the crafts is high; interest
on home mortgages is about nine percent; the average sale price on
new housing approaches $40,000; and housing starts have been cut in
half during the last two years.[1] While this period can be viewed as
one of inactivity and uncertainty, it can also be seen as an opportunity
to evaluate the housing process and to develop new strategies for the
future.

In the course of analyzing the way in which housing is made available, it is important to note that the requirements for residential units
in the next few decades will differ considerably from those of the past.
Birth rates have declined to historic lows as divorce rates have
increased, women are marrying at a later age, and they are assuming
roles other than those of wife and mother. By 1972, birth rates were
below population replacement and depression levels.[2] Because of the
birth boom after World War II, it may take several decades before the
U.S. population stabilizes or falls. There are so many potential
mothers in the population that, even with very low birth rates, large
numbers of children will be born in the near future. Approximately
1 million women in the United States now are 39 years old, while over
twice that number are 13 years of age.[3] In the long run, however,
the effect on the population will be apparent and the need for more and
more housing production should decline correspondingly.

While the birth rate has been dropping, older industrial regions
such as Detroit and Pittsburgh have experienced outward migration.
Many northern and eastern areas have declined as centers of economic
and employment opportunity, with industries that utilized semiskilled
and unskilled labor moving to smaller southern areas where labor is
cheaper and often not unionized.[4] Prospects for the future are that
growth-type industries will continue to be attracted to the South and
West and that labor-intensive companies that prospered along the
east coast and in the midwestern river towns increasingly will
substitute machines for personnel or, in some cases, simply cease
operations.

Based on these trends, conservation of existing housing would
seem to be a sensible strategy for older, nongrowth regions. Conservation does not imply that all housing would, or could, be saved.
Some units were constructed too poorly or have deteriorated too

extensively for rehabilitation. However, conservation does mean that residential wastage should be halted and housing should be valued as a resource. There ought to be an awareness of the relationship between excessive production and abandonment, and public policy should not encourage the premature elimination of structures.

The Case Against Production

Despite changing economic conditions and declining rates of growth in these older regions, there is still strong support for new construction of housing and also of schools, hospitals, stores, offices, and industries. Advocates perceive construction as a sign of progress and argue that the age of many structures makes the edifices obsolete. Their perceptions are far from valid. Progress is an illusion when the number of new housing units or amount of commercial floor space built in the suburbs is virtually equal to that being abandoned in the core. Developers' profits and the corporate and individual search for newness and fashion are motivating much of the construction. Completed structures are filled with occupants from vacated buildings that all too frequently are never utilized again. For example, office construction in the St. Louis central business district has not appreciably increased the number of tenants, but simply reshuffled those who were already located downtown. In September 1971, office space being used in the central business district totaled 5 million square feet—3.5 million for private business and 1.5 million for government offices. At the same time, the amount of vacant office space, 3.3 million square feet, was nearly as much as that which was occupied. [5]

In the St. Louis metropolitan area, housing eliminations from abandonment, demolition, fires, and other causes are approaching the increases in the regional housing inventory. [6] This trend is clearly evident in Table 1, which displays electricity user data provided by the Union Electric Company, a utility based in St. Louis. [7] From 1968 to 1972, the ratio of increases to eliminations has only been about two to one. This high percentage of eliminations-to-increases is consistent with the recent experience of many other urban areas. As contrasted with the 1930s, when most new construction added to the housing inventory, the decade between 1960 and 1970 found housing starts replacing units that were lost for a variety of reasons. This was particularly true in the northeastern and north central states, where only a small percentage of new units added to the housing supply. [8]

Advanced age often is used as an explanation for the increasing amount of housing abandonment in the St. Louis area. Neighborhoods

TABLE 1

Increases and Elimination of Housing Units
in the Union Electric Service Area,
St. Louis Metropolitan Area
(1964-1972)

Year	Customers	Increases	Eliminations	Percent of Eliminations to Increases
1964	549,278	17,041	5,218	30.6
1965	562,666	17,766	4,378	24.6
1966	573,363	17,425	6,728	38.6
1967	583,237	12,509	2,635	21.1
1968	592,415	15,274	6,096	39.9
1969	599,531	14,913	7,797	52.3
1970	604,220	12,196	7,507	61.6
1971	612,150	18,354	10,424	56.8
1972	620,161	17,492	9,481	54.2

Source: Union Electric Company, St. Louis.

with houses built in the 1910s and 1920s are considered old and less
attractive than their newer suburban counterparts. By this reasoning,
the older the housing the less functional it is and the sooner it should
be discarded. Like other consumer items in a disposable society,
the pattern is the same.

Citing age as the reason for abandonment is inadequate. By almost
any standard, American housing is not old. Most of the structures
built over 100 years ago have already been eliminated by code enforcement, urban renewal, highway construction, vandalism, fires, earth-
quakes, neglect, or abandonment. In the St. Louis area, which federal
housing officials have cited as a classic example of housing abandonment, only 42 percent of the housing was built prior to 1939.[9] Much
of the housing being abandoned in St. Louis is well-constructed, primarily of brick, and often with hardwood floors and hot water heating
systems. If the blighting process had not been so rampant, these
units could have been functional for many years.

The type of decay so evident in St. Louis is not the result of age
or shoddy original construction. Consider, for example, the "Hill"
section of the city. Much of the housing in that cohesive Italian
neighborhood is inferior, almost substandard in original design, yet
it is maintained in excellent condition because people want very much

to live there. As this example suggests, it is not physical, brick and mortar-type conditions so much as social fashion that make an older neighborhood attractive when occupied by the "right" people, but old and functionally obsolete when it has trickled-down to undesirables at the bottom of the social structure.

Another case in point lies on the west coast. San Francisco is considered one of America's most beautiful and desirable cities, yet as evidenced in the Census of Housing, its dwelling units are almost as old as those found in the city of St. Louis.[10] Without question, they are poorer in original construction and design, yet housing is conserved because people want to move to the San Francisco area and to the older parts of the city. Consequently, new residential building in the suburbs relates to the need for additional units, rather than fulfilling desires for fashion.

As a result, the flavor and heritage of San Francisco have been preserved. Older homes of cultural significance are not museum pieces, as in St. Louis, where they often stand alone among parking lots or abandoned structures. They are living examples of the past because the entire neighborhood where they are located has remained relatively intact. Older residential, commercial, industrial, and educational structures have comfortably adapted to modern times. Even loft buildings, which are considered unusable in many cities, have become furniture showrooms, warehouses, offices, and apartments in downtown San Francisco.

DESCRIPTION OF THE HOUSING PROCESS

Shortage or Surplus?

An article written by two Cleveland planners pointed out that important assumptions that have supported federal housing programs are not correct. "Chief among these is the notion of a housing shortage. Proponents of existing programs frequently state that there is a shortage of housing available to low-income families. This is not the case."[11] Only New York, out of 26 cities in the United States of more than 500,000 in population in 1970 had a vacancy rate for rental units under 4 percent. In seven cities, rental vacancies were above 10 percent; in 18, rental vacancy rates were greater for units under $100 per month than for more costly ones.[12]

The Cleveland planners argue that the problem is ineffective demand—that large groups in the population cannot afford rents that are sufficient to support new private construction and the maintenance and rehabilitation of older properties. Housing theorist George Sternlieb concurs. "The private operation of low-income central-city housing is dying. Consumer demand and need—yes; market, profitability, motivation for long term holding and improvement—no."[13]

Despite reports and articles describing surpluses of apartments and condominiums in many parts of the United States, the belief in the housing shortage persists.[14] Research projects and operating programs continue to be based on this premise. In 1970, Anthony Downs, a respected housing researcher, maintained that more and more units must be built to avoid severe housing shortages in the United States.[15]

Arthur P. Solomon approached the issue from a different perspective. Far from believing that there is a shortage of physical units, he argues that

> [t]he population of many of our older cities has declined
> faster than the removal of the older substandard housing
> stock. It is the loss of housing demand associated with
> an absolute decline in population, as well as more con-
> centrated poverty—rather than an inadequate supply of
> housing stock—which is at the heart of the older central
> cities' housing problems.[16]

Another astute observation concerning the housing situation was made by Henry Aaron of the Brookings Institution. Aaron suggests that societal values and norms determine our housing needs. What constitutes standard housing and the amount that should be paid for it is far more political than objective.[17] This means that supposedly "factual" evidence is far less important than political will and commitment in determining which goal—conservation or production of housing—is to be pursued.

It is not difficult to understand why belief in the existence of a shortage persists. Massive housing needs were generated by the migration to America in the late nineteenth and early twentieth centuries. More recently, the depression caused severe changes in housing markets, as units were shared and the size of habitable space severely restricted. When economic expansion began in the late 1930s, just prior to World War II, several conditions intensified the demand for low-, moderate-, and middle-income housing. As incomes increased and became predictable, those who were cramped began searching for larger units. They were joined in the search by rural migrants who flocked to the cities for employment. However, because of wartime scarcities of building materials, the supply could not be expanded to satisfy this demand. After the war, public programs were devised to alleviate actual shortages and to meet the needs of an expanding population. A production strategy was employed.

Only feeble attempts were made to incorporate objectives other than construction stimulation into federal programs. Public housing and interest-rate reduction provided a measure of income assistance to those with limited incomes, but they were intended primarily to build more units with the subsidy attached to the dwelling, not the individual or family occupying the structure.

Public resources have contributed to "excessive reliance on the subsidization of new construction."[18] As a result, federal policy has not squarely faced the issues of abandonment or neighborhood collapse.[19] Housing has been handled traditionally as a problem of inadequate production. This might be attributable in part to the pervasive notion that it is acceptable and even desirable to discard older and poorer neighborhoods. Housing abandonment and demolition have been traditional parts of American life. Our history is filled with accounts of mining, mill, and railroad towns that have prospered, grown, and then declined over a period of decades. Early housing reformers even believed that slum clearance and rebuilding were essential ingredients in changing the economic and social behavior of slum occupants. Structures were viewed as having increased functional obsolescence as they filtered down to poorer and poorer groups. This philosophy has permeated government housing programs to the present day.

Obsolescence or Taste?

For many years, housing has been described erroneously as functionally obsolete when the neighborhoods where the housing was located were no longer in demand. That the eliminated and abandoned housing could have remained in use for decades or even centuries, had it been conserved, was ignored. It had lost its attraction for those who were wealthy or middle-class, regardless of ethnic background or race. Those who remained in large parts of the urban core were the poor. When they inhabit a neighborhood, the housing is not considered functional by other groups.

Traditionally, residential movement to newer homes has been encouraged and viewed as upward mobility within the economic and social system. Even though this movement created instability and early retirement of neighborhoods, there were few, if any, constraints placed on individual behavior. If you were rich or near rich, you could move farther and farther into the suburbs and get away from those who were incapable of leaving. All that was needed was money, desire, and, until recently, acceptable race. Mobility was not to be restricted. It was synonymous with optimism, growth, and progress. To think about curtailing movement was considered unpatriotic. [20] There was no cause for concern that these actions resulted in abandonment. It was limited to the area where "they" lived.

Abandoned housing has become widespread in many central-city neighborhoods in the East and Midwest. As of three years ago, 100,000 units had been abandoned in New York and 20,000 in Philadelphia. [21] Since that time, these figures have increased considerably and are indicative of what has happened in Detroit, Chicago, St. Louis, and other cities. Given the extensive character of this phenomenon, it is difficult to believe that there is not tacit approval of the process by our society.

While suburban growth has been encouraged, large central-city districts have been abandoned. A study by Charles Leven and Murray Weidenbaum, Urban Decay in St. Louis, described this as "a process of wastage, an economic consequence of poverty coexistent with affluence in which the desire of the poor for decent housing is met through the exhaustion, the simple using-up, of an oversupply of devalued housing stock." [22] Residential units are prematurely eliminated in much the same way that other consumer items are discarded. Some researchers see this as good, because the level of the housing stock is being raised. According to Dempster Holland, "[t]he greater an old, large city's population decline, the more cause for rejoicing." [23] Others, like George Sternlieb, have noted that abandonment has swept away much good housing along with the bad. [24]

Our housing system is often referred to as a trickle-down or filtering process. As middle- and upper-income groups purchase new and larger housing or both, the housing that they vacate falls to socioeconomic classes beneath them. This continues until there are no takers for the neighborhoods vacated by those with the least income and class status. At that point abandonment occurs. This abandonment affects not only privately owned housing, but public housing, schools, commercial establishments and industrial facilities as well. In many instances whole neighborhoods cease to exist. In those metropolitan areas not experiencing population and economic growth, abandonment accelerates as housing production is increased. The greater the amount of new housing produced in the region, the faster the filtering process works.

Private Choices for Production

Housing construction proceeded rapidly for 25 years until 1973, when the combination of the Nixon moratorium on federal assistance, the credit crunch, and the recession took effect. Prior to that time, single-family homes and rental projects were being built despite surpluses in many midwestern and eastern urban areas. Only our lengthy prosperity since World War II and a series of public acts and policies were able to support the construction decisions made by builders, lenders, investors, purchasers, and renters. Individual and collective resources were sufficiently abundant to facilitate discarding older neighborhoods in Newark, Detroit, New York, and St. Louis. There was an availability of public funds for roads, sewers, housing construction subsidies, and the maintenance of secondary mortgage markets. Families were able to finance the move(s) from center-city neighborhoods, although sometimes at great sacrifice, and to readily accept increased transportation costs.

The end of World War II marked a dramatic change in the life-styles and attitudes of most Americans. For much of the population, it was the beginning of an era of optimism and material abundance. Gone were newspaper accounts of wartime deaths and injuries, clothing shortages, and gasoline rationing. Americans rushed to purchase new automobiles and limited amounts of new housing being built on vacant suburban land. There were indications that the doubling and tripling of families experienced during the 1930s and 1940s would soon be ended.

Large numbers elected to leave the central city. In the first place, they wanted to avoid real or perceived threats to their safety, inferior school systems, and long-term losses in property value. In addition, many partook of the shared aspiration for newness. Both of these factors brought about such a rapid exodus from the cores and older suburbs in the 1950s and 1960s that 15 to 20 percent central population declines were not uncommon, despite increases of births over deaths. Only race and lack of income slowed the process, and if there was any slight degree of stabilization, it was because the options to move of the poor or blacks or both were limited.

According to journalist Leonard Downie, Jr., the pressure to build has not been accidental.

In fact, it has been exactly as real estate speculators, builders, bankers, and even suburban homebuyers have wanted because it has been so profitable for them. They have forced government at all levels to plan suburban growth

their way through the administration of zoning laws, construction of highways, laying of sewers, writing of tax
laws, and supervision and subsidy of mortgage banking. [25]

A sharp contrast evolved in urban land-use patterns before and
after the war, particularly in housing. Before 1939, land uses were
often interspersed with schools, shops, recreation, and employment
often accessible by walking or minutes away by public transportation.
In the post-war suburbs, land uses were separate and distinct with
highways becoming the major connector for these activities. Densities
became considerably lower as much of the new housing was single-
family and detached on large lots.

Suburban development added income and life-style segregation to
the ethnic and racial segregation of the older cities. This meant a
change from the past when "homes 'on the other side of the tracks'
were . . . as accessible to the same community facilities and job
opportunities as the more affluent homes."[26] New neighborhoods and
even communities became inhabited primarily by one income class
whereas in the smaller and denser nineteenth century cities the wealthy
were only minutes away from those who were less affluent. Life-
styles became isolated, too. Large new developments of 20, 30, or
40 acres were created for couples without children, singles in pursuit of an active social life, and elderly, retired pensioners.

Movement to the suburbs with all that it implies in terms of new
housing, low density, segregation, and reliance on the auto has been
a clear preference for the majority of Americans. Nathan Glazer
commented in a 1965 article that the exodus from older cities was
the result of private decisions to acquire the free-standing house on
its own lot. He further stated that "when they [the people] have
choices, they create Los Angeles."[27] Glazer's reference to Los
Angeles is significant because it is the region that has epitomized
rapid suburban growth since World War II.

Between 1950 and 1960 the population of the Los Angeles-Long
Beach Standard Metropolitan Statistical Area grew by 45 percent,
from 4 to 6 million, as large numbers came westward in search of
climate, topography, and economic opportunity. It became an area
dominated by automobiles, big and sprawling with wide thoroughfares
and freeways servicing numerous residential, industrial, and commercial enclaves. An amalgamation of communities, Los Angeles
resembles a giant suburb that has a low residential density, the
absence of a strong central core, and a series of activity centers
spaced throughout the urban area.

To meet the demand for housing generated by the large immigra-
tion, homes and apartments were built on the fringes. Federal

mortgage insurance, developers' windfall profits, highway construction, tax shelters, and income deductions were a few devices used to promote this development.

Public Encouragement

Public policies and subsidies have aided construction of housing for over four decades. They have facilitated the movement of the middle- and upper-income classes to the suburbs and the retention of the poor in the central city. Direct programs include the amortization of capital costs, public housing, and interest-rate reduction, under Sections 221(d)(3), 235, and 236 of the U.S. Housing Acts. Less obvious ones are road construction, dewer and water grants, savings deposit insurance, and the maintenance of secondary mortgage markets.

Housing conservation has not received similar attention. About 90 percent of housing units subsidized directly between 1968 and 1972 were new construction. [28] Production has been emphasized even though there is evidence that it is a highly inefficient way to house low-income families. "Twice as many poor families can move from substandard to standard housing when the government leases existing units from private landlords than when it either sponsors new construction or guarantees the mortgage for a private developer to build new units." [29]

Important public programs have encouraged suburban development at the expense of stabilizing inner-city neighborhoods. From its inception in 1934, the mortgage insurance of the Federal Housing Administration (FHA) was obtained most easily in outlying areas. Prospective home purchasers gravitated to new residential locations where smaller down payments were required and longer-term mortgages were available.

With former real estate and mortgage professionals in key roles for many years, FHA's natural inclinations were to resist involvement in the central city, especially when there was a possibility that neighborhoods might experience socioeconomic decline. This was the agency that endorsed restrictive covenants in the 1930s based on the belief that homogenized neighborhoods, usually white and middle-class, would best preserve and enhance property values. Suburbs fit this bias. They were less diverse, with fewer blacks or poor or both than the core areas.

Perhaps these actions seemed rational at the time. Between 1934 and 1969, FHA was a ". . . business-type federal government agency functioning as a credit insurance company in the private market. "[30] It was only after FHA attempted to respond to the racial disorders of the 1960s that its effectiveness became impaired and the corporate nature of the enterprise was all but destroyed. Nevertheless, because of the agency's politices, central-city neighborhoods were often without FHA mortgage insurance—an important support of residential financing.

While federal policies aided the movement of middle-class whites to the suburbs, they encouraged lower-income blacks to stay in the core. Placement of public housing and interest-rate reduction projects have been, for the most part, in central-city locations where decline was evident and abandonment imminent. By concentrating the poor and near poor in the core and facilitating the movement of the wealthier classes to the suburbs, public policy contributed directly to a decline in the economic resources needed to maintain and renew the older cities.

Since the early 1930s, federal housing programs have been aimed at housing production while at the same time, establishing and protecting the dominant role for private entrepreneurs in the process. Public resources have been used to facilitate—not to substitute for— the private sector. [31] The rewards for businessmen over the past 40 years have been far greater in building houses and apartments than in conserving them. A recent evaluation of one federal program conducted by the General Accounting Office pointed out shortcomings of the production emphasis: "Inducements to participate in the Section 236 program [interest-rate reduction on rental projects] are directed toward achieving project construction; there is a need to restructure the inducements to encourage long-term ownership and efficient management. "[32]

Builders and developers, logically, favor new construction. Through their trade organization with over 50,000 members, the National Association of Home Builders (NAHB), they have created one of the most effective lobbies in Washington. [33] They fight hard for the availability of mortgage money and for FHA subsidies. Philosophically, the NAHB favors growth. Zero population growth means fewer customers in the future and less need for new housing, so the builders oppose it.

Federal housing legislation in 1934, 1937, 1949, and 1954 was intended to provide housing and jobs through construction, to stabilize the lending industry, and to enable cities to renew themselves. By the 1960s, it was apparent that many urban centers were deteriorating rapidly despite passage and implementation of these laws. It was confusing to see housing production encouraged in precisely those metropolitan regions where abandonment was the greatest or to find urban renewal funds spent to keep people in the central city while far more resources were put into highways to take them out.

As the magnitude of the urban housing problems increased, the federal capacity to cope with them diminished, and there was a growing tendency to disavow any involvement in the fate of our older cities. By 1972, an assistant secretary of the Department of Housing and Urban Development, the federal agency concerned with housing, commented that the government could hardly be held accountable for the implementation of poor or inadequate housing policies. He stated that:

> Nobody foresaw the abandonment of whole areas of the
> city. Since the riots of 1966-67, people have been leav-
> ing many of the areas, just abandoning property. Nobody
> wants to live there. We didn't recognize this until fairly
> recently. Most of these troublesome mortgages were
> written in 1968-69 before this problem [large numbers
> of central city foreclosures and abandonments] surfaced. [34]

It seems difficult to imagine such lack of awareness when it was evident for years that federal policies had stimulated private investment in housing production in the suburbs while avoiding comparable participation in conserving central-city neighborhoods.

BENEFITS AND COSTS IN THE SYSTEM

Winners

Housing production has been emphasized because powerful groups profit from the system. Since contractors, tradesmen, title companies, lawyers, lenders, planners, and architects profit from new construction, it is natural that they advocate openly continuation of the system and resist changes that diminish their benefits.

Clients of new housing also receive advantages. They can buy or rent the most fashionable and modern units in neighborhoods distantly removed from the problems of the central city. Purchasers of suburban homes have often found that the upward spiral of construction costs has resulted in quick appreciation of their property values.

Benefits are greatest for the wealthy. They are part of a shrinking group, estimated at less than one-fourth of American families, who can afford to purchase new homes averaging nearly $40,000 and lease new apartments costing upwards of $200 per month. [35] Because of the high cost of land and construction, their neighborhoods are protected from intrusion by those with lower incomes who are unable to buy or rent new housing on the open market without subsidy. They can keep the poor concentrated and distant. Wealthy communities are clusters of affluence with abundant resources for municipal and educational services and very much in demand. Property values are high and respond quickly to periods of inflation.

Upper-income homeowners also receive a major share of the largest housing subsidy—the $6 billion in mortgage interest and property taxes deducted annually from taxable income. Since their rate of taxation is higher, the wealthy can deduct larger actual amounts from their income than those who pay taxes at lower rates. While a large share of the $6 billion goes to middle-income homeowners, the percentage of the benefits to the wealthy far exceeds their numbers in the population. [36]

Generators of new housing—developers, lenders, and investors—are frequently wealthy and clearly beneficiaries of policies supporting construction. Often public assistance is so critical to their enterprises that housing is built in areas where surpluses exist if federal and state subsidies and mortgage insurance are available and/or the project can be sold to rich investors as a federal income tax shelter.

Because of the significance of tax law on the production of rental housing, developers were concerned several years ago by Nixon administration tax proposals. These proposals were designed to prohibit the losses on real estate projects—taxes, interest, and depreciation—from being used to offset other unrelated income-producing activities. No longer would physicians, business executives, or lawyers have been able to diminish their income tax liabilities by investing in new housing projects and receiving accelerated depreciation. [37] Fortunately for these groups, powerful opposition to the proposed change prevented it from becoming law.

Legislation to encourage production of housing units was designed when there were national shortages and provided wealthy investors with mechanisms for sheltering income by purchasing interests in new projects. In the case of a well-known St. Louis development, the Mansion House, Henry Ford of Ford Motor Company, Harold Geneen of ITT, and 18 other entrepreneurs invested for the acknowledged purpose of saving federal income taxes. These investors had no personal liability for payment on the mortgage. Their only real stake in the success or failure of the project was to avoid foreclosure so that tax savings resulting from accelerated depreciation would not be recaptured by the federal government. [38] In recent years, the project has been rife with scandals involving favoritism for the rich and influential.

While the wealthy have received many of the benefits from the housing delivery system, they have not shared proportionally in the costs. Federally assisted housing for low- and moderate-income families has rarely been located in wealthy communities. Theoretically, these communities should be those most capable of accepting a small influx of poor people, but wealthy suburbs have powerfully resisted economic and racial integration. Many public housing units

and even 221 (d) (3) and 236 moderate-income projects have been
placed in or near blighted neighborhoods. When site selection battles
over federally assisted housing were fought in the suburbs, there was
never even a contest in the affluent communities of Ladue, Beverly
Hills, Winnetka, or Grosse Pointe. For the most part, the fights
have been confined to working-class, lower-income communities.

Public policy has encouraged the concentration of low- and
moderate-income housing in the central cities and older suburbs.
Traditionally, local government approval has been required for the
placement of public housing and rental subsidy units, and only those
local governments already having a large proportion of their residents
with incomes sufficiently low to qualify for this housing ever grant
approval. Dispensing or withholding federal grants has never proved
to be an effective stimulus to induce wealthy communities to accept
poor families, for those cities have enough local funds to avoid requesting federal aid if it is conditioned on the acceptance of low- and
moderate-income housing. Zoning, too, has been utilized for years
to promote income and racial homogeneity and advantage. Although
"snob" or large-lot zoning is under heavy attack in the courts, it has
been used by many communities to block construction of housing units
at densities greater than one or two families to the acre.

Losers

The urban housing system, while distributing benefits, also
inflicts costs. Individuals, families, neighborhoods, communities,
and regions all pay a heavy toll when housing construction is encouraged
while comparable rewards are unavailable for conservation. There
are various costs to individuals. Sometimes repeated moves are made
from central-city and older suburban housing to avoid real or perceived destructive encroachment, threats to personal safety, and inferior
schools. Aside from the turmoil generated by this continual change,
it is an expensive process and places severe hardships on those with
only limited funds.

As housing filters down to lower-income groups, the market
forces work progressively less smoothly. Selling costs increase and
in some neighborhoods become so excessive that it is cheaper and
easier to sell to dealers at very low prices. Sales commissions, financing charges, and rehabilitation to meet local and FHA standards
can easily amount to 30 or 40 percent of the selling price in economically and racially transitional neighborhoods.

For those who own property in neighborhoods where there
are problems of vandalism, vacancies, arson or abandonment, the
financial costs are staggering:

One of the primary functions of home ownership in
our society over the last generation has been for
the purpose of capital accumulation. For most of
the lower and middle socioeconomic groups, it is
the long term holding of a house—the paying down
of a mortgage and the building up of equity, coupled
with increasing value through inflation, which has
provided the major form of securing a nest egg.
The black home buyer in Newark [New Jersey] of
the 1960s has seen his investment at a standstill
(or evaporate), while suburban equivalents doubled
and tripled over the same length of time. Are government home ownership programs therefore in the central city dooming their nominal beneficiaries to an
equivalent dead end? Are there alternatives?[39]

Incentives for homeowners to improve property in declining neighborhoods disappear when funds spent on rehabilitation cannot be recovered
through stabilization or appreciation in market value. Once wholesale
and retail prices of housing start downward, they frequently move
rapidly and discourage real estate investment.

Numerous examples can be cited of houses and flats that
sold for $15,000 to $20,000 ten years ago and now trade for $2,000
to $3,000 or less. One central-city landlord bought a four-family flat
in the northern part of St. Louis 15 years ago for $16,000. Last year
he purchased an identical building, which was not vandalized, on the
same block for $1,600. Many resident owners of central-city property
with marginal credit and little to lose have simply quit paying on mortgages after five or more years when they realized that their debt was
twice the price of comparable housing down the block.

Abandonment destroys the advantages ascribed to relatively
high density neighborhoods—convenience, mutual help, security, and
cohesiveness. In addition, necessary commercial institutions close or
move away from blighted districts because of the loss in population
and the declining incomes of those who remain. Employment drops
as vandals, robbers, and arsonists attack industrial structures, and
school enrollments become so low that physical plants, whether new
or old, cannot be operated efficiently. Many neighborhoods which
were once cohesive and well defined with strong social, cultural, and
commercial institutions have been altered by abandonment into a series
of isolated structures without supporting facilities.

At the city level, abandonment results in the loss of assessed
valuations or ratables, thus diminishing the ability to raise revenues
for ever-increasing municipal and educational service demands. In
addition, the image of the city becomes tarnished and it becomes less

attractive for investment. Entrepreneurs, lenders, and residents
seek long-term stability when they make investments in property.
When there is a decline in the real estate market, renewal is quickly
replaced by deterioration.

When property values and profit expectations are falling,
development cannot be produced merely by large-scale land assemblage. There are numerous examples of federally aided urban renewal where land aggregation and write-downs were insufficient to generate redevelopment. Recent legislation provides authority for the
city of St. Louis to acquire tax-delinquent properties and combine
them into investment packages. Original hopes for the program anticipated new industry, employment opportunities, and increased
sales and property tax revenues. The results have been far less
than expected with the outcome that the city has become a major
landowner and landlord, operating at times in violation of its own
housing codes.

Costs to the region entailed in the production-abandonment
process can also be estimated. Construction of suburban housing and
the concurrent elimination of denser central-city neighborhoods have
resulted in abandonment and inefficient usage of costly service systems. Streets, sewers, power lines, and parks are hardly used in
some parts of a metropolitan area while in others there is a pressing
need for comparable facilities. A recent study estimated the costs of
development for a hypothetical 10,000-unit suburb. Schools totalled
approximately $45 million and public facilities totalled $16 million.
Depending on the residential density of the new community, streets
and roads cost from $23 to $38 million and utilities between $22 and
$62 million. [40]

Because the exodus from the urban cores has been so large
for the last 25 years, massive extension of public services has been
required. The cost of these services, which were needed to make
suburban fringes accessible and attractive, have not been borne entirely by the new users. Residents of older suburbs frequently pay a
major share of the principal and interest on county-wide bonds issued
to extend facilities. Not only do they receive few benefits in return
for their tax payments used to retire bonds, but their communities
increasingly become less able to compete with the new developments
for industry, residents, or commercial facilities. Suburban residents
have also received more than their share of benefits from state and
federal highway systems while central-city neighborhoods have become
fragmented and even destroyed.

As populations have declined in central cities, municipal and
local service needs have not dropped correspondingly. In fact, because
of inflation and greater dependency of the populations left behind, they
have increased.

There are hidden costs of suburbanization. Transportation systems, for example, have become dysfunctional and obsolete. Low suburban densities, reliance on the auto, decreased inner-city populations, and declining importance of central business districts have contributed to the demise of one form of fixed transit—streetcars—and made the financial cost of new rapid rail systems almost unsupportable. Still, it is currently fashionable for many planners and other urbanists to promote the construction of rail transit as a cure for urban core problems. One transit proposal for the St. Louis region was estimated to cost $2 billion and require an annual public subsidy of about $50 million. [41] The center of the system was a weakened business district and a large number of stations were designed for neighborhoods with extensive abandonment.

One other cost of the production-abandonment process deserves mention. Foreclosures of central-city properties have not only jeopardized the federal mortgage insurance system but have increased the difficulty and expense of financing the purchase of property in older neighborhoods. In the last decade lenders have foreclosed on hundreds of thousands of urban mortgages. Many of the structures have been turned over to the Federal Housing Administration for reimbursement on the mortgage insurance. By early 1974, FHA had taken back 5,000 housing units in Detroit alone and an estimated 20,000 others conceivably face the same fate. For the first time since its inception in 1934, FHA reserves, amounting to $1.7 billion accumulated through insurance premiums on economically sound mortgages, are threatened by gigantic losses in high risk programs, $467 million in the year ending June 30, 1973. [42] Large sums have been allocated by the U.S. Treasury during the last few years to reimburse lenders for their losses. Mortgage lenders have withdrawn from many older cities, because they see them as centers of declining residential demand.

CONCLUSION

Conserving existing housing is a prudent alternative to wastage, particularly because new construction is so costly. This approach is especially sensible in many parts of the East and Midwest, which simply don't need larger quantities of residential units.

Firstly, it is less costly to subsidize existing housing as compared to new. [43] Secondly, by shifting assistance from the producer to the consumer through the payment of cash allowances, demand can be made more effective for inner-city housing. [44] This might result in the upgrading of neighborhoods—a goal that housing allowance

proponents feel has been neglected by past federal housing programs.[45]
Because public housing and federally assisted projects virtually have
been barred from the suburbs, improvement of the quality of inner-
city housing stock is vital to low-income groups.

Implementing a policy of conservation is not without risks or
negative side effects. Some housing specialists still believe that the
physical housing shortage is acute and will worsen unless the national
goal of building 26 million new units between 1968 and 1978 is attained.[46] Others discount this position, stating that only a residual role
should be given to production subsidies. In this view, for example,
new towns might be constructed to meet the needs of those who are
neglected by the system, like black, low-income families.[47] Critics
have also assailed housing allowances as a conservation strategy by
arguing that the cost of housing for the poor and near-poor will be
raised and a windfall will be provided for the absentee owner or "slumlord."[48]

The prospects of conservation are further clouded by the
phenomenon known as "unslumming," a trickling-up process in which
middle and upper-income housing consumers acquire properties previously occupied by low-income families who are displaced. Unslumming is taking place in some central cities and older suburbs and may
become more pervasive if the price of gas increases and its availability
declines, or if older neighborhoods become increasingly fashionable.
Although most central city mayors and planners believe that some, and
often much, unslumming is essential for economic stabilization and
renewal, critics in the press tend to assail it. "For all its appeal to
the elite who can afford to enjoy it, unslumming may be the cruelest
of all forms of slum real estate speculation. Old, run-down housing
and neighborhoods are brought back to life, but there is no benefit
for those who had to endure what had been those areas dying years."[49]
A more balanced, yet still critical view is "that whatever the long-
range benefits for the city of upgrading neighborhoods, the change
presents immediate and sometimes tragic problems for the low-income
families who are squeezed out by economic forces they cannot control."[50]

Housing is political because inevitably it distributes costs
and benefits unevenly and is an important determinant of access to
the social opportunity structure. For every reason to proceed in
one direction, there seem to be five to go the other way. However,
it has been a long time since our nation has tried conservation, and
there should be strong motivation to do so now.

NOTES

1. "As Millions of Americans Search for Homes—The Outlook Now," U.S. News and World Report 72, no. 24 (December 9, 1974), pp. 53-54.

2. Jack Rosenthal, "U.S. Birth Rate Falls to a Record Low But Zero Growth Is Said to Be Far Off," New York Times, March 2, 1973.

3. U.S. Bureau of the Census, Census of Population: 1970— General Population Characteristics, Final Report PC(1)-B1 (Washington, D.C.: Government Printing Office, 1972), p. 265.

4. Gerald Meyer, "St. Louis Economy Lags . . . What Are the Reasons?" St. Louis Post-Dispatch, May 13, 1973, p. 1. Sally Bixby Defty, "Labor Cost One of the Factors in Flight of Plants from St. Louis," St. Louis Post-Dispatch, May 14, 1973, p. 1.

5. Summary: Space Use Survey—Central Business District, St. Louis, Mo. (St. Louis: City Plan Commission, September 1971).

6. Elimination of units results from public action in highway construction, urban renewal, and code enforcement. In the private sector, elimination occurs through abandonment, fires, and vandalism. Increases in units were primarily attributable to new construction but include, in a few cases, subdivision of existing units.

7. The Union Electric service area includes the city of St. Louis, St. Louis County, St. Charles County, and major portions of Jefferson and Franklin Counties on the west side of the Mississippi River in the St. Louis metropolitan area. East St. Louis, Cahokia, and smaller industrial cities in St. Clair County and Alton, Roxana, and a few other Madison County communities comprise the east side service area.

8. "Most Housing Starts Soon Replacements," Washington Post, October 9, 1974, p. 34E.

9. U.S. Bureau of the Census, Census of Housing: 1970— Detailed Housing Characteristics, Missouri, Final Report, HC(1)-B27 (Washington, D.C.: Government Printing Office, 1972), p. 128.

10. Ibid., p. 110; and U.S. Bureau of the Census, Census of Housing: 1970—Detailed Housing Characteristics, California, Final Report, HC(1)-B6 (Washington, D.C.: Government Printing Office, 1972), p. 257.

11. John Linner and Douglas Wright, "The Housing Moratorium," Planning, 39, no. 4 (May 1973), p. 23.

12. Ibid.

13. George Sternlieb, Robert W. Burchell, and Virginia Paulus, eds., Residential Abandonment: The Environment of Decay, Exchange Bibliography, no. 342 (Monticello, Ill.: Council of Planning Librarians, December 1972), p. 2.

14. Michael Jett, "The End: Apartment Builders Watch Boom Sputter as Lenders Get Wary," Wall Street Journal, November 28, 1972, p. 1.

15. Anthony Downs, "Alternative Forms of Future Urban Growth in the United States," Journal of the American Institute of Planners 36, no. 1 (January 1970), p. 8.

16. Arthur P. Solomon, Housing the Urban Poor: A Critical Evaluation of Federal Housing Policy (Cambridge: MIT Press, 1974), p. 11.

17. Henry J. Aaron, Shelter and Subsidies: Who Benefits from Federal Housing Policies? (Washington, D.C.: Brookings Institution, 1972), pp. 26, 39.

18. Solomon, op. cit., p. 2.

19. Ibid., p. 7.

20. Leonard Downie, Jr., Mortgage on America (New York: Praeger Publishers, 1972), p. 208.

21. George Sternlieb, "Abandonment: Urban Housing," HUD Challenge, 111, no. 5 (May 1972), p. 12.

22. Charles L. Leven, and others, Urban Decay in St. Louis (St. Louis: Institute for Urban and Regional Studies, Washington University, 1972), p. 57.

23. Andrew Wilson, "Urban Ghost Town," St. Louis Globe-Democrat, June 9, 1972, p. 4B.

24. George Sternlieb and Robert W. Burchell, Residential Abandonment: The Tenement Landlord Revisited (New Brunswick, N.J.: Center for Urban Policy Research, Rutgers University, State University of New Jersey, 1973), p. xii.

25. Downie, op. cit., p. 87.

26. Ernest Erber and John Prior, "The Trend in Housing Density Bonuses," Planning 41, no. 10 (November 1974), p. 17.

27. Nathan Glazer, "Slum Dwellings Do Not Make a Slum," New York Times Magazine, November 21, 1965, pp. 55-64.

28. Solomon, op. cit., p. 15.

29. Ibid.

30. Horace B. Bazan, The Fragmentation of FHA (Washington, D.C.: Mortgage Bankers Association of America, June 1974), p. 6.

31. Saul B. Klaman, "30 Years Later, Where Do We Go Now in Housing?" The Mortgage Banker 26, no. 6 (March 1966), p. 30.

32. U.S. Department of Housing and Urban Development, Office of Audit, Report on Audit of Section 236, Multifamily Housing Program (Washington, D.C.: Government Printing Office, 1972).

33. William Lilley III, "The Homebuilders' Lobby," in Jon Pynoos, Robert Schafer, and Chester W. Hartman, eds., Housing Urban America (Chicago: Aldine Publishing Co., 1974), p. 30.

34. "Why So Many Mortgages are Being Foreclosed," U.S. News and World Report 72, no. 1, January 3, 1972, pp. 52-64.

35. Housing Is Everybody's Problem (St. Louis: Leagues of Women Voters of St. Louis and St. Louis County and Regional Forum of the East-West Gateway Coordinating Council, 1972); and Edward C. Burks, "Survey Shows that Most New Yorkers Cannot Afford Unsubsidized Housing," New York Times, July 11, 1972, p. 37.

36. Anthony Downs, Federal Housing Subsidies: How Are They Working? (Chicago: Real Estate Research Corporation, 1972), pp. 11-12.

37. U.S. Department of the Treasury, Proposals for Tax Change (Washington, D.C.: Government Printing Office, April 30, 1973), p. 15.

38. See the St. Louis Globe-Democrat, March 16, April 18, May 6-7, June 10-11, 12, 15, 19, and July 26, 1972; and the St. Louis Post-Dispatch, June 14 and 15, 1972.

39. George Sternlieb, Robert W. Burchell, and Virginia Paulus, Residential Abandonment: The Environment of Decay, Exchange Bibliography, no. 342 (Monticello, Ill.: Council of Planning Librarians, December 1972), p. 43.

40. Real Estate Research Corporation, The Costs of Sprawl: Detailed Cost Analysis (Washington, D.C.: Government Printing Office, April 1974), pp. 8-10.

41. St. Louis Metropolitan Area Rapid Transit Feasibility Study Long-Range Program (St. Louis: Bi-State Development Agency and East-West Gateway Coordinating Council, August 1971), pp. 65-72.

42. See Brian D. Boyer, Cities Destroyed for Cash: The FHA Scandal at HUD (Chicago: Follet Publishing Company, 1973), pp. 6-13; "Major Scandals Rock HUD's Big Subsidized Housing Programs for the Nation's Poor," House and Home 42, no. 5 (February 1972), p. 9; and Bazan, op. cit., pp. 38-39.

43. Aaron, op. cit., p. 166.

44. Solomon, op. cit., p. 186.

45. "The Federal Government and Neighborhood Change," speech by William Lilley 3d, deputy assistant secretary for policy development, HUD, and Rudolph G. Penner, deputy assistant secretary for economic affairs, HUD, at the American Real Estate and Urban Economics Association and the Federal Home Loan Bank System, Mayflower Hotel, Washington, D.C., May 24, 1974.

46. Downs, op. cit., p. 24.

47. Solomon, op. cit., pp. 197-198.

48. For further discussion of housing allowances, see the essay in this work by James Zais.

49. Downie, op. cit., p. 41.

50. Thomas W. Lippman, "Prices of NE Slum Houses Skyrocket," Washington Post, December 14, 1974, p. 1.

CHAPTER

2

FEDERAL HOUSING PROGRAMS, LOCAL POLITICS, AND A STRATEGY FOR PUBLIC ACTION: THE ST. LOUIS STORY

S. Jerome Pratter

The United States is passing through another period of re-flection about federal housing policies. Despite the passage of the Housing and Community Development Act in August 1974, program reevaluation continues and housing policies remain in a state of flux. The administration's recent moves toward leased housing and cash allowances may the opening notes of yet another chorus of housing "solutions."

No matter how you approach it, housing is money. The abundance and distribution of dollars determine whether low-income families are located in good or bad structures and neighborhoods. The federal government plays an essential role in housing because it has the capacity to redistribute funds from the wealthy to the poor. Although local conditions exert a significant impact on housing initiatives, we should emphasize that local action alone cannot produce the resources needed to carry out the construction, rehabilitation, or subsidy functions. Without the catalyst provided by a substantial input of federal dollars, those with limited incomes will see further decline in their already meager residential opportunities. Although the need for this sort of assistance becomes increasingly acute in the face of inflation, it is questionable whether there will be any effective involvement over the next few years.

Of course, the availability of dollars from Washington does not insure that urban housing problems will go away. The St. Louis case studies presented in the first part of this chapter illustrate the difficulties encountered in the attempt to implement subsidized housing programs at the local level. Major themes are bureaucratic insensitivity, the encouragement of unrealistic expectations, and the fierce hostility of most local residents to any suggestion that poor families be housed in the residents' neighborhoods.

What emerges from these melancholy tales is that housing markets in our older cities and suburbs operate in a very uneven manner. The wealthy and the powerful reap a disproportionate share of the benefits. In addition, the case materials clearly demonstrate that in the absence of a receptive local enviornment federal dollars will produce little or no housing for those who cannot compete effectively on the open market.

In the second part of the chapter, I want to go beyond the case studies and outline a public action strategy to deal with housing investment in older urban areas. The suggested approach, which avoids some of the major shortcomings described in the case studies, grew out of my experience as a housing and renewal consultant in the St. Louis region. Hopefully, these recommendations will contribute constructively to the continuing debate aimed at development of an approach to the conservation of older urban neighborhoods which is both realistic and humane.

HOUSING AND CASE STUDIES

Belle Lane: Community Development Against the Grain

One of the saddest housing failures in my experience occurred in a neighborhood adjoining Gas Light Square, an entertainment area in central St. Louis that flourished in the early 1960s and died by the time the group I was working with was organized in 1968.[1] At the height of Gas Light's popularity, Lenny Bruce, Elaine May, Mike Nichols, Alan Arkin, and the Smothers Brothers, among others, played at bistros in the four-block area.

To the south of Gas Light Square was "faded elegance." These were the once magnificent residences of prominent S. Louisans of an earlier era; some had been converted into rooming houses, while others, though zoned for one-family dwellings, retained only modest value. To the north was a neighborhood where a group called the Belle Neighbors lived. Their organization was composed predominantly of elderly blacks who lived in apartments and residences which fifty years before housed upper middle-class whites. Around World War II, this area was considered a very desirable black neighborhood in a city that was highly segregated.

The years had taken their toll on the neighborhood. Decline and abandonment were evident. When the Belle Neighbors formally came together in the late 1960s they decided to push for new housing. For more than a year the residents tried on their own to put a project

together. They went to developers with their Belle Lane project, as
it came to be called, and asked them to build housing. Each time,
they were turned down. Developers told them that the neighborhood
was slipping, that more money could be made elsewhere, that it was
easier to work without community groups, that they wanted no part
of black militancy, and that it was difficult to house the elderly. This
has been the classic introduction of low-income citizen organizations
to the housing game.

I met with the Belle Neighbors early in 1969. Shortly thereafter I was initiated into the workings of the federal housing bureaucracy by attending my first meeting with the Federal Housing Administration (FHA). In looking back, I don't know whether to be happy or
sad. There we were on an upper floor of an old office building in downtown St. Louis—a young white lawyer who had no firsthand experience
in housing, a group of white bureaucrats, and a delegation of poor,
old and mostly black people who were trapped in a neighborhood that
was being abandoned by everyone but them. These residents were
believers. They had read about great federal programs designed for
those with low incomes. Since they were honest and dedicated, they
felt that there was no reason they would not qualify for benefits under
the programs.

We should have realized that something was wrong, because
everyone at FHA was exceptionally nice. It was the sweet, fast treatment designed for those whom you don't take seriously. We were in
and out of the office so quickly that I don't think the elevator door
closed. We all came out with those little blue handbooks that describe
the programs. It didn't matter that we had them when we came in,
because these were "newer" editions. When we had explained our proposal, the FHA officials said they liked the idea of a neighborhood
association trying to improve housing conditions. Their advice was
given with sincerity and a smile. "Go home, study the programs in
the booklet, and we will be happy to work with you. "

It would have been fairer and more humane if they had told
the Belle Neighbors that the project was impossible, that it would
never go, and that they should give up. What they did was nurture a
dream by people who had already had more than their share of dreams
punctured by reality. By feeding their fantasy, the bureaucrats encouraged them to waste their time in a never-ending round of meaningless activity.

In the process of working on the project, the Belle Neighbors
merged with the Union-Sarah Economic Development Corporation, a
community development agency sponsored by the Office of Economic
Opportunity. After the merger, Union-Sarah took charge of the stalled
project. A short time later, it was agreed that instead of going the
tortuous FHA route as a nonprofit group, the joint venture would try
to put together a turnkey public housing project.

Ralston-Purina put up a $110,000 loan for seed money to demonstrate that it wanted to encourage black capitalism and urban revitalization in St. Louis, the city where it is headquartered. It was difficult not to want to help the people of Belle Neighbors; they were so persistent and so honest. Without detracting from the motives of those who put money into the project, it also was good public relations.

Over the three years that the project was being evaluated, processed, and reviewed for federal assistance by the Department of Housing and Urban Development (HUD), Belle Lane became a classic example of how to apply project selection criteria and arrive at different answers each time. First the project was on. Then it was off. Then the local housing authority said they would take the project when it was built. Then they said that they would not.

By the end of 1973, five years after the Belle Neighbors had come together to build one simple project using federal aid, HUD's Washington office said no, absolutely not. Today the land lies fallow, and a faded sign and a weedy lot are the only reminders of the Belle Neighbors' hopes for better housing. All of the participants in the project are confused, angry, and tired. Between $200,000 and $300,000 had been invested in a project that is no longer feasible because of increased costs of construction and interest rates.

Other aspects of the Belle Lane venture also are tragic. The proposed project site lies in a neighborhood that has become so abandoned that it would probably be foolish to put new housing there, where it would surely be overwhelmed by the surrounding blight.

Belle Neighbors tried to do everything correctly. They paid relocation costs and helped people move. They demolished structures to avoid vandalism. Maybe the humane approach doesn't work. One thing is certain—without money and experience you are in trouble in the housing game. The bureaucratic maze is very hard on professionals, but on groups like Belle Neighbors it is disastrous. Is there a realistic place for neighborhood residents as housing developers in an industry that is so highly sophisticated, so risky, and so fragmented as to defy comprehension? I seriously doubt it.

Gast Place: Urban Irony

The lure of low-and moderate-income housing development has not been restricted to amateurs. Professionals have been down the same road. About the time that Belle Lane was beginning in the fall of 1968, I received a phone call from a developer friend. He had optioned a five-acre, multiple-family site. He was enthusiastic. He felt that HUD would be crazy about it too. It was one of the few re-

maining unbuilt properties in a predominantly white, older section of
North St. Louis known as Baden. Located beautifully on high ground,
the riverfront Gateway Arch was visible seven miles away.

During the months that followed, the developer nursed the
project along through the local housing authority for a general occupancy (family) turnkey public housing project. He also took it through
the city building commission reviews. Preliminary plans were approved and only the valuation of the site was in question for HUD acceptance.

After learning of the proposal, the local alderman wrote the
Plan Commission requesting a downzoning of the property. Without
any fanfare, the Plan Commission and Board of Aldermen approved
the rezoning. It was months later that the developer learned for the
first time, and then indirectly, that his site had been quietly rezoned
to single-family use. He filed suit in Circuit Court of the City of
St. Louis, attacking the rezoning on four grounds:

- that the initiation of the rezoning violated city
  ordinances because it was done by an alderman;
- that insufficient notice was given to the owner;
- that a vested right in the original zoning was
  created by the series of municipal assurances
  and administrative approvals; and
- that the city should not be permitted to enforce
  the rezoning ordinances since the city, through
  various agents, had encouraged the development
  of the site for multiple-family use. [2]

Judge Nathan Bloom, in ruling for the plaintiff-owner, relied
upon the fourth argument. He also referred to the lack of adequate
notice and stated that "minimum fairness" would dictate that the city
apprise owners of proposed zoning changes. The court found from
the evidence that the rezoning of the property was arbitrary and unreasonable. It was not a reasonable exercise of the police power of
the city, nor was the action founded upon any desire or necessity to
protect the general welfare of the entire community. Rather, the rezoning had been designed to protect the residents of one street, Gast
Place, from alleged depreciation in their property values as a result
of the establishment of the adjoining federally assisted apartment project. Even if a material factor in justifying the rezoning, the court
held that there was no competent evidence that such depreciation in
value would occur. [3]

There were two ironic footnotes to this victory. First, the
same firm had been the original developer for the controversial Park
View Heights housing project in Black Jack, Missouri, a suburban

area in the northern part of St. Louis County that had incorporated
and used its newly found zoning powers to sidetrack the proposed
federally assisted development for nearly five years. When suburban
resistance to subsidized housing in Black Jack threatened the developer's firm with legal suits and financial reprisals, he redoubled his
energies in the city and found himself in yet another battle with local
residents. The second irony to the Gast Place chronicle is that the
developer's legal victory turned out to be pyrrhic. He gave up on the
project and sold the ground to another firm, which subsequently developed a housing project for the elderly on the site. Gast Place on
top of the Black Jack confrontation completely traumatized the developer. He quit building altogether, moved to another city, and went into
the career development business. It was safer.

In Gast Place, a professional developer tried to do what
HUD wanted—build housing outside blighted ghetto neighborhoods—but
fierce local resistance and legal battles effectively torpedoed development efforts. By not having neighborhood residents involved in the
project at the outset, chances of success were diminished. But, unfortunately, subsidized family housing means poor blacks to many
people, and nobody wants them nearby.

River Bend: The Art of Obstruction

Other subsidized projects have been subjected to neighborhood harassment in St. Louis. Of all the cases that I have read about
where communities fought housing, one in particular stands out as a
model of innovation in the fine art of obstruction.

Across town from the Gast Place site along the Mississippi
River Bluffs, one of the city's most successful developers proposed
building an eight-story apartment tower to be called River Bend. The
project was to contain 98 units and to be financed under the Section
236 general occupancy program. In addition, the Rouse-Wates Building System, one of those being tested by HUD in the St. Louis Operation Breakthrough development, was to have its first regular run.
Recognizing the futility of attempting a rezoning, the developer chose
to purchase a tract already zoned for multi-family use.

Located in the southern part of the city, the site covered
about two and a quarter acres, a small part of which was Missouri
Pacific Railroad right-of-way at the foot of the hill adjacent to the
river. Topographically, the land featured a gently rising surface
grade from the western property line for 400 feet, at which point a
limestone bluff fell abruptly to the Mississippi. A magnificent view
of the river and the farms on the Illinois flood plain enhanced the
site's attractiveness.

Multi-family zoning was established for this property and other adjoining sites in a ten-block area in 1950. It acknowledged existing land uses and permitted their expansion. This zoning went unchallenged until 1966 when a group of surrounding owners first attempted to rezone the River Bend location to a single-family category. The St. Louis City Plan Commission denied the petition because it felt that the higher density usage was superior.

No single-family homes had been built on the bluffs since World War II, but there grew up a number of unattractive, multi-story nursing homes which obstructed the view of the river. In 1960, a 20-family apartment complex was constructed nearby. As late as 1967, the Plan Commission advocated retention of the large existing single-family residences that dotted the bluff, and the inclusion of well-sited multi-family units that would enhance rather than block the magnificent vista from high ground.

Opposition to River Bend intensified in mid-1971 when the proposed federally subsidized project was announced in the newspaper. Indignant outcries from local residents prophesied that the area would become traffic congested and that schools would become overcrowded. It also was argued that the proposed development would be completely out of character with the surroundings.

Sophistication in fighting subsidized housing reached new heights at River Bend. The city Landmarks Commission designated the site and the entire ten-block stretch along the bluffs in south St. Louis as an official city landmark, citing its unmatched natural beauty as the reason. This action enabled the commission to exercise design review over the project. It was hoped, and even voiced by the vice-chairman of the commission, that this would stop construction of the proposed project.[4]

Another attempt was made to downzone the adjoining three-block area which included the River Bend parcel. This effort was rejected by the Plan Commission, which may have been concerned over the Gast Place suit that was pending at the time. Despite Plan Commission denial, the local alderman, responding to a petition signed by 2,100 local residents, introduced an ordinance to override the Commission's recommendation and the downzoning bill was passed. This move set up a veritable cat-and-mouse game between the city and the area HUD director.

After learning of the aldermanic action, the regional HUD director immediately ordered a review of all proposed subsidized projects in the city. Noting recent court decisions in the Shannon and Gautreaux cases,[5] which he interpreted as prohibiting HUD approval of subsidized housing in ghetto areas, he stressed the need for regional housing solutions. He stated further that his office viewed the River Bend rezoning as the first critical test of the city's new housing plan, which endorsed the use of scattered sites for low- and moderate-income housing. If the mayor signed the rezoning ordinance, the HUD director was in fact threatening to cut off federal housing to the city. The mayor, caught in the middle between the Board of Aldermen and HUD, said bravely that he would not be intimidated by anyone. A few days later he vetoed the rezoning. Threats of suits by area residents and countersuits by civil rights groups associated with the Black Jack effort were hurled about, but none were filed. Months later, the developer received final HUD approval and proceeded with the project.

Although finally successful where Gast Place had failed, the River Bend case illustrates the enormous difficulty that professional developers face in attempting to locate subsidized housing outside deteriorating center-city areas. In many cases, projects are tied up in legal battles that consume large amounts of resources that might otherwise be channelled in socially useful directions. In a business where time is money, the mere prospect of delays caused by litigation is enough to undermine the feasibility of most federally assisted developments. This classic Black Jack pattern was repeated after a fashion in Gast Place and only narrowly avoided by the courageous action of the mayor in the River Bend case. Given the likelihood of "blackjacking," it is hardly surprising that few developers are interested in trying to put subsidized housing outside the ghetto. [6]

While the maintenance of segregated housing patterns is one painfully apparent consequence of local opposition to federally assisted housing, there is another side effect which is far more subtle. This is the tendency to engage in planning that substitutes rhetoric for reality by playing on the fantasies of those who view integrated housing as a worthy goal.

The Gateway Plan: A Regional Fantasy

In the spring of 1971 at the height of the national debate over appropriate locations for subsidized housing, the St. Louis area office of HUD approved an application by the East-West Gateway Coordinating Council (EWGCC), the regional council of governments, to draft a community development plan for housing. The agency had already tied itself into knots over taking an official stance on the Black Jack controversy. The council had resolved to do nothing about that project. Now it was to prepare by June 30, 1972, a comprehensive regional housing plan.

HUD instructions to EWGCC were that specific housing targets, actions, and innovations be stated explicitly. It was clearly indicated that another traditional planning study and a series of general recommendations were not desired. HUD wanted significant implementation of the region's planning efforts.

EWGCC assembled a special staff to undertake this charge. The Danforth Foundation, anxious to see an effective regional housing strategy developed and put into action, sponsored six mini-conferences and a major conference on housing. In September and October 1971, the regional housing question was discussed at the six sessions, each aimed at a particular sector of the St. Louis community such as finance and insurance, or planning agencies and government officials.

The major conference was held in the first week of November. A number of national speakers, including Dale Bertsch, Executive Director of the Miami Regional Planning Commission (Dayton, Ohio); Anthony Downs of the Real Estate Research Corporation, and Paul Davidoff, Director of the Suburban Action Institute, spoke to a variety of concerned citizens about their views on the state of the housing planning art and the success and failure of other regional efforts. Coming away from the session, everyone wondered what the St. Louis region would produce.

The Dayton "Fair Share" Plan and the effort that it involved seemed inappropriate in St. Louis, partly because the major conference did not include the real decision makers—the mayors, supervisors, business executives, labor leaders, or even the board members of EWGCC. They went about their business while those already working for the dispersal of low- and moderate-income housing exhausted each other with talk.

As the months went by, murmurs of concern grew about how EWGCC was approaching the plan. In May, only days before the initial draft of the plan was presented to the EWGCC Board of Directors, the St. Louis Post Dispatch carried a lead editorial questioning the plan. The plan, said the editorial, "reads more like the rules of a Monopoly game than an effective program to improve housing conditions in the St. Louis area."[7] Brushing aside last-minute complaints from its own citizen-based regional forum that had been ignored in drawing up the plan, the staff presented the plan to the council's board on May 24, 1972.

In his brief introductory remarks prior to the staff presentation, the EWGCC executive director, as if to convince everyone on the board that nothing dangerous was on tap, assured them that EWGCC was not an implementing agency; implementation was up to others. The staff also led off by noting that numerical assignments or quotas on subsidized housing were not in the plan. The plan only set forth guidelines for implementation by others, if they saw fit to follow through.

What emerged was hardly a plan, and the guidelines were nonexistent. There were three sections: first, a series of general goals; second, policy recommendations for various levels of government and private housing groups; and third, descriptions of a variety of hypothetical neighborhoods in the region, dubbed typologies, with recommendations on how to improve conditions in them. There was no section on implementation.

The 33 regional goals in the plan touched all the bases: rehabilitation of sound housing, the use of new technology, tax incentives to encourage private industry to build housing in deteriorated areas, and elimination of unreasonable zoning and codes that prohibit balanced and orderly growth. Then, the draft proposed general policy recommendations for everyone from the federal government to private industry. The laundry list of ideas ran from ending discrimination, to homeowner training programs, to better zoning controls. The only fresh approach was the "typologies," which grouped the region's residential areas into 14 types based upon common street patterns, regional locations, land-use allocations, and building conditions. Each typology resembled actual neighborhoods that, with few modifications, appeared in the region. The recommendations for each typology were to be merely "a useful point of departure during the implementation phase," whenever that might occur. [8]

Once revealed, the draft plan left everyone bewildered. No one knew what the thing was, but everyone who read it agreed it certainly was not a plan. There was no effort at quantifying housing needs or resources or at identifying goals for any political jurisdiction. The amorphous document was filled with vague ideas and impossible dreams. It had no measurable targets, not to mention any way of seeing that the targets would be realized.

Immediately after the unveiling, the Post-Dispatch commented that "anyone attempting to apply such a plan to reality is automatically involved in a complex guessing game."[9] In addition, it noted that the six-month period for review and public debate requested by EWGCC was just enough to get by the November 1972 elections, thus giving all those involved in the plan "a chance to mix into their last-minute calculations the nature of the national administration for the next four years."[10]

Sensing the rising criticism from the press, planning professionals, and concerned housing groups of their almost $200,000, 18-month effort, EWGCC's staff rallied to redraft the document. A revised edition appeared in July 1972. Everyone agreed that at least this draft was more readable. A new format was used. Yet the underlying premise of the plan was appalling in its naivete. The planners believed that " . . . subsidized housing is acceptable to most communities within the region . . . if everyone understands the rules."[11]

The fourteen typologies, which were now grouped into five "policy sets," would serve to show people the expected impact on housing in their neighborhoods. Hidden within the second effort were two major additions: first, a clear statement that if such a plan were accepted, compliance with it would be used as a means of evaluating requests for federal funding normally reviewed by EWGCC; second, the revised plan proposed that subsidized units be limited to five percent of the existing stock in all neighborhoods, except those requiring major redevelopment.[12] Despite the improvements, there was still an absence of numbers or a well-developed means of seeing that the housing impasse would be broken. Even the plan's drafters felt that they were powerless without substantial support.

The new draft was not received with much more favor than was the first effort. Generally, it was ignored since most concerned persons felt that EWGCC either could not or would not do anything about providing increased housing opportunities. The only strong objections came from the city of St. Louis, which feared that it would continue to get the bulk of subsidized housing under the plan, and from the professional planners, who were anxious to distinguish the EWGCC report from their conception of planning.[13] Most of the planners' criticisms were aimed at the methodology of the report. For the most part, even they doubted whether the regional agency had the ability to improve the housing situation.

After the initial comments, the issue was dropped by the press, and many of those who were originally concerned wondered if the whole issue was meaningless anyway. The plan was poor, but the blame couldn't be placed solely on the agency. Hadn't they produced what the larger community and EWGCC's board wanted—a plan that would forestall federal funding cutoffs against the region, but do little more? Without a substantial power base in the metropolitan area, EWGCC's regional housing plan could not help but appear more sham than substance.

AN ALTERNATIVE STRATEGY FOR PUBLIC ACTION

It is not likely that those working for dispersal of low and moderate income families will succeed in developing a constituency with sufficient clout to achieve their objective in the foreseeable future. It is far more reasonable to expect a continuation of the patterns observed in the case studies. Those with money will move to the suburbs and those without will be confined primarily to older core-city areas because of their severely limited purchasing power and of the hostility of recent emigres to encroachments by subsidized housing. Meanwhile, housing bureaucrats and planners will continue to raise hopes unrealistically in the absence of a workable strategy for dispersing federally assisted projects.

Despite my lack of optimism, there are public actions that can be taken to improve living conditions in older core areas. Even with the constraints imposed by the uncertain federal funding picture and the limited possibility of political acceptance at the local level, there are things that can be done to stabilize and redevelop older areas.

In suggesting a public action strategy for conservation and redevelopment of older urban neighborhoods, I am not suggesting that public officials and citizen groups should drop all attempts to scatter housing opportunities for low- and moderate-income people. Indeed, the actions proposed in the following comments presuppose a continuation of these efforts at dispersal, at least on a moderate scale. At the same time, experiences in Black Jack, Gast Place, River Bend, and the East-West Gateway Coordinating Council suggest that it would be foolish to rely principally on the dispersal strategy as a means for improving the housing chances of those with limited incomes. Like it or not, both political prudence and the disastrous effect of the current economic recession on the housing construction industry point to the desirability of neighborhood conservation and reuse as strategies for public action.

The problem with the way urban redevelopment has been practiced to date derives chiefly from the overly simple way in which the city has been approached. Public officials and planners have lacked the courage to suggest that neighborhoods with different characteristics require different public policy approaches. Most of our older urban areas should be viewed not as one city, but as numerous neighborhoods or action areas having unique attributes and opportunities.

For purposes of discussion, we may distinguish three kinds of neighborhoods based on such things as age of dwellings, stability of residents, market attitude and physical appearance, as well as the quanitity and quality of public services required. The three action areas which deserve special attention are:

- Conservation Sectors
- Redevelopment Sectors
- Depletion Sectors

Whatever one might feel about classification schemes of this sort, some such set of distinctions will be necessary if we hope to come up with a realistic public action strategy to deal with investment in our older urban areas. Hopefully, the following suggestions will contribute to the formulation of such a policy.

Conservation Sectors

These are established residential, commercial and industrial
areas that are well maintained, attractive, and have economic vitality.
They have an ability to attract continued investment, from simple
home repairs to massive renovation of industrial properties and new
commercial construction. In these neighborhoods, public and private
sectors work well together. The public sector maintains a high level
of services, including garbage collection, schools, street paving,
and police protection.

Conservation sectors are the base upon which a city can
build, and the primary goal of public involvement should be to maintain their long-term stability. City, county and regional resources
should be devoted on a priority basis to these areas in an effort to
avoid private disinvestment. A line must be drawn to demonstrate
that a community will neither allow blight to proceed unchecked nor
will it abandon those investors and resident owners who have taken
a stand.

Good schools, police protection, and code enforcement are
vital in these neighborhoods. If the schools cease to be vehicles for
upward mobility, the crime rate increases, or housing standards are
not maintained, there will be outward movement and decline.
cline.

Code enforcement is not a strategy which works in all parts
of older urban areas. Often, compliance is difficult or even impossible to obtain. Enforcement becomes a game ranging from polite
request to judicial coercion. It may be ineffective in older, poorer
sections of a city where the original construction or design of buildings
makes them unadaptable to changing business or social patterns. In
addition, a tough policy on codes can mean automatic displacement
of those who financially are unable to comply.

The key to the problem lies in enforcing the code effectively,
not in the regulations themselves. If the code is enforced effectively
in conservation sectors as new investments are made, it can prevent
blight from spreading. Code enforcement must be undertaken in these
areas on a large-scale systematic basis and in cooperation with other
public and private activities. It must also have the full support of those
who are within the target area.

An occupancy-permit program should be considered in conservation sectors. The occupancy-permit method of code enforcement
is now being successfully used in a number of cities in the St. Louis
region. Instead of inspections on a general city-wide basis, or merely
relying upon complaints to discover code violations, the occupancy-
permit system requires a certificate issued by the building commission-
er before any person can occupy an existing unit or new addition to a

dwelling. The permit is not issued until the minimum housing standards in the code have been met. Such an ordinance should not be applied retroactively and should be administered in a flexible manner in order to maximize compliance in specific neighborhoods.

If the occupancy-permit system is adopted by a community for selected conservation sectors, there must be a commitment of public improvements and services to upgrade the neighborhood and maintain confidence in it. Further, the entire effort will fail without owner access to improvement capital. Once the individual decision to comply with the code is made, financing for repairs may be too costly for the owner, or even totally unavailable. A city, therefore, may have to assist some owners in coping with home improvement costs. Every effort must be made to inform financial institutions about the program and secure their support. Neighborhood financial institutions, which are more directly affected, must be given special attention and encouragement. The city must anticipate the need to establish a loan guarantee and high-risk fund for qualifying homeowners in conservation sectors.

Local government and lending institutions in Pittsburgh, Cincinnati, Oakland, and a number of other cities, have an excellent opportunity to assist with and guarantee home improvement loans that have been offered by the Federal Home Loan Bank Board. The program combines loan commitments from the local banking industry with municipal and federal funding. Ideally, it offers all the capital needed to assure code compliance. If used in a concentrated way, such assistance should prove to be a wise investment since code compliance can be expected to increase the market value and stability of property in conservation sectors.

Conservation in urban areas is the only alternative to all-out production. While there may be a political consensus to continually discard older areas, we no longer have the resources as a nation to do so. Maintenance of older housing is the only way to reduce the need for new highways, sewers, and building materials. In the long run, our cities will be better off, too, because there will be a greater range of environments from which to choose as well as greater stability of neighborhoods.

Redevelopment Sectors

These are areas of advanced deterioration where potential for redevelopment, as measured by the interest or private investors, would appear to exist. In some, federally assisted urban renewal is already under way. These are major efforts characterized by either clearance and reuse or extensive rehabilitation.

Since passage of urban renewal legislation in 1949, there are numerous examples of overaggressiveness and undue optimism in relation to redevelopment. Often, designation of a neighborhood for renewal has merely accelerated its decline and downfall. In addition, federal funds for renewal and housing are scarce. It is foolish, then, to designate mile after mile of the older urban cores for redevelopment. There is neither the market for the land nor enough money for the acquisition, demolition, and write-down costs. Despite the fantasies of most aldermen that their wards can become new-towns-in-town, reality dictates only limited possibilities.

Public action strategies in redevelopment sectors should be aimed at inducing concentrated private investment. Naturally, the chances of obtaining this investment are better in some areas than others. Those neighborhoods that have little possibility of capturing private investment should not have a heavy input of public dollars. With limited public money, a city must be prudent in allocating its resources and legal powers; it must use them as leverage.

No portion of a city should be considered for redevelopment unless there is a good probability of achieving success with implementation tools that are readily available. Even with the continuation of urban renewal under the guise of special revenue sharing in the Housing and Community Development Act of 1974, local committees should conduct a realistic reappraisal of their renewal policies. The redevelopment process should become more selective, and increasing reliance will probably have to be placed on state and local initiatives and sources of support.

Attention and care must be given to the designation of redevelopment sectors in order to avoid raising false hopes. This, of course, has been a valid criticism of past programs. In much the same way that the Belle Neighbors were sorely disappointed by the FHA, residents of renewal areas have had their expectations dashed by cruel and lengthy processes in which both they and the city were worse off than before the area was designated for renewal.

With the growing scarcity of federal funds for redevelopment, other public tools may have to be substituted for the federal write-down incentive. One of these used by the largest Missouri cities is called the Section 353 Development Incentive Program. It is intended to encourage private sector construction and rehabilitation by transferring the public powers of eminent domain and long-term tax abatement to developers. The state of Ohio has recently enacted similar legislation for "impacted cities." To be effective, use of these incentives should be limited. When they are used, they should be tied to a carefully sequenced program of public improvements and selective enforcement of codes.

Public funds and powers are merely catalytic. Under our economic system, they are not substitutes for private investment, as many disillusioned antipoverty and model cities' planners have learned. Unless local programs like Section 353 or the placement of public office buildings, schools, and parks can encourage private sector activities, they should not be used. Scarce funds should only be applied in redevelopment sectors where reuse is reality, not a dream. Renewal cannot be willed by a planner's magic marker.

Depletion Sectors

While conservation and redevelopment sectors are tough to handle both politically and economically, they are easy compared to those sectors of neighborhoods that have been worn out with the passage of time and, at present, have no development potential. These are the areas where aldermen remember wistfully when there were many residents, lots of votes, and lots of money. They are the sites of urban nostalgia turned by a cruel twist into block after block dotted with burned-out buildings, rubble-strewn lots, and boarded-up businesses. Given the nature of the forces at work in these areas, they can only be called depletion sectors, for chances of private reinvestment in the foreseeable future are practically nil. Abandonment and disinvestment are likely to continue for some time.

The nature of this wasteful process, which has become commonplace recently in many older American cities, presents public officials and planners with two difficult dilemmas. First, depletion sectors are clearly in need of massive redevelopment efforts. But vigorous public actions designed to promote redevelopment, such as strict code enforcement, rigid building demolition, and the assembly of vacant parcels are only likely to accelerate the eventual collapse of the area.

The second dilemma arises from the fact that some people and businesses are trapped in these areas. For reasons both political and humanitarian, city officials cannot totally ignore the continuing needs of these people for public services. Given the conflicting imperatives involved in this difficult situation, it is not strange that cities have attempted to go both ways at once. While continuing to funnel limited funds into these areas with the express intent of maintaining their livability, contrary efforts are made to encourage total clearance and redevelopment efforts.

Politics makes it tough to deal honestly with the residents of depletion sectors. In one example, a neighborhood group in St. Louis was encouraged by one set of HUD officials to acquire properties for scattered-site 235 housing while, at the same time, the planning departments of HUD and the city were working on a plan for the area which had as its major goal redevelopment for unassisted, middle-income housing. While the neighborhood group was spending limited resources to acquire properties, the federal and local governments were working quietly in the opposite direction. Even if politically necessary, it can be questioned whether this type of accommodation is either the fairest treatment for the residents of that district or the most desirable for the city.

This implicit policy of calculated dishonesty needs to be set aside. Efforts should be made to assure that essential services and public investments are provided those who remain in these depletion areas. Yet these efforts should be pursued without encouraging new investment until a city determines that major redevelopment is truly possible. Continual reassessment of service needs and marketability is required. In addition, a clear linkage of public services and invest-ments to the phased approval of new development should be established for central cities as had been done in some expanding suburban areas.

In the case of Golden v. Ramapo, the New York Court of Appeals linked suburban residential growth to the availability of pub-lic services. [14] The Ramapo concept was based upon the township of Ramapo's legal requirement that all residential development areas meet predetermined service standards before a special construction permit could be issued. The development area was evaluated on its available services by a system of points, 15 points being necessary to receive a building permit. The novel and critical part of this ser-vices test was that Ramapo had a six-year capital improvement bud-get and a 12-year capital improvement plan during which time it ob-ligated itself to provide the entire community with, for example, roads, sewers, parks, and firehouses. Until the town provided these essen-tial services, the developer could not build. He could, however, pro-vide the services necessary for approval at his own expense and there-fore speed up the development process.

Ramapo and subsequent rulings have upheld the notion that the public sector may, under certain circumstances, regulate and control growth. While judicial attitudes remain in a state of flux, there is a growing realization that public investments should be made only when a market potential is reached which will pay for the invest-ment within a reasonable period of time. Unless a positive program of this sort is adopted in the city, the residents of depletion sectors will continue to be the marks of a political con game.

Those who now live in depletion sectors are trapped. Many are elderly. Most are frightened because they have little security. Some often have everything tied up in their houses, and they can ex-pect to get nothing for them. Others have their homes paid off. All are trapped at the bottom of the filtering process. Know that it is only a matter of time for them, they are locked in because they do not have money to relocate. They are being kidded while slowly, but surely, abandonment proceeds and services are being curtailed as the city's resources are spread even thinner. I propose to be honest and take the next step. Help these people out of these areas, buy their homes with fair compensation, and put the land aside to lie fallow until it can be redeveloped.

Public financing of relocation is not cheap, but it is humane and it redistributes some benefits from suburban homeowners who gain rapid real estate appreciation to those who pay dearly for suburban expansion and central city abandonment. Maximum effort should be made to find federal and local resources to finance the movement of people out of these badly blighted areas.

My planner's bias leads me to believe that controlling growth is an appropriate function of the public sector. This notion is being accepted in some suburban areas and I advocate it for central-city depletion sectors. Tax dollars should be used to bank land and to relocate those who are trapped. Land banking in core areas is now receiving considerable national attention. It is already happening in a city like St. Louis, where tax delinquent properties are being acquired by local government. This land aggregation process should be extended to abandoned buildings, HUD foreclosures, and other parcels which are needed as fill-ins for development packaging. By subjecting this land banking procedure to conformance with an overall plan and local legislative sanction, its operations would be controlled. If undertaken only in designated areas, such action would clearly meet any legal challenge of "public purpose."

We should recognize that federally assisted urban renewal has been a process of land assembly and in this regard it has been useful. It failed in that, until recently, it did not provide realistic options for relocatees and it often forced development when market forces were not working. Realistically, depletion sectors should not be considered for reuse or for homesteading. They should become land inventories for future private and public investment.

Irate critics of this idea point out that it is socially insensitive and that abandoned areas should be renewed into habitable neighborhoods for the poor. However, the poor want no part of these sections of the city, and there is no way to make them desirable until the demand for inner-city land changes. The question then becomes: How are those who are trapped to be compensated fairly and how do you make these areas more marketable? It can't be done with doctrinaire rhetoric.

One warning should be voiced for those concerned with intervention in depletion sectors. Of all the public services that affect these areas, none has greater negative impact than code enforcement. With our without an occupancy-permit system, strict code enforcement can and will accelerate abandonment, because the private financial resources necessary for compliance are not available. For humanitarian reasons, this is not an acceptable strategy since enforcement churns the market and places the burden of reinvestment and relocation upon those least able to bear it. It is not acceptable for businesses either. Those located in these exhausted neighborhoods are already experiencing great difficulties, and to push them harder either causes them to leave the area or to close down permanently, thus adding further impetus to the deterioration and abandonment cycle.

In addition, strict code enforcement is a poor investment of city funds in these areas. Strict code enforcement should be given priority only where reinvestment can accompany it. Thus, we have emphasized that code enforcement in conservation sectors should be linked with such devices as the Federal Home Loan Bank insurance guarantee program. In depletion sectors, enforcement must be more superficial, with standards and procedures reflecting the market and capabilities of the area. Enforcement should not become a mechanism to accelerate abandonment and land banking. Abandonment will come soon enough in these areas as a natural consequence of population and investment migrating to more desirable locations.

CONCLUSIONS

In the first part of this chapter, much time was spent analyzing the problems associated with attempts to locate low- and moderate-income housing in areas outside blighted and decaying neighborhoods. Expected payoffs from this approach to housing improvements are likely to suffer from fierce citizen hostility to encroachments by subsidized housing. In the absence of a workable local consensus, federally assisted programs aimed at "opening up the suburbs" for occupancy by those with limited incomes are perversely tantalizing; expectations are alternately raised to unrealistic heights and then dashed against the hard realities of grass-roots opposition. [15] For this reason, proponents of housing improvement for low- and moderate-income families can only be sorely disappointed if they rely heavily on dispersal strategies.

The recommendations for public action outlined in the second half of the paper avoid the major difficulties observed in the case studies presented in the first part. The suggestions emphasize conservation and phased reuse of the existing housing and neighborhoods found in older urban areas. Given the growing scarcity of resources for new construction and the ever-present barriers to the systematic dispersal of subsidized housing, public action strategies stressing the need for conservation and renewal in the natural state appear to be a reasonable course of action.

To some extent, of course, the conservation and redevelopment strategy that we have outlined depends upon the creation of housing opportunities for the poor and minorities outside the ghetto. In fact, if there is a legitimate political purpose for emphasis on the production of new housing outside center-city areas, it is to expand the opportunities of those who traditionally have had options denied to them. While it would be foolish to rely excessively on any single approach, concern both for fairness and for the feasibility of center-city conservation and redevelopment point to the necessity of continued efforts to disperse housing chances for those with low and moderate incomes. From this perspective, both dispersal and conservation-redevelopment can be viewed as part of an overall housing improvement package. To a large degree as well, the perverse patterns of frustration observed in the case studies may simply be a product of overemphasis on the dispersal approach to the neglect of a well-thought-out set of guidelines for conservation and redevelopment. These we have attempted to provide in the second half of the essay.

In closing, one final point needs to be made with regard to the chances of bringing about planned change in the housing system. I find that it is impossible to get full control of the housing process, which at best is highly complex, fragmented, and subject to the influence of unforeseen factors. If planners were to plot and scheme for 50 years to conserve the housing resources of the central city, they might not equal the impact of an unforeseen event like a continuing energy crisis. If energy shortages do persist for some years to come, this might force urban conservation and redevelopment into a new ball game. The rising transportation costs of such a continuing crisis might bring many of the affluent back to center-city areas increasing private demand for urban land. The impact of this hypothetical scenario on those with limited incomes would be rather more difficult to predict. Hopefully, they would not be priced entirely out of the market as happened in the Georgetown section of Washington, D.C. when that area was reborn some years ago.

In the event that there is no sudden resurgence in the demand for center-city real estate, we can confidently expect a continuation of the politics of housing as we have come to know it over the past 20 to 30 years. When the poor are denied access to better neighborhoods and at the same time are forced to bear the costs of disinvestment in abandoned areas, then certainly they cannot be considered

winners in the housing game. But we are all losers because we are
abandoning what was once a highly functional system of shelter, employment, and transportation for one that is both costly and wasteful. In
our preference for newness and disposability in housing, we also are
forsaking an important part of our cultural heritage in the city, and
this will lead to irreparable damage. As the years pass, conservation
sectors may become increasingly less viable until the time will arrive
when housing 15 or 20 years old is considered obsolete. At that time,
our society will likely be even more woefully short of resources for redevelopment than it is at present.

These thoughts may be overly pessimistic, and I sincerely
hope that they are. Still, it is only by making an unsentimental, hard-
headed assessment of the deficiencies of the present housing system
that a solid foundation can be established for corrective action. I
hope that these remarks have contributed something toward that end.

NOTES

1. Much of the material used in preparing the case studies
is from my article "Gateway to Frustration—Housing in St. Louis,"
The Urban Lawyer 4, no. 4 (Fall, 1972), pp. 746-756.

2. Creative Communities, Inc. v. City of St. Louis, in
Circuit Court of the City of St. Louis, Cause no. 19002F.

3. Ibid., p. 32.

4. Louis J. Rose, "Landmark Status Linked to Housing
Opposition," St. Louis Post-Dispatch, October 6, 1971, p. 1A.

5. See Shannon v. Romney, 436 F. 2d 809 (3rd Cir. 1970),
and Gautreaux v. Chicago Housing Authority, 296 F. Supp. 907 (N.
D. Ill. 1969).

6. For details on the Black Jack case, see "Dispersed Housing
and Suburbia: Confrontation in Black Jack," in Land Use Control Annual, 1971 (Chicago: American Society of Planning Officials, 1971).
After nearly five years of legal battles, the developers of the Black
Jack project may finally get to build some subsidized units. In late
December 1974, a federal appeals court unanimously reversed a
lower court ruling which upheld the city's ban on multi-family housing
as a reasonable use of the zoning power in United States v. City of
Black Jack, 508 F. 2d 1179 (8th. Cir. 1974). Subsequent to this reversal, the Supreme Court refused to review the appeals court decision.
Rejoicing by subsidized housing advocates was tempered by the realization that challenges to other discriminatory zoning ordinances would
have to proceed piecemeal, one at a time and at considerable expense.
Despite the obvious importance of the legal precedent established by

the reversal, the mere thought of lengthy legal action is likely to deter most housing developers. In the Black Jack case, the greatly increased costs caused by delays will force the developers to scale down the number of units foreseen in the original proposal should they decide to go ahead and build the project. However, they are appealing to HUD for special assistance to overcome this final hurdle.

7. "Abstract Regionalism," St. Louis Post-Dispatch, May 13, 1972, p. 4A.

8. East-West Gateway Coordinating Council, "Recommendation for St. Louis Community Development," mimeographed. St. Louis, May 24, 1972, p. 24.

9. "Delay Realities," St. Louis Post-Dispatch, May 30, 1972, p. 2B.

10. Ibid.

11. East-West Gateway Coordinating Council, "Recommendation for St. Louis Community Development," mimeographed. St. Louis, July 13, 1972, p. 2.

12. Ibid., pp. 5-7.

13. See comments by A. J. Wilson, Jr., executive secretary to Mayor A. J. Cervantes, "Scatler Housing Plan Criticized as 'Too Vague,' " St. Louis Globe-Democrat, July 18, 1972, p. 6A.

14. For an extensive discussion of the issue of controlled growth and the Ramapo case, see Nongrowth as a Planning Alternative, Planning Advisory Service Report No. 283 (Chicago: Planning Advisory Service, American Society of Planning Officials, September 1972).

15. For an interesting, if overly sanguine, discussion of problems and prospects of dispersing low-income people in suburban areas, see Anthony Downs, Opening Up the Suburbs: An Urban Strategy for America (New Haven, Conn.: Yale University Press, 1973).

"Once upon a time 'politics' was described as 'who
gets what, when, and how.' Today it seems that
politics centers about 'who feels what, when, and
how.' The smoke-filled room where patronage and
pork were dispensed has been replaced by the talk-
filled room, where rhetoric and image are dispensed."

—Thomas R. Dye, Understanding Public Policy.

Dye's observation applies with particular force to the politics
of urban housing because people tend to become uncommonly emotional
about housing questions. Residential concerns are not just a matter of
survival. Where a person lives, next to whom, and in what circumstances are important determinants of identity and status. As these
matters are closely connected with strong feelings and human value
considerations, discussions about housing policies and problems often
are particularly heated. Players in the urban housing game regularly
employ pointed, one-sided arguments that are designed to identify and
condemn opponents, enhance the morale of supporters, and persuade
the uncommitted. In other words, political debate in the housing policy
arena involves a good deal of rhetoric.

One of the prevailing myths about political rhetoric is that
it makes no difference to public policy outcomes. In this view, words
are just so much hot air. Nothing could be further from the truth, at
least insofar as urban housing is concerned. One of the most important
ways oratory makes a difference is by frustrating attempts at reasoned,
balanced analysis. For better or worse, understanding the policy-making
process in this area hinges on being familiar with the slanted arguments
voiced by the players in the urban housing arena.

In the first essay in this section, Michael A. Quinn analyzes
the main arguments and consequences that follow from the oratory employed by actors in what he calls the urban housing drama. According
to Quinn, both liberals and conservatives engage in rhetorical overkill.
Liberals vilify the "slumlord," while conservatives "blame the victim."
Although rhetoric is an important device for calling attention to problems, Quinn argues that it also obscures group interests and reduces
the flexibility of actors in their approach to housing problems. Actors
sometimes lose sight of stated objectives because rhetoric has a way
of capturing those who use it.

Quinn's argument is illustrated by case materials involving
three urban housing issues: the lead-paint poisoning of small children
residing in dilapidated city housing; the Federal Housing Administration scandals; and the debate surrounding a recent research report on
St. Louis by the prestigious RAND Corporation. The facts suggest
that prospects are not good for a happy ending. Nonetheless, Quinn
concludes by offering a few modest suggestions designed to improve
the performance of actors in the urban housing drama.

Quinn's discussion of the RAND controversy is especially
interesting because it shows that scientific researchers, too, are
players on the urban stage. The expects have a stake in the housing
game just like everybody else. Specifically, they compete for research
funds, publications, and prestige within the academic community.
Whether the expert comes down on the side of change or the status
quo is a question best answered by reference to these practical considerations rather than abstract formulations couched in the language
of scientific objectivity. As one seminar participant noted, you pay
your nickel and buy your expert.

Brian D. Boyer also criticizes academicians in his essay,
"Bad Dreams in the Night: The American Housing Con Game." In
his view, scholars should leave their ivory tower to teach the "true
nature" of the housing industry. Boyer argues that Americans are
being exploited systematically by a conspiracy of mortgage lenders,
real estate speculators, and construction interests. In the process,
our cities are being "destroyed for cash." Boyer refers to himself
as a "prairie populist," and in many ways he does exemplify the American populist reformers of the late nineteenth and twentieth centuries,
especially in their zeal for moral crusading and expose journalism.
Boyer closes his discussion with several provocative suggestions for
dealing with our urban housing problems. Most notably, he would
promote direct federal housing delivery, closely regulate mortgage
capital sources, and provide federal insurance for the house buyer
instead of the lender.

In the question-and-answer period that followed Boyer's
seminar presentation, the "prairie populist" got into an extended
discussion with Michael Quinn. In the process, some of the major
characteristics that distinguish reformers like Boyer from many
housing policy researchers and practitioners were revealed. Boyer's
reformist zeal was apparent in several remarks that he made about
the necessity of viewing human acts in morally significant terms.
Those who resist this moral imperative, he claimed, are deluding
themselves. American cities are being ruined by the actions of im-
moral and greedy people who must be held accountable. Boyer warned
that unless housing policies change and are implemented in a responsible and honest fashion, " . . . we will have more housing riots and
they are going to be fierce."

Quinn countered with a plea for a more reasoned analysis. He argued that the Federal Housing Administration's ill-fated entry into the slums in the 1960s was related in a major way to the inflamed passions that touched off the riots of that period. More specifically, it was rhetoric like Boyer's that pressured the FHA into policies that led to disaster in many inner-city neighborhoods. Quinn's point was that there may be heavy costs in approaching housing problems in a highly moralistic way. Moralizing tends to promote rigidity in the participants' positions, thereby reducing the changes for compromise and " . . . for small, pragmatic gains."

The debate became more intense when Boyer suggested that Quinn was arguing for " . . . a continuation of corrupt policies as somehow being more efficient than honest ones." The issue, he declared, was " . . . a question of fundamental justice and law." Housing programs had been administered dishonestly and were filled with scandal. When compared with the magnitude of human need, Quinn's preoccupation with short-term gain was deemed irrelevant. Boyer's position received support from a seminar participant who said that she felt Quinn was wrong in suggesting that the use of rhetoric created a problem for poor people living in slum housing. To this criticism, Quinn responded by pointing out that oratory may be a useful device for spotlighting shortcomings in the system, but it is only a political tool and not a public policy solution. Negotiation and compromise also are needed to deal with complex housing issues and there is little to be gained by " . . . going off and tilting at windmills like Don Quixote."

When the discussion subsided, it was doubtful whether either of the principals had been persuaded by the logic of the other. Boyer's moralizing and Quinn's pragmatism were like two ships passing unseen in the night. While each view has some plausibility in its own right, it is only with great difficulty that the two can be reconciled. More important, perhaps, this kind of communication gap appears with regularity in the politics of urban housing, where it undermines possibilities for fruitful cooperation toward the solution of common problems.

3

MUCH SOUND AND LITTLE FURY: THE PLACE OF RHETORIC IN THE POLITICS OF HOUSING
Michael A. Quinn

"There is a great deal of ferment in the housing field at present, but not much action. Rhetoric has far outrun (and in a sense diverts attention from) any corresponding commitment to allocate resources. "[1]

Unhappily, these words are just as true today as they were when Chester Hartman wrote them in 1967. The politics of housing in our older cities and suburbs exhibit much sound and little fury, much talk and little significant action designed to treat the many problems that continue to plague urban housing. Like it or not, housing ills excite the passions of men of words like problems in few other policy areas. This makes it important to have a clear understanding of the character and uses of oratory in the politics of housing. Accordingly, the central purpose of this essay is twofold. It seeks to outline some of the major rhetorical themes and images put forward by actors in the housing arena, and to explore the consequences of rhetoric for those engaged in the politics of housing. Although general in scope and intent, the argument draws for illustrative purposes on three recent controversies in the housing field—the lead paint poisoning of children residing in dilapidated housing, the scandal at the Federal Housing Administration, and the debate surrounding the prospects for revitalizing of one large midwestern city, St. Louis, Missouri. Before referring to specific cases, however, it is necessary to begin with a few general remarks on the role of rhetoric in the politics of urban housing.

Introduction to the Urban Housing Drama

The key point that must be recognized in this context is one that many housing specialists would rather forget. Words are important in the politics of housing. For better or worse, people respond intensely to the potent symbolism of the spoken word. Language specifies the boundaries and content of public debate, thereby shaping the outcomes of the policy-making process. Rhetoric, which is the art of using words to persuade and convince others, performs several functions for people active in the housing policy arena. First, it provides a way for them to simplify a very complex and often perplexing subject matter. Whether consciously or otherwise, people screen out information that they consider trivial or irrelevant. If simplifying increases the probability of error, perhaps this is the risk that must be assumed if one is to act convincingly in the political process. Participants in the housing policy arena cannot afford the luxury of the ivory tower. They must quiet their doubts in order to act forcefully in the so-called "real world."

Besides simplifying and ordering information on housing problems, rhetoric also provides its advocates with a persuasive philosophy to aid in recruiting people to their cause. Myths provide a valuable source of identity and personal fulfillment for the "true believer," who may, by comparison, find his private life barren and meaningless.[2] Similarly, oratory is useful as a weapon in the political arena, where it provides a convenient formula for exorcising demons who dare to withstand its appeal. For example, it is used frequently to shame lawmakers into action that they might not otherwise take.

Finally, rhetoric is important to actors in the politics of housing because most of them come to believe intensely in the images that they project in the policy arena. Though the premises of their beliefs may be little more than figments of imagination, they are embraced as reality. Thus, the scientific basis of public oratory is a moot question. Saying and believing may result in a self-fulfilling prophecy. Politics, then, boils down to selling your definition of particular problems to the public.

In additon to these positive functions, rhetoric also may produce negative consequences, both for its proponents and for the overall efficiency of the housing delivery system. Significantly, it often tends to obscure facts, issues, and motives, thereby making it difficult to formulate effective approaches to housing problems. Rhetoric has an emotional logic that resists cold calculation and measured response. Confrontations in the housing policy arena frequently assume the form of a morality play in which the forces of good and evil are locked in bitter struggle. Competing social myths or ideologies

serve to escalate the conflict and give the appearance that any one
actor's gain is, necessarily, his opponent's loss. In situations of
this sort, accommodation is very difficult because the moral principles
projected by adversaries do not lend themselves to compromise. One
important consequence of this pattern is that housing improvement
strategies calling for cooperation among actors often are ruled out,
with frustrating results for everyone involved.

Unfortunately, the rhetoric that provides the script for the
housing drama undermines the objectives that the actors have set for
themselves. The irony of these situations is especially apparent when
specific practical goals are sacrificed in favor of taking a strong moral
position against living conditions that are considered intolerable. If
the following remarks have a central theme, it is that where rhetoric
dominates, as it does frequently in the politics of housing, political
activity is likely to be futile and its effects exceedingly perverse. As
we shall see, the politics of housing in our older cities and suburbs
confirm a variation on the old theme: "It's not whether you win or lose,
but how you place the blame."

The Slumlord, Arch-villain

Scapegoating is a prominent motif in the urban housing drama,
a kind of real-life theater that is not noted for heroes or happy endings.
Perhaps the most notorious of all villains on the urban stage is the slumlord, an often maligned figure who has furnished a convenient target
for irate community groups and public officials since the time of the
tenement house reforms that began in the middle of the last century.
Former Mayor Robert Wagner of New York City provides a classic
definition of the slumlord: " . . . that small body of landlords who are
out to squeeze every last dollar out of the property as quickly as they
can, regardless of the consequences in terms of human life, suffering,
and sickness."[3] As suggested by this characteriziation, owners and
managers of slum property are supposed to be greedy, callous individuals who " . . . look [in Julius Horowitz's terms] as though they
had spent their childhood drowning their playmates."[4]

The slumlord often is often cast as a real estate speculator
with extensive property holdings. He seldom resides in his buildings,
preferring instead to work his influence from a distance, more than
likely an expensive suburban location or a well-fortified center-city
realty office. By milking his units, the slumlord allegedly earns excess profits and causes structures to deteriorate to the point where
human health may be imperiled, even to the extent of causing death
or injury to tenants. When such cases come to light, the judgment of

the famous tenement house reformer, Jacob Riis, is brought to bear
against the villain. In one of his many works, Riis wrote that " . . .
murder is murder, whether it is done with an axe or with a house. "[5]

Occasionally, these rhetorical themes of human insensitivity
and greed are embedded in an undercurrent of prejudice, especially
anti-Semitism. In the historical development of large cities in the
Northeast and Midwest of the nation, neighborhoods served as staging
areas for successive waves of immigrants. Tensions were inevitable
as ethnic groups displaced one another over time. In the years since
World War II, blacks and Puerto Ricans have come to reside in formerly white areas, many of which were owned and occupied by Jews.
A sensitive racial dimension is thereby added to the friction inherent
in the traditional relationship between landlord and tenant.

All of these characterizations are, of course, open to question.
In an interesting essay, Michael Stegman goes to great pains to debunk
what he calls "the myth of the slumlord. "[6] Citing the best data available from recent studies, he argues convincingly that most owners
of low-income rental property are small holders who spend the bulk
of their time in other pursuits. He also presents evidence that suggests slumlords are not earning fantastic profits. Hard pressed by
rising operating expenditures, vacancy rates, vandalism, and tenant
militancy, many owners appear to be breaking even or losing money
on their slum properties. In many older urban areas, the bottom has
dropped out of the market leaving numerous center-city real estate
investors holding the proverbial bag. [7]

Though obviously relevant, in a sense these protests are
academic. The myth of the slumlord will continue to persist as long
as it serves a useful function for its proponents that cannot be satisfied
by alternate means. Belief in the existence of a villain who is held
respondible for admittedly deplorable housing conditions may be mandatory in the absence of a firm, substantial commitment to deal with
the realities of the problem at hand—a commitment that no one has
been willing or able to make. In the absence of material efforts to
match the magnitude of the problem, inner-city housing conditions
inspire a highly symbolic kind of politics. Public officials and politicians who find it difficult to fulfill existing financial commitments can
hardly be indicted for attempting to make their constituents feel better.
They often do this by lashing out at suitable scapegoats.

The slumlord fits perfectly the dramatic requirements for
the proper villain. While usually an individual of sufficient stature to
be a credible target, he often is marginal to the city's social and economic establishment. He is thus without substantial capacity to re-
taliate effectively against the politicians who attack him. The villain
also must be an individual for whom it would be difficult to gain much
sympathy, a person who will play the role of the heavy and thereby

provide the media, community groups, and tenants with the opportunity to vent their emotions against the sorry living conditions of the slums. The struggle in the city of St. Louis against the lead-paint poisoning of small children in dilapidated housing provides an excellent case in point. The liberal press and protest groups focused their outrage on a tough, 75-year old landlord, who looks as if he played lineback for the city's football team in his heyday. Here was a man who could be expected to fight, an expectation he more than fulfilled, both in the press and the courts. For example, when questioned about conditions in some of his apartments, the man once had the audacity to suggest that tenants today have it soft, what with hot water and indoor toilets instead of the cold-water flats and outhouses that were common in his time.

This sort of script would be amusing were it not for certain costs implicit in ritual attacks on the slumlord. Late in 1970, when the lead-paint controversy had been raging for about one year, a turning point was reached. The executive vice-president of the Real Estate Board of Metropolitan St. Louis, the local realtors' association, offered to cooperate with community groups in dealing with the problem. If tenants would provide the labor, the realtors would try to supply brushes and lead-free paint for detoxifying rental units where the hazard was found to exist. The realtors' organization also offered to aid in the preparation and distribution of educational literature designed to alert parents whose children might be exposed to lead poisoning.

The board did not have long to wait for an answer. Within a few days, the offer of cooperation was rejected by the leaders of one of the groups that had been protesting local housing conditions. The protesters called for stern enforcement of all aspects of the city's housing code, arguing that "[i]t is criminal negligence for realtors and landlords in this city to perpetuate genocidal conditions and aid urban decay."[8] It would be difficult to imagine a clearer case of dramatic irony. Community groups, in effect, undercut their explicit objective to get the lead out by their unwillingness or inability to depart from the script of the morality play. Instead of working with "genocidal" slumlords when the opportunity arose, they opted for the course of theatrical protest and urged compliance with a strict local ordinance that, if enforced, would result in reduction of the supply of low-cost housing by the route of rent increases and building abandonment.

Heaping public scorn on the slumlord may provide psychological gratification for some people. By providing an emotional release or catharsis, it may even forestall serious forms of political disruption or violence. The price of admission to the housing drama, of course, is that some tenants may be more poorly housed than might

have otherwise been the case if protesters had been able to maintain
a degree of tactical flexibility. Even allowing that the slum landlord
is no do-gooder and that it would be foolish to take the pressure off
him altogether, this conclusion holds. Some possibly useful policy
measures are not initiated because of their negative symbolic value.
To cooperate openly with the landlord, even if only 10 percent of the
time, is to betray the cause and commit political suicide. It simply
is not done. [9]

Speculators, Con Men, and Other Villains

     In addition to the slumlord, many other actors with a role in
the production and delivery of housing have been blamed for the numerous problems associated with substandard housing in our older cities
and suburbs. Builders and labor unions, speculators and developers,
bankers and mortgage lenders, as well as government bureaucrats
and planners have all been identified as villains in the urban housing
drama at one time or another. A couple of examples should serve to
illustrate the script of the drama and some of the supporting cast.
     Woody Klein's study of a slum tenement in the East Harlem
section of New York City provides a perfect case in point. His purpose
is stated succinctly at the outset, where he tells us that his book is
" . . . an attempt to find out where the guilt lies. "[10] In the first part
of his study, Klein conducts a preliminary investigation into the crime
against the building at 311 East 100th Street. He then develops the
evidence against the suspects in the case, beginning with landlords
and ranging over tenants, public officials, and a variety of social-
welfare advocates, whom he calls "soul-makers." Finally, the case
goes to a jury of uncertain composition that returns a guilty verdict
against all of the accused. Significantly, after spending nearly 260
pages allocating guilt, the author devotes a mere seven pages to the
matter of bringing about change in public policy toward the slums. In
place of reasoned argument and practical guidelines for action, Klein
gives us a few pages of undeveloped suggestions and exhortation.
     Many of the substantive themes that emerge frequently in the
housing drama are nicely illustrated by Brian D. Boyer in a recent
expose on the Federal Housing Administration's ill-fated venture into
low-income housing. [11] The National Housing Act of 1968 authorized
the FHA to use its mortgage insurance in conjunction with various
direct subsidy programs to promote homeownership and apartment
construction in the inner city.
     Normal underwriting practices for FHA insurance were re-
laxed in order to increase mortage production in older, blighted areas.

Poor families, including many on public assistance, were put into housing that they could not afford. The shabby quality of much of the new and rehabilitated housing provided under the program combined with slipshod administrative practices and questionable activities on the part of real estate speculators and mortgage companies to produce a near total disaster. The facts of the case make for a beautiful polemic. In Boyer's words,

> Let me say that the disaster known as the FHA scandal was not caused by ignorance or unsophistication. Instead, it was a deliberate program of urban ruin for profit. The destruction of the cities can be understood if put in old-fashioned cops and robbers terms—there were a bunch of bad guys who stuck up the cities and rode away with the gold. [12]

This melodramatic approach, with its insistence on the notion of conspiracy, is typical of the morality play that often substitutes for balanced analysis in this area. An overpowering sense of guilt and rage comes through clearly at several points in his discussion. These strong inner emotions are resolved by a puritanical morality that is displaced on selected scapegoats, especially real estate speculators and mortgage companies. In the author's words, "Too many men, from the exposure of vice, learn the devil's tricks and not what should be done."[13] The response to moral weakness is harsh: punish the bad guys.[14] Like Klein, Boyer is much more concerned with placing blame than he is with practical suggestions that might alter the status quo. Of the 249 pages in his Cities Destroyed for Cash, only the last 10 deal with proposals for policy change.

In a sense, this lack of concern with detailing strategies for change is hardly surprising. Critics of the status quo are seldom charged with running an organization on a daily basis, so naturally they are less concerned with how you move from point A to point B. Also, the notion of conspiracy renders trivial such practical matters. Given the high degree of knowledge and power implicit in the idea of a system-wide conspiracy, the question of policy change is reduced to the status of an insubstantial consideration. Remove the bad men and all else will take care of itself.

If these remarks seem too harsh, we should acknowledge that under certain conditions the expose may be both useful and necessary for bringing about change. It is hard to imagine, for example, that the Progressives at the turn of the century could have succeeded in enacting their tenement house reforms without the likes of Jacob Riis' muckraking book, How the Other Half Lives.[15] At the same time, the political tract designed to raise consciousness of social problems leaves much to be desired as a guide to public policy. This is especially true in areas like housing, where solutions are extremely complex, require an extraordinary degree of coordination of diverse and often conflicting groups, and are likely to threaten vested interests. Boyer's treatment of the FHA scandal is a good case in point. By his own admission, the riots of 1966-68 and the impassioned rhetoric that accompanied them were largely responsible for the decision to send FHA into the slums. [16] Ironically, rhetoric like Boyer's helped push decision makers into a series of ill-conceived and poorly executed actions that aggravated the very problems they were intended to solve. FHA could be criticized no matter what it decided to do.

Though liberals will not find the idea appealing, their political oratory often is counterproductive. The notion that there are no problems without quick, easy solutions is an implication that comes through repeatedly in the urban housing drama. We are frequently confronted with the man-in-the-moon argument. If America can put a man on the moon, why can't she eradicate the slums?[17] The logic of this analogy cannot help but raise expectations to great heights. The cynicism and frustration so apparent in Boyer's polemic is the product of a situation in which expectations outpace accomplishments in the housing sector, and where change comes about slowly. [18]

The rhetoric of the urban housing drama often is perverse in its effects. Although the scapegoating of selected villains may be necessary to attract public attention to particular housing problems, it will likely raise expecations unrealistically and, in the long run, produce cynicism and demoralization. The notion that urban housing ills are exclusively the work of evil men, rather than complex, perplexing problems that would be difficult to deal with even assuming the best of intentions, makes for frustration and bad public policy.

The Legacy of Lincoln Steffens

The sad fact is that many actors in the housing drama have significant stakes in the rhetorical approach to the slums. Although the morality play may make for bad public policy, it is good politics. The media provide a case in point. The urban housing drama could not be presented without the nurturing provided by the media generally and the newspapers of our larger metropolitan areas in particular. In fact, many recent exposes regarding housing conditions have been written by journalists. For example, both Woody Klein and Brian Boyer were reporters who turned to the housing expose as a result of assignments that brought them into close contact with problems of the inner city. Klein was employed by the New York World-Telegram

and Sun, and Boyer has worked for both the Detroit Free Press and
the Chicago Sun-Times. Recent exposes on housing by Joseph Fried
and Leonard Downie, Jr. also were written as a consequence of experiences they gained as reporters for their respective papers, the
New York Times and the Washington Post. [19] While it might be tempt-
ing to believe that these individuals were moved solely out of concern
for the public interest, such an interpretation overlooks the system
of practical rewards available to investigative reporters.

The legacy of moral outrage that turn-of-the-century muck-
raker Lincoln Steffens left to later generations of journalists has
blinded many people to an important point—the investigative reporter
has a practical stake in life like everybody else. The moralizing
tradition of The Shame of the Cities with its exposure of human greed
and corruption functions as a powerful ideology that makes it difficult
to perceive reporters' vested interest. [20] Indeed, this whole area of
practical interest in journalism has been little studied by scholars,
who generally are respectful of the Steffens mystique. A May 1970
conference on "Muckracking: Past, Present, and Future" held at
Pennsylvania State University provides an excellent case in point.
Throughout the proceedings, hardly any mention is made of the benefits that accrue to the practitioners of expose journalism. [21] Aside
from the emotional rewards associated with crusading, one gets the
distinct impression that investigative reporting is a thankless task
that only brings hardship to those who practice it. The public gets an
occasional glimpse behind the moral facade, when Pulitzer Prizes
are awarded or when one learns for instance, that the reporters who
uncovered the Watergate affair will receive nearly $1 million in
magazine, paperback, and movie rights for their bestseller. [22]

These remarks do not mean that investigative reporters and
their employers are never harrassed for their exposes, for they sometimes are. Nor are we trying to suggest that muckrakers do not perform a valuable public service when they uncover corrupt practices
and refer them to appropriate law enforcement agencies. At the same
time, it is also true that many reporters and their papers reap substantial practical payoffs from the journalism of exposure. Newspaper
publishers solidify and extend their hold on the reading public. Successful exposes earn reporters prestige and literary awards from their
colleagues; promotions, pay increases, and bonuses from their employers; and, sometimes, as in the case of Bob Woodward and Carl Bern-
stein of the Washington Post, lucrative contracts from book publishers
and film producers. The moral appeal of the Steffens tradition inac-
curately portrays the stakes that underlie the role of expose journalism
in the urban housing drama. Professional disclaimers notwithstanding,
investigative reporters play a major part in the politics of urban housing.

The art of expose journalism presents critics of the housing
drama with a very real quandary. Although there is much in urban
housing that should be exposed to intelligent public debate and remedial
action, the moral categories employed to make the issues comprehensible to the public inevitably oversimplify, limit flexibility, and sometimes even compel policymakers into reckless measures that make
problems worse than they were initially. From this perspective, one
can understand Roger Starr's suggestion that " . . . nothing could
serve American city government better than putting the works of
Lincoln Steffens on specially restricted shelves in the journalism
schools of the nation."[23] Of course, this deceptively simple solution
begs the real question. How does one attract public attention and
create pressure for action without the rhetoric of moral outrage? No
one has developed any very good answers for this question.

The key role of the media in the housing drama should not
lead us to overlook the fact that numerous other groups also have a
stake in the rhetorical approach to the slums. Community groups
protesting local housing conditions often resort to exalted oratory.
In part, this behavior is a product of how you define "all the news
that's fit to print." Protest grows stale, and groups that employ un-
conventional tactics must escalate their verbal assaults and assume
increasingly bizarre postures if they hope to attract continued news
coverage and keep their issues before the public.[24] At the same time,
it seems clear that many protest leaders have found threatening oratory a useful device that may win them specific, tangible payoffs like
jobs from the establishment.

Other groups receive symbolic rewards from the morality
plays occasioned by urban housing problems. Emerging minority
groups are an example of this phenomenon. The status deprivations
imposed historically on blacks, Mexican-Americans, and other minorities produce intense needs for self-esteem and public expressions
of group identity and unity. These are exactly the kinds of needs for
which exalted rhetoric and public drama are good therapy. From this
perspective, it may even be rational to curse the slumlord rather
than assume a flexible, pragmatic posture which would not totally close
the door on possibilities for cooperation.

Many established interests also receive symbolic gratification from the rhetoric which attends the urban housing drama. As
pointed out by James Q. Wilson, for example, big city mayors have
become increasingly sensitive to demands for appropriate oratory imposed by the media, federal agencies, the foundations, and liberal
voters.[25] A certain amount of faddish rhetoric masquerading as
relevant, forward-looking policy is mandatory for many local elected
officials.

The convergence of these diverse group interests serves to maintain the highly symbolic rituals of the housing drama in our older urban regions, thereby reinforcing two important dilemmas. First, the short-term needs of politics and group psychology militate against the formulation of effective housing strategies. Second, although the drama often may be necessary to raise issues and get action on housing problems, it tends to lock the actors into inflexible, adversary roles, even in those situations where a different approach would increase the likelihood of payoff. As a result, the frustrating logic of the morality play often substitutes for improved housing conditions.

The Villain's Retort: Blaming the Victim

If these remarks seem to place the burden for the morality play exclusively with liberal actors, it should be noted that conservatives also are active on the urban stage. Indeed, the housing drama could scarcely be played without the balance provided by a conservative rhetoric. Conservative actors engage in what their liberal opponents call "blaming the victims."[26] Next to the villain, the victim is the most important figure in the urban housing drama. In the normal course of events, the number two role is choreographed by the same players who initiate action against the bad guy. If the villain is accused of doing evil, the audience cannot react until it has some conception of the party that has been wronged. The making of the villain and the casting of the victim go hand in hand. By contrasting the powerful, inhuman villain with helpless victims, a dramatically effective situation is established that inclines the audience in favor of the underdog.

The victim in the housing scenario invariably is cast as a meek, powerless individual without substantial capability to respond to insult or injury on his own behalf. If women, the elderly, the infirm, or small children can be recruited for this role, the villain is likely to be condemned by the audience. A good case in point is provided in the work of Jacob Riis, a master choreographer of the urban housing drama who left us many unforgettable portraits of the victim. There is, for example, his story about little Susie Rocco. Riis tells us that little Susie was " . . . as good a girl as you can find in Philadelphia."[27] She and her mother had been abandoned by a no-good father who left them to the impoverishment of marginal employment in a slum area of the city, where they soon fell on dark days. The author's development of the plot is worth citing at length:

Everything went to the pawnshop, last of all the
mother's wedding ring. . . . [The mother] had to
go to the hospital then; the doctor said so. Susie
wept. . . . could not bear the thought. She cast
about in the house for something that was yet of
value enough to take to the pawnshop, so that she
might stay the evil day, and she found [her] doll.
It was not a nice doll by that time; it was very much
in need of the hospital itself. But to Susie it was beyond compare, for was it not her doll baby? She did
it up in a newspaper and carried it to the pawnshop
with tears, for she was bringing the greatest sacrifice
of all. And that bad man, when he unrolled the bundle
and saw what it held, smashed the doll angrily against
the stove and put little Susie out into the street. There
she stood and wept, as if she would cry her eyes
out. . . . [28]

This sort of melodrama, although perhaps a bit heavy by today's standards, nonetheless compels sympathy for the helpless victims while
directing fury at the villain of the piece. The latter, for his part, ad-
heres to the script by engaging in the conservative practice of blaming
the victim. In the case of little Susie, one can imagine the pawnbroker
blaming the poverty of his clients on weak moral character or laziness.
Riis himself acknowledges that Susie's father was "a loafer" and that
both mother and daughter were forced to repair whiskey flasks in
order to make a living. [29]

Conservative rhetoric also is apparent on the contemporary
scene in a problem we dealt with earlier, the lead-paint poisoning of
small children. In this scenario, defenseless toddlers living in old,
dilapidated housing are poisoned by eating flaking chips of toxic lead
paint that was used widely in housing up until the 1950s. As we have
seen, the liberal press and community groups blame the slumlord for
this tragedy. Landlords, in turn, accuse the victims, the parents of
the poisoned children, who fail to watch their offspring and keep a
sanitary apartment. The distinctive feature in all such cases of blaming the victim is an insistence on the personal responsibility of the
injured party for his own sorry state. While liberals may curse the
privileged and "the system" that serves them, conservatives search
for flaws in the personal character or life-style of the victims.

Some conservative commentators have refined their moral
judgments about the victims into full-blown social theories. Edward
Banfield's conception of "lower-class subculture" is a noteworthy
example:

> The lower-class forms . . . a single problem: the
> existence of an outlook and style of life which . . .
> attaches no value to work, sacrifice, self-improve-
> ment, or service to family, friends, or community.
> Social workers, teachers, and law-enforcement
> officials—all . . . "caretakers"—cannot achieve
> their goals because they can neither change nor
> circumvent this cultural obstacle. [30]

In this view, the solution for difficult urban problems rests not in
attacking the privileged or in radically changing "the system." The
only adequate answer is to be found in a combination of social control
and moral reeducation of the lower-class individual. As Banfield
argues at one point in The Unheavenly City, " . . . the problems pose
by the lower class can be solved fundamentally only if the children of
that class are removed from their parents' culture."[31]

In fairness to Banfield, it should be noted that some liberal
scholars have subscribed to the notion of a lower-class subculture,
especially the so-called "culture of poverty" thesis popularized in
the work of the late well-known anthropologist, Oscar Lewis.[32] Still,
liberal and conservative views on the subject differ considerably.
While the former tend to empathize strongly and adopt a permissive,
almost romantic attitude toward the poor and oppressed, conservatives
like Banfield emphasize the "pathologies" of lower-class life styles
and the subsequent need for social control and moral indoctrination.

The basic problem with conservative doctrine is that it con-
ceals motives and distorts issues every bit as much as does liberal
rhetoric. For example, parental neglect, presumably a major short-
coming of lower-class subculture, only touches on one possible source
of the lead-paint poisoning problem. Other factors are perhaps more
important. Attention might be paid to the weak enforcement of housing
codes or the unhealthy tendency to ingest non-food substances that
affects many small children, regardless of the social class standing
of their parents. The point that must be stressed here is that this
distinctive problem of slum housing has many causes, and oversimp-
lification necessarily does injury to what is, in fact, a most perplexing public health problem. One-sided interpretations also are suspect
because they conceal the practical interests of their advocates. In the
case at hand, it is useful for the landlord to blame tenants for their
poisoned children because it conveniently diverts attention from his
own role in producing the problem.

Whether viewed from the conservative or the liberal angle,
whether you elect to blame the victim or pillory the landlord, it should
be apparent that the rhetorical approach inevitably distorts the am-
biguities of difficult problems while obscuring the role of self-interest

In so doing, rhetoric makes it exceedingly difficult to find effective solutions for pressing housing problems.

Prophets of Doom versus Civic Promoters

If further proof is needed of the power of words to shape the politics of our older urban areas, one only has to recall the furor surrounding the pessimistic 1973 report on St. Louis by the RAND Corporation, one of the nation's foremost research organizations.[33] The RAND controversy is instructive because it provides a current example of an old theme in the urban housing drama—the conflict between the detractors and the promoters of the city. The anti-urban sentiment rooted in our agrarian heritage extends back to colonial times and, perhaps for this reason, it appears to be the stronger of the two currents of thought. Writings by Thomas Jefferson, Alexis de Tocqueville, and, more recently, by Edward Banfield suggest that the city is a sordid, evil place threatening to the moral character of the citizen and the stability of our system of government.[34] This philosophy has functioned at various times to channel national energies away from the problems of the city. The Nixon administration policy of "benign neglect" is only the most recent example of this traditional antiurban bias.

The "city beautiful" theme, on the other hand, was rather late in developing because it had to wait on the emergence of the industrial city and the urban planning profession in the late nineteenth century, when Walt Whitman celebrated the strengths of urban America. In recent years, Ada Louise Huxtable, Jane Jacobs, and others have attempted to project a positive image of the big city as a fascinating, rewarding place in which to live.[35] The ideals of this school of thought provided the vital force behind the urban renewal program in the 1950s and 1960s until it became apparent that the "city beautiful" rhetoric was distorting what the program actually was doing. In place of the decent home and suitable living environment for every American family that had been promised by the Housing Act of 1949, urban renewal substantially decreased the supply of low-cost housing, while benefiting upper-income and large commercial interests at the expense of urban minority groups.[36] For a period during the 1960s, this concern with the plight of minorities and the poor led many of the city beautiful" crowd to sympathize with the liberal rhetoric of the "urban crisis," in hopes that it would bring more positive attention to bear on the problems of the city. As suggested by the RAND controversy, however, the promoters of the city soon realized that continual crisis-mongering was only playing into the hands of those who wished to portray the city as a nasty place.

Though couched in cautious academic language, the RAND report on St. Louis, issued in October 1973, was widely interpreted as sounding the death knell for the city. The document emphasized the marked decline in population and economic activity experienced by the city during the 1960s, along with the rapid rate of housing abandonment that accompanied this process. After examining the impact of public policies on these trends and a number of alternatives open to local decisionmakers, the report concluded that deterioration of the city was likely to continue.

Despite the trite character of the RAND findings, public recitation of the city's many economic and housing woes by so renowned an institution made the city fathers turn red with rage. Expressions of wounded civic pride were forthcoming from many local leaders. The Board of Aldermen passed a resolution condemning the report. The city's planning director promptly labeled the RAND document " . . . a sort of gloom and doom report," and the president of Downtown St. Louis, Inc. admitted that it made him "damn mad."[37]

Specific criticisms of the RAND document were numerous. Many objected to the statement that the city of St. Louis had slipped from a position of primacy in the metropolitan area to that of being one suburb among others. Some critics were unhappy with the conservative label that the report affixed to the local banking community. Others felt that adequate attention had not been paid to recent plans for commercial and residential construction in the city. Finally, the St. Louis report was part of a larger study financed by the National Science Foundation for more than $1 million. For this amount of money, critics argued, the document contained few practical suggestions that local leaders could use to improve the plight of the city. Instead, the report suggested that many important decisions affecting the city's future were outside the control of local authorities. St. Louisans were cast as sorry victims of circumstance, who could do little on their own to significantly counter the long-term decline of their city. Ultimately, it was probably this suspicion of impotence that elicited the most indignant responses from community leaders.

The city fathers were outraged partly because the gloom and doom of the report undermined the image of civic rejuvenation that they hoped to promote. Spokesmen for the new city administration, the large downtown banks, and the recently created Regional Commerce and Growth Association (RCGA) were especially active in the attempt to create a renewed sense of pride and confidence in the future of the city. In spring 1974, the civic promoters launched a public relations counterattack called "St. Louis has it! A to Z." This $2 million effort is designed to sell St. Louisans on a new, positive image of their city. The executive vice-president of the RCGA explained that "St. Louis is like an awkward adolescent girl who must 'feel pretty' before her

charms will work on potential suitors."[38] The St. Louisan must be
made to believe that he is happy living in the city. If he is told that
he is happy often enough, he may begin to believe it and, believing,
he may begin to act in ways that actually enhance the character of
the city as a place in which to live, work, and, most importantly, do
business. As suggested by Norton Long, civic leadership today requires highly developed skills with bell, book, and candle. In large
part, leadership is a matter of driving out unclean thoughts and ex-
horting people to a greater sense of civic purpose and community. [39]

Of course, a moment's reflection will suggest the difficulty
in destroying Edward Banfield's frightening conception of the unheavenly city. The difficult problems of housing, economics, and social
welfare that afflict our older urban areas will not give way easily, if
at all, before a wave of oratory and wishful thinking. Moreover, city
promoters have to contend with the prophets of doom, who will continue to project visions of urban horrors like the public housing ghost
town at Pruitt-Igoe.

On the positive side, words do count for something, and
neither the power of public relations nor the possibility of self-fulfilling prophecy should be discounted. If the urban housing drama
has any single lesson, it is that, for better or worse, people respond
intensely to political rhetoric and symbolism. If good public relations
can create the climate of civic boosterism necessary to revitalize
the city, then rhetoric can have a positive impact. At present, it is
too early to tell whether the civic promoters or the doomsday crowd
will succeed in establishing their definition of the city.

The Curtain Falls: Prospects for a Happy Ending

In closing, we have seen that the urban housing drama is not
noted for heroes or happy endings. Instead, the script of the morality
play that typifies the politics of housing in our older cities and suburbs
features victims and villains locked into an apparent no-win situation.
Although rhetoric may perform positive functions, more often it pro-
duces distorted, pathetic caricatures of complex realities. Inflamed
oratory also tends to push actors into rigid positions and unproductive
actions that serve to undermine many of the goals that they have set
for themselves. In particular, actors in the morality play frequently
sacrifice small, pragmatic payoffs in favor of the diffuse, emotional
satisfactions that the muse of the drama allots to those who follow
the course of no compromise.

The structure of the urban housing stage where the drama
takes place makes it difficult for those who would write a happy ending

to the play. Most importantly, the drama is neither written nor choreographed by a single person. Housing conditions are determined by the disjointed and often contradictory choices made by thousands of individuals acting in their own self-interest. This highly fragmented situation makes it impossible for any single actor, whether governmental or private, to impose solutions for pressing problems.[40] Perhaps this perplexing fragmentation also helps to account in part for the highly rhetorical sort of political activity discussed in this essay, a politics of much sound and little fury, much noise and little significant movement.

Barring the possibility of basic structural change or revolution, which is unlikely, what are the prospects for a satisfactory conclusion to the housing drama? Without some change in the orientation of the actors to their respective roles, the prospects probably are not very good. Exalted oratory will more than likely continue to play a major part in the politics of housing. As noted earlier, many groups have both practical and symbolic stakes in the rhetorical approach to housing problems. Unfortunately, it also is true that these problems sometimes might be ignored altogether were it not for the incentive provided by inspired rhetoric. Despite these gloomy observations, it is possible to conclude on a hopeful note by offering a few common-sense suggestions for upgrading the performances of players in the drama.

Actors should attempt to avoid situations in which rhetoric forecloses the possibility of fruitful cooperation with opponents when opportunities present themselves. This is most important. Protest theatrics may help to create the leverage necessary to get to the bargaining table.[41] At some point, however, protest must give way to practical politics if concrete gains are to be registered. At no time should flexibility be sacrificed to empty rhetoric and ideology. This is basically an argument for a more pragmatic, instrumental approach to oratory. Admittedly, this will not be easy to achieve, especially for minority groups searching for a new, positive identity in a rapidly changing society. Still, the tangible payoffs likely to follow from a more pragmatic approach would justify the effort involved.

Next, the players in the urban housing drama might benefit by simply trying to view themselves in the place of their opponents. In the process of empathizing, the link between ideology and practical self-interest is clarified, thereby offsetting the tendency of rhetoric to obscure this very important relationship. With improved understanding of group interests, it may then be possible to approach the issues in a more constructive, practical fashion.

Finally, no amount of rhetoric or wishful thinking can eliminate the differences in self-interest that separate political actors and give them their distinctive identities. These differences must be confronted honestly and with knowledge that much patience and hard work are required to reach an accommodation. The incentive for such an undertaking can only be that it is better to get part of what you want than nothing at all. This is precisely the sense in which it is better to have less sound and a little more fury.

NOTES

1. Chester W. Hartman, "The Politics of Housing," Dissent 14 (November-December 1967), p. 701.

2. Eric Hoffer, The True Believer: Thoughts on the Nature of Mass Movements (New York: Harper & Row, 1951).

3. Quoted in Woody Klein, Let in the Sun (New York: Macmillan Co., 1964), p. 201.

4. Quoted in David R. Hunter, The Slums: Challenge and Response (New York: Free Press, 1964), p. 10.

5. Jacob A. Riis, The Peril and the Preservation of the Home (Philadelphia: George W. Jacobs & Co., 1903), pp. 141-142.

6. Michael A. Stegman, "The Myth of the Slumlord," American Institute of Architects Journal 53, no. 3 (March 1970), pp. 45-49.

7. See Michael A. Stegman, Housing Investment in the Inner City: The Dynamics of Decline, A Study of Baltimore, Maryland, 1968-1970 (Cambridge, Mass.: MIT Press, 1972); and George Sternlieb, The Tenement Landlord (New Brunswick, N.J.: Urban Studies Center, Rutgers, State University, 1966).

8. "Assails Realty Unit on Lead Poison Codes," St. Louis Post-Dispatch, December 20, 1970.

9. This does not mean that some slumlords aren't guilty of the charges that liberals have made against them. Our point is a relatively modest one: (1) it is doubtful whether all landlords fit the stereotype of the slumlord; and (2) advocates of change should not allow their rhetoric to lock them into inflexible positions in dealings with opponents, regardless of the truth or falsehood of moral judgments.

10. Klein, op. cit., p. xv.

11. Brian D. Boyer, Cities Destroyed for Cash: The FHA Scandal at HUD (Chicago: Follett Publishing Company, 1973).

12. Ibid., p. 4.

13. Ibid., p. 238.

14. In Boyer's words, "Since the automobile industry didn't get 'enlightened' until it was kicked in the ass a time or two, the same favor should be paid to the construction, real estate and mortgage industries." Ibid., pp. 248-249.

15. Jacob A. Riis, How the Other Half Lives (New York: Charles Scribner's Sons, 1892).

16. Boyer, op. cit., p. 20.

17. See Klein, op. cit., p. 259.

18. Overall, there has been improvement in the quality of the American housing stock since World War II. Census data show a steady decline in the percentage of substandard units since 1950. See Edwin S. Mills, Urban Economics (Glenview, Ill.: Scott, Foresman & Co., 1972), p. 166.

19. See Joseph P. Fried, Housing Crisis U.S.A. (New York: Praeger Publishers, 1971); and Leonard Downie, Jr., Mortgage on America (New York: Praeger Publishers, 1974).

20. Lincoln Steffens, The Shame of the Cities (New York: McClure, Phillips & Co., 1904).

21. See John M. Harrison and Harry H. Stein, eds., Muckraking: Past, Present, and Future (University Park: Pennsylvania State University Press, 1973).

22. See "The Woodstein Papers," Newsweek 83, no. 15, (April 15, 1974), p. 79.

23. Roger Starr, The Living End: The City and Its Critics (New York: Coward-McCann, 1966), p. 69.

24. See Michael Lipsky, Protest in City Politics: Rent Strikes, Housing and the Power of the Poor (Chicago: Rand McNally & Co., 1970), pp. 169-172.

25. James Q. Wilson, "The Mayors vs. the Cities," The Public Interest, no. 16 (Summer 1969), 25-37.

26. See the interesting study by William Ryan, Blaming the Victim (New York: Pantheon Books, 1971).

27. Riis, Peril and Preservation of the Home, p. 102.

28. Ibid., pp. 102-103.

29. Ibid., p. 102.

30. Edward C. Banfield, The Unheavenly City: The Nature and Future of Our Urban Crisis (Boston, Mass.: Little, Brown and Co., 1968), p. 211.

31. Ibid., p. 229.

32. For an interesting discussion and critique of this thesis, see Charles A. Valentine, Culture and Poverty: Critique and Counter Proposals (Chicago: University of Chicago Press, 1968).

33. Barbara R. Williams, St. Louis: A City and Its Suburbs (Santa Monica, Calif.: The RAND Corporation, 1973). Originally set up in 1946 as a defense-related research organization sponsored by the U.S. Air Force and Douglas Aircraft, RAND has diversified and become involved in a variety of domestic and urban-related projects in recent years.

34. The anti-urban theme in American intellectual history is documented in Morton and Lucia White, The Intellectual Versus the City: From Thomas Jefferson to Frank Lloyd Wright (Cambridge, Mass.: Harvard University Press, 1962). Also see Banfield, op. cit.

35. See Ada Louise Huxtable, Will They Ever Finish Bruckner Boulevard? (New York: Macmillan Co., 1970); and Jane Jacobs, The Death and Life of Great American Cities (New York: Vintage Books, 1961).

36. See Martin Anderson, The Federal Bulldozer: A Critical Analysis of Urban Renewal, 1949-62 (Cambridge, Mass.: MIT Press, 1964); and Scott Greer, Urban Renewal and American Cities (Indianapolis, Ind.: Bobbs-Merrill Co., 1965).

37. See Robert Cassidy, "St. Louis Tunes Out the Blues," Planning 40, no. 3 (March 1974), p. 14.

38. "Get with it, St. Louis, and Spread the Good News: You!," St. Louis Globe-Democrat, April 27-28, 1974, p. 1A.

39. For Long's position, see Norton E. Long, The Unwalled City: Reconstituting the Urban Community (New York: Basic Books, Inc., 1972), Preface and Chapter 1.

40. See the useful piece by Nathan Glazer, "Housing Problems and Housing Policies," The Public Interest, no. 7 (Spring 1967), 21-51.

41. See Lipsky, op. cit.

4

BAD DREAMS IN THE NIGHT: THE AMERICAN HOUSING CON GAME
Brian D. Boyer

American housing policy today is among the most regressive, careless, stupid, and destructive of any free government in the world. I intend to tell you some of the reasons why I think this is so and why I fear that at least half of the American population is in the process of being evicted or foreclosed by both the private and the governmental sectors. I'll tell you about my concern for the fabric of our society in a time of housing chaos, and as an unlettered and unappointed prophet I will present some solutions to the housing problems that give us bad dreams in the night. I speak not only for myself but also for 50 million or more for whom decent housing is a dream being betrayed in American life.

My knowledge of housing was miniscule until early 1972, when as night city editor for the Detroit Free Press I became alarmed about what appeared to be the steady destruction of the city. Investigation revealed that at least 10 percent of the city's housing was being deserted, burned, and bulldozed down. Further questioning led me to the conclusion that the decline of Detroit was the direct product of misadministration by the Federal Housing Administration (FHA), and the involvement of the federal government with a series of gangsters, speculators, and mortgage bankers, many of whom wore all three job titles simultaneously. Finally, it became apparent that the blight and abandonment that were devouring Detroit were not isolated phenomena but a widespread epidemic of FHA, a crippling disease that strikes at the heart of American cities, usually causing death or permanent disfigurement. I finally became aroused enough to write a book entitled Cities Destroyed for Cash, which describes in grim detail the largest, most profitable criminal conspiracy in American history. [1]

How did the scandal get started? Quite simply, our elected representatives were duped by the powerful Washington housing lobby that is headed by the guys in the home loan business. Congress had its conscience pricked by the riots of the 1960s; it wanted to do justice to urban blacks and to throw water on the flaming cities. But the congressmen listened to the professionals rather than the people. The housing boys sat down together, carved the turf and emerged with a set of programs that would make them all filthy rich. The result was the National Housing Act of 1968, the piece of legislation which authorized a $70 billion raid on the U.S. Treasury by the housing professionals.

In simplified terms, the great housing confidence game worked this way. A suede-shoe artist buys a dilapidated house at a low price, makes a few cosmetic repairs, and then bribes an FHA official to appraise the structure for twice its value. The speculator seeks a poor, naive buyer, often a black mother with children on welfare, and arranges an FHA-insured loan through a predatory mortgage outfit. Nobody accepts the responsibility when the house deteriorates and its market value falls faster than the amount of the mortgage outstanding. The surprised owner is soon forced to abandon the dwelling and the mortgage company forecloses. In addition to points on the sale and a commission for servicing the loan, the lender gets his money back from the government, and the speculator gets his windfall profit. Nobody cares about the shattered dreams of the homebuyer, or the abandoned hulk that destroys the quality of life in our cities. The vultures feast on the innocent and the poor, while lawmakers sleep. Nationwide, this confidence game will result in the foreclosure and eventual destruction of at least a half million houses and apartment units.

Needless to say, it was difficult to uncover the facts of this scandal. Getting accurate information from the FHA is like getting the proverbial blood from a stone. The agency's operations are concealed from view by a dense shroud of secrecy. FHA officials give you either the runaround or misleading information. It is a strange, ironic situation, to say the least. Initial inquiries concerning the scandal were met with disclaimers of wrongdoing and accusations of yellow journalism and muckraking directed at this investigator. At the same time, government officials steadfastly refused to furnish the accurate information necessary to do a thorough job of reporting the situation.

Here is a case in point. In 1972 the Department of Housing and Urban Development, which is FHA's parent agency, announced officially that it had an inventory of 7,574 houses in Detroit. This figure represents the number of foreclosed mortgages or bad investments that had been made by FHA in that city. What this statistic does not reveal is that there were an additional 3,000 houses locally that the agency was holding in limbo by placing them in a category called "redemption," a semantic subterfuge that refers to the final phase of the foreclosure proceeding. Worse yet, there were another 23,000 houses with mortgages in serious default. If we take the estimate of the government's General Accounting Office that roughly 75 percent of the dwellings in serious default will be foreclosed, the Detroit inventory should have been placed at some 28,000 houses either foreclosed or certain of foreclosure. You do not have to be an expert at statistics to recognize that there is a significant difference between 7,574 and 28,000. The FHA's figures are clearly intended to mislead the average citizen and to put a rosy glow on a thoroughly wormy apple. The government lies to the public in an effort to conceal its own incompetence.

The incompetence of HUD personnel is legendary. Even former HUD Secretary George Romney admitted that it takes a federal bureaucrat nearly a year to learn what a clerk in private business masters in a couple of weeks. I am not suggesting that this ineptitude exonerates government personnel from responsibility in the scandal. To the contrary, many FHA officials were in league with confidence men in the real estate speculation and mortgage banking business. Sometimes the vultures even assume the mantle of government authority. For example, in 1974 the former chief of a large mortgage banking firm, Mortgage Associates, was HUD's Assistant Secretary for Housing Production and Mortgage Credit. Obviously, the operating philosophy for housing programs under the Nixon administration was to put the wolf in charge lest some of the lambs escape. In addition to Watergate crimes, Richard Nixon should be indicted for his misadministration of the 1968 National Housing Act that has caused so much destruction in our cities. Romney ought to be tried along with him for incompetence. [2]

I firmly believe that problems in American housing always begin with the mortgage capital source because town planning in the United States starts not with a plan, but with a mortgage. This fact was brought home recently to the writer by a not so rare personal experience.

I've always been a renter, not a homeowner, so the problems of buying a house have always belonged to somebody else. Recently, I found a little stone house and 15 acres of land that I wanted to buy near Galena, Illinois, as a retreat and a fail-safe home in reserve for the end of the world, so I did what a person usually does in these situations. I called my friendly banker, American National Bank, in downtown Chicago.

The receptionist told me the mortgage loan officer wasn't in and, furthermore, he couldn't return my telephone call because he doesn't return anybody's telephone calls. Mortgage officers have an

especially high opinion of their own worth. Humbly I called back
several hours later and reached the mortgage loan officer himself.
I explained that I had a savings account and several checking accounts
at the bank, and I wondered what the procedure was to apply for a
mortgage loan at American National. "Do you have a second floor
banker?" the man asked suspiciously. "No," I admitted, "I don't."
"Is a second floor banker necessary to get a mortgage?" "Yes," he
told me. Well then, I allowed, I wanted one of them. "How do I get
a second floor banker?" I asked him. "To begin with," he replied in
somewhat superior tones, "You have to have at least $75,000 in non-
interest-bearing deposits." Lately, I've had a little better luck. I
haven't found a mortgage yet, but I was offered a land contract if I
put down $10,000 cash, only 40 percent.

The 40 percent figure reminds me that the number of mortgages now being given in the greater Chicago area is down 40 percent
this year over last. It's virtually impossible to get FHA insurance in
any circumstances except when the government itself is selling previously repossessed property. Today, five to seven points and more
are being charged at the front end of conventional mortgages for persons
with good credit and financial track records. FHA sales cost up to
12 points.

Recently, I talked with a man who was unfortunate enough to
get hit by points on both ends of a transaction in which he sold one
house and bought another. In the first instance, he sold FHA and had
to pay eight points to the mortgage company. When he went to buy
the new house, he was charged seven points up front by the savings and
loan association. That totals up to 15 points the poor fellow paid, or
$4,500 in order to purchase a new $30,000 home with 25 percent of his
own money down. He complained to me that he felt as though he had been
run over by a truck. He said something else, too, that is more significant. He declared, "I was in the Navy during World War II, and
I've raised my family and kept my nose clean, paid my taxes and
saved my money. Now I'm getting [the worst] because of it. I'm not
sure who's at fault. But when I find out, they're going to pay." This
man's plight is atypical only in that he had both the cash on hand to
pay the points, and he found a conventional mortgage to buy a new house.
He was lucky to get a new house at all, let alone one for under $30,000,
which is rock bottom on new houses being built in most parts of the
country. At this price, about half of all American families cannot afford to purchase a new house under any circumstances.

We are building new housing only for the powerful, the influential, and the rich. The private sector of our economy, which
traditionally has been responsible for 98 percent of all home building
in the country, has abdicated outright the construction and delivery
of housing to half of the American public. At the same time, the

mortgage bankers, savings and loan associations, and commercial
banks are engaged in ferocious lobbying to remove the usury limit on
mortgage loans. Recently, the money lenders in Illinois succeeded in
pushing this limit up from 8 to 9.5 percent. Their ultimate goal is to let
mortgage rates rise, presumably to prime or above, in the name of
free enterprise, but mortgage rates of 10 to 12 percent are usury,
which is by definition, tradition, and law, a crime. It is a crime that
once carried the death penalty. If we allow usurious interest rates to
become the prevailing interest rates, we are insuring extraordinary
rates of inflation, social discontent and disturbance, and eventually
the death of our society. Certainly, the incredible facts of the FHA
scandal indicate that the desctruction is going on now.

Mortgage capital is also engaged in a number of other socially
destructive practices. By "red-lining," or refusing to make loans,
in wide areas in our older cities, mortgage-writing institutions cause
urban blight and racial segregation. Recently, research by the Chicago
Title Insurance Company showed that savings and loan associations
located in the city of St. Louis have been siphoning the dollars of city
residents into affluent St. Louis County, while making only token
amounts available for mortgages and home improvement loans in the
city. [3] As if this were not bad enough, the data suggested that the
scarce city dollars were going to promote the blockbusting tactics of
speculators in racially changing neighborhoods. If there is anybody
who still believes that housing segregation in our cities is simply the
product of choice by large numbers of black and white citizens, I
would suggest a simple experiment. If the skeptic is white and he has
good enough credit to qualify for a mortgage, he should try to buy a
house in a black or changing neighborhood. He will find the experience
at least as frustrating as a black in the same position who is trying to
buy a house in the largely white suburbs of any major city in the United
States.

The mortgage capital sources in our country are a plague
on the older cities. The facts of the case lend credence to an updated
version of the colonial exploitation thesis. Mortgage capital sucks the
life blood out of the increasingly black center-city areas to fatten the
already welathy, white suburbs and it's being done in the name of free
enterprise.

Real estate speculators and the building trades also are involved deeply in the destruction of our cities. The speculators provide
the motive energy for the disinvestment in our cities and the unplanned,
jerry-built housing developments that have made a shambles of our
countryside. They are the suede-shoe boys whose unethical hustle and
scare tactics in racially changing areas promote white flight and de-
stabilize residential patterns. They are the interface that enables
mortgage capital to flee the cities and they pay off suburban officials

to make zoning changes that lead to windfall profits. All speculators
may not bribe officials, but I can pick any rapidly growing suburb and
find consistent patterns of zoning payoffs and graft. Without exception,
my friends in the homebuilding and land industries tell me that 5 to 10
percent of project costs are budgeted for graft. When we talk about
land and housing speculation, we are discussing what may be the most
corrupt business in the United States. The building trades have their
own hustle going. Not only are their wage demands outrageous, and
getting worse, but their craftmanship is poor. A group of Scandan-
avian builders recently came to Chicago to look at home buildings.
They were uniformly shocked at the shoddy workmanship by carpenters,
tinners, plumbers, and other tradesmen. Their comment was that
such workmanship, commonly found in American home building, would
be subject to immediate disciplinary actions in their own countries,
including the revocation of the workman's trade and union cards.

     In the face of all this, federal housing policies have been and
continue to be a massive failure. The situation is getting worse at a
time when private housing development is also in serious trouble. It
seems as though the housing crisis our black citizens have lived with
for half a century is now spilling over the economic lowlands of white
society. As blacks have bitterly resented bad housing, whites resent
it too. Crisis is a strong word, and we have recent, dismal experience
to tell us what it means. The urban riots that scorched our cities in
the 1960s have been variously defined as a social problem, and as an
economic one, but in large part, they were a housing problem, a
housing crisis if you will. Unless drastic and massive changes are
made, we will have new riots, and the participants will not be limited
to black and brown citizens. White housing groups in Chicago, New
York, Philadelphia, and other major cities are ethnic, conservative,
and very, very angry. Direct action in the form of demonstrations,
picketing, and other expressions of rage are the commonly chosen
methods of bringing their plight to public attention. If the legitimate
complaints of these people are not solved, their protests will escalate
and take more militant forms. They will join their protests with those
of citizens of darker skins.

     In facing up to severe housing problems, other western demo-
cracies take a direct role in the construction and financing of housing
for their citizens. J. S. Fuerst, assistant director of urban studies
at Loyola University in Chicago, points out in an important new book
that 35 percent of all housing in Great Britain is under government
auspices. [4] One-third of all housing units in West Germany and Den-
mark are either under cooperative, union, or public auspices. In
France, the public housing figure is 15 percent of all housing, plus
about 33 percent of current production. The figure in Israel is more
than 50 percent.

The figure in the United States is statistically negligible, 3 percent of the nation's total housing units. And the percentage is dropping, when we need about 26 million new homes within the next decade. If we are to have any chance of meeting this goal and averting the growing restiveness of our ill-housed citizens, both the federal and state governments must become involved in the direct provision of housing to a far greater extent than they are now. The argument that direct delivery can't work falls down in the face of the experience of almost every other western democracy.

The character of federal subsidies for low- and moderate-income housing programs also must be altered drastically if Cities Destroyed for Cash is to become a library curiosity rather than a recurring drama. The government should insure the mortgage holder against foreclosure and the house against substantial defects rather than insuring the lender as is done presently. It is most important. In practice, this would mean that FHA insurance would become operative when the homeowner missed mortgage payments for reasons beyond his control, such as for sickness or work layoffs. Coverage should also extend to major structural defects, guaranteeing items like the foundation and roof, wiring, plumbing, and heating systems. These changes in FHA policies would benefit everyone involved in housing transactions, stabilize deteriorating neighborhoods, and frustrate the sort of confidence game that characterized the recent scandal. Also, the money saved by insuring the owner rather than the lender would provide a valuable source of capital for supporting related federal efforts in housing.

In addition to these measures, there should be no more interest subsidy programs of any kind. They are too expensive and have a serious inflationary effect on the national economy. Instead of abandoning the philosophy of helping the low-income individual, the government should make available direct mortgages with very low yields, down to 1 percent, the same interest rate presently being paid by people under the 235 and 236 federal housing programs. This change in policy would lower the cost of homeownership or rental effectively without costing any money. The mortgage loans will be paid back with interest, making dollars available for reinvestment in housing for the needy. By placing competitive pressure on private lenders, direct federal mortgages would also have the salutary effect of containing interest rates in the private market. I might add here that the argument that direct government mortgage loans are inflationary is absurd. High interest rates are one of the key inflationary forces. Low rates exert a stabilizing influence. The government need not print more money in order to make these loans, for it is now rolling in money harvested from windfall tax income produced as a result of inflation.

One other point should be entered in this context: FHA should be thoroughly reorganized with a view toward eliminating the possibility of corrupt practices. The FHA ought to be separated from the patronage pork barrel at HUD and its personnel should be upgraded by instituting appropriate training programs and hiring procedures. The cookbook approach to insuring should be discarded in favor of a review process that looks at applications in their entirety. A small team of qualified people should go through all of the insuring process together. By working as teams rather than individuals, FHA personnel will find it much more difficult to accept bribes and keep it secret. Under no condition should the agency be sold out to private business, which is always sniffing around for a fast buck. Properly administered, the FHA can be one of the most valuable of all federal "social" programs.

Earlier, I noted that all city planning in the United States begins with a mortgage rather than a plan. My final substantive recommendations for realigning American housing policy deal with these two areas. All housing, whether for urban redevelopment or suburban construction, should come about only after legally binding land-use plans are established at the state and municipal levels. Obviously, I feel the need for more and better housing is critical, and I don't want to fall into the traditional trap of years of planning without any construction. But we need autonomous governmental planning units that are accountable to the people and not to other governmental units. Presumably, a great deal of confusion would exist as these planning units get under way and absorb the present planning functions of city and state governments, but since they will function with the force of law, their creation will soon bring some semblance of order to the chaos of our current housing patters.

I must admit that I do not know how to ensure that the planners will be good, in both senses of the word—skillful, even inspired, as well as honest. But I am enough of a prairie populist to believe that our native stock still contains the seeds of genius, decency, and democracy. The planners will find it difficult to be dishonest if we establish confiscatory economic sanctions against speculators and others who have the audacity to bribe these hardworking officials. Jail isn't good enough for the greedy speculators or public officials who hold the public hostage to schemes of profit and ruin, but confiscatory economic sanctions are.

The private mortgage industry also must be regulated carefully, preferably at the state level. Officials of the mortgage industry, which now operates with few legal restrictions of any kind, and none at all in the case of the mortgage banker, protest that they are regulated, but they never explain what those regulations are. I would suggest a few new laws.

One of them would be for the annual disclosure of the amount and geographic location of all mortgage loans. Such a regulation now is being discussed in Illinois and in the city of Chicago. The twin practices of disinvestment and red-lining should be forbidden by law and replaced by a policy of affirmative lending that requires a certain percentage of mortgage investment in the home area of all mortgage sources. I would suggest a figure of 75 percent for savings and loan banks, and perhaps 50 percent for commercial banks, except where no mortgage opportunities exist. The problem is tougher for mortgage bankers because their money does not come from savings depositors but from loans drawn from other sources. But a new law requiring equal mortgage borrowing on a first-come, first-served basis ought to solve part of the problem. Although affirmative lending would not wipe out the ghetto, which is economically based, it would quickly reduce its size. It would also put an end to the blockbusting tactics of the real estate scavengers, thereby exerting a stabilizing effect on residential patterns.

Mortgage loans ought to be regulated on the state level because the federal government has proved itself wholly incompetent or unwilling to take action against mortgagees who have abused the FHA programs. In addition, Watergate, the Small Business Administration scandals, the milk producers scandals, and the defense contract scandals, have shown without a doubt that when the federal government goes wrong it pollutes both oceans and the nation in between.

State corruption has geographic limits. We have the pattern of state insurance regulation to guide us. Although that has not been without flaws, it is one of the bright success stories in American government since World War II. Even the billion-dollar Equity Funding insurance scandal has been managed well by the Illinois Department of Insurance. A state reorganization plan now before the courts will make all policy holders whole despite Equity Funding's massive losses. The same cannot be said for Equity Funding's stock owners, but that is a federal, not a state problem.

The role of the federal government in the regulation of mortgage capital would consist of strict limits on overseas investments, and equally strict limitations on foreign capital investments in American land and property. This sounds like, and is, a protectionist attitude. But it's necessary, because the federal government also will be charged with the national limitation of mortgage interest rates, and we don't want domestic capital to flee. Just because some South American and European countries have been struggling with mortgage rates of 12 percent and higher doesn't mean that it's a good idea. Interest rates that close off home ownership and necessary building and construction of living units are a bad idea, no matter who has tried them first. I would suggest that a mortgage limit of no more than 8 percent is a good idea.

The opposition to this idea comes from capital sources that declare petulantly that if they can get only 8 percent, they'll take their investment elsewhere. Savings and loan associations, commercial banks, insurance companies, and other major sources of capital, however, generally pay less than that to their depositors. They can make a profit at 8 percent. If they cannot, then it is up to the federal government to make available directly mortgage loans to persons who want to buy houses, mortgage loans with interest rates of perhaps 5 or 6 percent or even lower in the case of the poor. As suggested earlier, the government won't lose money on the deal. The capital will be returned, and the taxpayers will even experience a profit, something rare in modern goverment.

Finally, I have a recommendation for the community of scholars who are concerned with the housing industry and housing patterns. They should put their energies to work to identify and teach the true nature of the mortgage and housing industries in the United States. We all must stop repeating the old, blind, cliches about racial prejudice, broad social forces, and ignorant fate that have so obscured our perceptions of the economic forces that shape our lives. It's the individual lust for profit, not chance that has led us to our present housing crisis. The concept of blind fate has not been an operative one except in housing circles since the Protestant Reformation.

As I reflect on these comments, they seem controversial and sometimes harsh, but they are not without hope. I think I am not an incurable optimist to believe that men can be good, laws just, and government fair. I think that our people can be well-housed. I think that this objective is a major job for our society, one that stands second to no other social concern. World resources are running short. The time of scarcity for all peoples and all nations is drawing near. Unless we start building now we may have nothing to leave our successors on this earth and on this continent. The time to begin is now. We are the people to begin this job. We are the hope, the best and last chance to forestall the impending peril and dispel those bad dreams in the night.

NOTES

1. Brian D. Boyer, Cities Destroyed for Cash: The FHA Scandal at HUD (Chicago: Follett Publishing Company, 1973).

2. These opinions are Brian Boyer's and are more fully substantiated in his Cities Destroyed for Cash (Chicago, Ill.: Follett Publishing Company, 1973).

3. Richard Goldkamp, "Loan Activity Much Heavier in County than City," St. Louis Globe-Democrat, July 13-14, 1974, p. 11A.

4. J. S. Fuerst, ed., Public Housing in Europe and America (New York: John Wiley & Sons, Inc., 1974).

INTRODUCTION
TO PART III

The main offerings in this section are written by and about intermediaries in the urban housing game. The intermediaries or middlemen, as they often are called, are go-betweens who become involved because owners and tenants, builders and buyers do not always combine easily in the marketplace. Their role is to bring the producers and consumers of housing closer together.

Whether public or private, intermediaries in the housing process usually maintain a low profile. Nobody has much sympathy for the man in the middle. As a consequence of his low visibility— violated ordinarily only when some enterprising reporter or state's attorney turns up what promises to be a juicy scandal—the role of the go-between is little understood. The papers presented in this section attempt to remedy this lack of comprehension by describing the operation of selected intermediaries in urban housing markets.

In the first essay, Charles Liebert provides a detailed account of his 25-year career as an entrepreneur in housing. The chronicle of events that he recounts says a great deal not only about his own life, but about the operating code of most successful middlemen in the housing business. The basic requirements is that the intermediary remain highly flexible and move with changing market conditions. In this sense, and without negative connotations, the successful middle-man is an opportunist. At one time or another during his long career, Liebert has functioned as a buyer and seller of real estate, an owner and manager of rental units, director of urban renewal for the city of St. Louis, a land speculator, housing developer, contractor, and syndicator for subsidized apartment projects. He is now in the luxury housing business in St. Louis County. Sould the distribution of payoffs in the market change once again, we may expect to see Liebert "go where the action is."

Given the low esteem in which the middleman is usually held, it is perhaps worth noting some of the positive functions that Liebert sees private entrepreneurs performing in the marketplace. His discussion of real estate speculators in St. Louis after World War II is especially informative. In the early postwar era, speculators performed a valuable service by rehabilitating dilapidated buildings that otherwise might have been eliminated from the housing inventory when demand for them was greatest. They also provided a cash market for residential investments and secured financing for families in areas where FHA and savings and loan associations would not lend. By

emphasizing these positive roles, Liebert is not denying that speculators ever engaged in shady deals or confidence games. He is merely
trying to tell a side of the story that is seldom acknowledged and without which a balanced appraisal is not possible.

Liebert's presentation also is interesting in its discussion of
the problems and prospects associated with central-city redevelopment in the St. Louis area. Although not totally pessimistic, Liebert's
long years of experience in this geographic region suggest that the
prospects for substantial revitalization of older core areas are not
good. Even armed with the powers of eminent domain and the tax
abatement incentives provided to area developers under Missouri law,
Liebert asserts that some core neighborhoods may be too far gone to
redevelop without a substantial change in market conditions.

In the third essay of this section, James E. Murray, senior
vice-president and general counsel of the Federal National Mortgage
Association, (FNMA or Fannie Mae), provides a succinct and very
readable account of the historical development and operations of the
secondary market for residential mortgages in this country. Authorized
to act as a public intermediary during the New Deal period, Fannie
Mae helped to restore liquidity to the badly depressed housing industry
by providing a market for federally insured mortgages. In 1968, FNMA
was transferred entirely to private ownership and its special assistance (direct subsidy) programs were turned over to a newly-created
entity, the Government National Mortgage Association (GNMA or Ginnie
Mae). Since that time, the liquidity-enhancing functions of Fannie
Mae and the special support provided by Ginnie Mae have been brought
together in formal agreements called Tandem Plans, which are designed to subsidize the construction of housing, especially for low-
and moderate-income families.

In the final offering in this segment, the editors comment
briefly on the politics of the secondary mortgage market, with special
attention to the question of who benefits from the operations of Fannie
Mae and Ginnie Mae. In general terms, they conclude that a variety
of private intermediaries, especially mortgage bankers and originators
of home loans, benefit from FNMA and GNMA secondary market operations. At the same time, mortgage loans for single-family homes
and apartment projects are made both more available and at lower
rates of interest as a consequence of the actions of these agencies.
Thus, homeowners and, to a lesser extent, renters receive payoffs
from the system. In this case, at least, the politics of housing assume the characteristics of a positive-sum game, with many actors
receiving some sort of payoff from FNMA-GNMA support of the mortgage market.

Taken as a whole, several interesting themes emerge from
the presentations in this section. First, intermediaries in the urban

housing game are a varied lot and their interests do not always har-
monize. For example, in his essay Liebert expresses a view charac-
teristic of many private entrepreneurs—public bureaucrats, though
middlemen in their own right, are bumbling incompetents more concerned with rules and regulations than they are with housing production. Although this perspective can surely be questioned, it suggests
nonetheless that intermediaries do not represent a single, monolithic
force in the competition for payoffs from the urban housing market.
In general terms, the housing delivery system in the United States is
highly complex and disjointed, and middlemen often compete for benefits among themselves as well as against producers and consumers.

    Of course, intermediaries also have certain basic common
interests that supersede their disagreements. In this regard, all of
the contributors in this section are united in accepting the private
housing market as the primary device for allocating costs and benefits
in the housing game. As a private entrepreneur, Liebert adjusted his
behavior to conform with the demands of the marketplace. Although
perhaps not as apparent, public intermediaries also accept the basic
logic of the private market. Murray suggests that Fannie Mae was
established to compensate for market defects, but the fact of the
matter is that Fannie Mae, and Ginnie Mae as well, function to shore
up or assist the private market, not to replace it. In this sense, all
middlemen, both public and private, accept the basic rules of the
game as defined by the ebb and flow of market forces.

    This brings us to another important point about the inter-
mediaries in housing. In accepting the basic framework of the market, middlemen feel that they are working within a system whose
ground rules are established by the decisions of others, in this case,
consumer preferences and producers' choices regarding the supply
of housing. Liebert's essay, in particular, leaves the impression
that the intermediary is an amoral actor reacting to market conditions.

    To the extent that middlemen will not assume responsibility
for the consequences of market operations, it seems clear that they
cannot be relied on to police themselves. This became quite apparent,
for example, in the FHA scandals cited in the editor's comments. No
one was willing to assume responsibility—not the mortgage lenders,
nor the speculators, nor the FHA appraisers, nor the Secretary of the
Department of Housing and Urban Development. Obviously then, the
intermediaries are not capable of regulating their own activities.
Some other force is needed to moderate their pursuit of self-interest.
But who? While periodic newspaper exposes or consumer advocates
like Ralph Nader perform this role to some degree, a full-time, dis-
interested monitor is lacking. Even if such an agency were found, it
too would probably develop a practical stake in the status quo that
would keep it from performing its function to the fullest.

There is no easy answer to the age-old question "but who will guard the guards themselves?" Meanwhile, in our complex society there is no way that housing can be built, financed, and delivered to the consumer without somebody playing the part of the intermediary. Therein lies the dilemma. Perhaps we should accept this fact and re-frame the question altogether: "Granted that the intermediaries will always profit from the housing game, how do you get a greater piece of the action for those consumers most in need—the low- and moderate-income families?"

CHAPTER

5

THE ROLE OF THE MIDDLEMAN
IN THE HOUSING MARKET
Charles B. Liebert

The many faces of the private intermediary in the housing field can be illustrated by my 25-year career in the real estate, renewal, and construction fields. As a middleman, I have had to remain flexible and respond to shifts in the market. Those of my colleagues who were unable to switch their operations ran into serious trouble. Private intermediaries cannot be successful, that is, make profits, unless they respond quickly to new opportunities. Often, these opportunities are of such short duration that failure to act precludes chances for survival.

From 1948 to 1956, I brokered and speculated in real estate. Between 1956 and 1960, I continued to buy and sell and broker property, but I also acquired housing units as investments. In 1960 and for seven years thereafter, I speculated in land, first in Las Vegas (1960-64) and then in Missouri farms and Lake of the Ozarks acreage (1964-67). For the next three years, I worked for the St. Louis Redevelopment Authority, where I became director of urban renewal. Finally, in 1970 I moved into the building business, specializing in the construction of luxury single-family homes and, to a lesser extent, in turnkey public housing and federally assisted rental projects. These dates and activities are significant because they correspond to changes in the market and in government policies that forced an adjustment of my behavior as a housing entrepreneur.

Real Estate Broker, Dealer, and Investor

I entered the real estate business when I finished college in 1948. My father had been in the business for about 30 years and it

93

seemed natural for me to go in with him. He started as an office boy
when he was 21 years old and always liked real estate. Through the
years, he began gradually buying and selling in the city of St. Louis.
By the late 1920s, just prior to the stock market crash, he employed
about 20 salesmen, many of whom became very successful in later
years as real estate dealers, builders, and in other occupations. His
operations occupied almost the entire fourth floor of a downtown office
building, where the business remained for over 50 years. Rent was
so cheap that one room was reserved specifically for a dice game for
the salesmen.

Business was very good in the 1920s. The, the Great Depression hit. Real estate men threw away the second mortgages that they
had accumulated as profit from their buying and selling activities. They
threw them away, that is, until the Home Owners Loan Corporation
(HOLC) came into existence in 1933. The HOLC was enacted by federal
legislation to prevent owners from losing their property through foreclosure by refinancing home mortgage debt, but it turned out to be a
profit opportunity for real estate men who were going broke.

None of the real estate dealers had any intention of foreclosing
under their mortgages during the Depression. First, the owners of
the property on which they had mortgages didn't have any money, so
there was nothing to get from them through foreclosure. Second,
buildings were encumbered for more than they were worth. Suddenly,
however, dealers became aware of the government-sponsored windfall
and scurried through their basements and closets to find old mortgages,
which they could take to an HOLC office and receive 20 or 30 cents on
the dollar. The program was intended to save the private homeowner
but it also helped us. It was like found money and kept our family eating
during the Depression.

My memory of the 1930s was that our family obtained many
items through barter. We would go to a gas station and my dad would
tell the owner to fill the tank and inform him later that the money for
the gas was coming off the mortgage payment. The same thing was
done periodically at a grocery store, despite protests by the owners
that they needed money worse than a reduction in their mortgages.

I always liked real estate. Buying and selling was exciting,
because I'm a gambler. I have always been thrilled to draw up a contract of sale, whether for a wholesale, retail, or new construction
deal. It is difficult to be successful as a middleman unless you like
the excitement of the market. Naturally, the profits taste better than
the losses.

Back in the 1948-56 period, the atmosphere of real estate
speculation in the city of St. Louis was very different from what it is
today. All property in the city had some value. It was never abandoned; even the most dilapidated structures were worth rehabilitating.

There was much trading between dealers, and there was an informal
wholesale real estate market. The hub of activity was the corner of
Eighth and Chestnut Streets and some 200 dealers were engaged in this
activity. They would walk up and down the street looking for a building
to buy and sell. Many times a building was purchased at the corner
and sold 20 paces away, 15 minutes later, for a profit. Frequently,
buildings were bought and sold without a contract. If a man didn't
live up to his word, he simply wasn't trusted again.

     To understand the entire process, it must be remembered
that values of real estate were rising rapidly in the postwar period.
Neither the listing agents, those who acted as brokers for others, nor
the owners of real estate were as close to the market as the dealers,
or speculators, who engaged informally in a process of setting prices.
Buildings would originate from listing agents who did not speculate or
buy real estate. Dealers would visit the listing agents daily and ask
to see the new listings. They would find what they considered a bargain, inspect the property, and then give the agent a check for earnest
money and a contract for purchase. Some of the speculators didn't have
an office. They operated with a checkbook and an answering service
and would close their deals at a title company.

     If the building was bought and closed by the speculator and he
wanted to peddle it, or if the speculator wanted to make a profit without actually completing the purchase beyond providing earnest money,
he would enter the wholesale market. This meant that he was trying
to sell it to another speculator. If the original speculator who purchased the real estate from the listing agent or the ultimate speculat-
or who bought it after one or more wholesale profits remodeled the
property and sold it on the open market, he was considered a retailer.
I rarely bought a building directly from an individual owner. Generally,
my purchases came from other dealers and I acted primarily as a retailer. Sometimes I would make wholesale profits when I needed cash
or when the wholesale mark-up was almost what I could make if I re-
tailed it. It was common for buildings to turn over three or four times
on the wholesale market within a matter of hours or days. Sometimes
the profit was $50; other times, $1,000. There were even losses when
you made errors in judgment or bought a structurally unsound building
with a bad wall or broken furnace.

     Legitimate purposes were served by the wholesale market.
Anything could be sold for cash, although at discount prices. An offer
could be obtained by merely telephoning a dealer. This was particularly
useful in the case of estates where beneficiaries could not agree on the
value of the real estate. It functioned like the over-the-counter market
in stocks. In looking back, the concentration of so many men on Chestnut Street resulted from a great demand for housing in the postwar
period and rapidly rising prices for residential real estate.

During those years, there was an influx of people to the cities, and very little construction of new homes. Buildings in the late 1940s and early 1950s were sold not only because people desired to own a home, but simply because they needed to find a place to live. The government had controlled rents through the Office of Price Administra tion and many homes were purchased because there was nothing avail- able to rent. There were many two- and four-family flats in the city of St. Louis, and purchasers could move into one unit and rent out the balance to assist in their monthly payments. Today, people don't want anything to do with much of the older city housing; everyone wants a new place. In 1943, four rooms, bath, hot water, and stove heat were acceptable, but life-styles and aspirations have changed.

Speculators also performed another useful function. They ac- quired rundown properties and made them habitable and saleable. Some buildings were in such deplorable condition that there was no way that they could be sold from one private owner to another. No one would finance them because they were dilapidated and no one would buy them because they required too much money to be repaired. They were in violation of local codes and required too much work to meet the stand ards of the Federal Housing Administration (FHA). When a speculator bought a house, it was not uncommon to spend between $3,000 and $5,000 on it. Typically, the costs of new electric services, furnaces, tuck-pointing, and decorating amounted to 25 percent of the retail sales price although, in some instances, repairs went as high as two or three times the dealer's original purchase price.

When I started in real estate, almost all financing was done through private capital. FHA was not active in the city; in fact, it had red-lined many core areas. Private mortgage money was available through the savings of individuals who were interested in getting a yield of approximately 6 percent by buying first mortgages. These residen- tial loans were usually for a period of three or five years, payable with interest only, or with a small principal payoff every six months. Purchasers of real estate with whom I dealt usually had a down pay- ment of not more than 10 percent. The first mortgage was approximate ly 50 percent to 60 percent of the sale price, and a second mortgage was taken back by the seller who, in my case, was a dealer.

Let me describe a hypothetical transaction. A five-room brick house with a bath and furnace might have sold for $8,950 with $950 down and principal and interest payments of $80 per month. This meant that $8,000 in financing would be needed. Assume that a first mortgage of $5,500 could be obtained from an individual investor and that the balance of $2,500 in the form of a second mortgage was ac- quired by the dealer. The payment schedule might be as follows:

Total Monthly Payment

Payment on first mortgage:
interest only with no
principal reduction
(5,500 x 6% ÷ 12)   = $27.50

Payment on second mort-
gage:
principal and interest
with amortization in
approximately 5 years   = $52.50

Total $80.00

Those who lent money on first mortgages tried to protect
their investment by keeping the loan-to-value ratio as low as possible.
This was done because there was no real retail market for many of
the properties that we bought and sold and the lenders did not want
to risk more than the wholesale value. Because of the class, race,
and income of the purchasers, no single financing instrument was
available for 75 percent or more of the sales price. As a result,
the second mortgage or second deed of trust, as it is sometimes
called, was a very important financing instrument in the 1940s and
1950s enabling many people to buy homes who ordinarily couldn't
afford them.

There were abuses in the second deed of trust business and
a few unscrupulous dealers gave a bad name to those who were more
honorable. The worst practice, which for some reason was never
publicized, was the 36-month "balloon note" in which owners were
charged a renewal commission when the second mortgage came due.
Sometimes this charge was nearly equal to the original down payment
at the time of purchase. It was a bad practice that was employed by
only a limited number of dealers.

Often, those private purchasers of first mortgages that I
mentioned before were friends and relatives of dealers. The buyers
were not in the real estate business but they had faith in us to protect
their investment. Today, when so many of the buildings that were
used as collateral for these mortgages have been vandalized and abandoned, this faith has come back to haunt us. Although I avoided personal guarantees for the principal and interest on first mortgages,
there were situations where this was not possible. Other dealers
guaranteed mortgages with regularity. When properties became impossible to rent or sell, payments on the mortgages on abandoned
buildings often wiped them out or threw them into bankruptcy. However,

the written agreement to protect the loan holder was not the only reason many dealers kept "going into their pockets" to try to protect their investments. Many of us felt a moral obligation to those who had come to us or whom we had asked to invest their money at 6 percent on inner-city properties.

Today, it seems strange that people would actually seek out 6 percent investments when banks pay over 7 percent and government bonds 8 percent. Twenty-five years ago, however, prime real estate mortgages carried 3 percent interest and banks and savings and loan associations paid only 2 percent on their deposits. Actually 6 percent then would be the equivalent of 12 percent now. In that respect, it could be said that the private mortgage buyers were paid to take a risk, but you have to be callous to look at it that way, especially when friends or relatives are involved.

When the housing shortage was acute in the late 1940s and early 1950s, attached houses were frequently bought and sold. St. Louis had a large number of row houses in parcels of 6, 8, or 12 units in older areas that were conducive to conversion from rental investments to ownership of single units. Since the federal government would not allow rent increases, and tenants could not be given notice to vacate unless for possession by the owner, these buildings became more profitable for buying and selling as individual parcels than for retention, in their entirety, as a rented investment. With the pent-up demand for housing, it seemed logical to convert these rows from tenantry to home ownership. As an indication of the dire housing shortage in 1950, I bought a row of seven attached brick houses on the 1400 block of Dolman Street in an old neighborhood adjoining Lafayette Square. There were tenants in six of the seven units and I renovated the vacant one. By showing customers the remodeled unit and promising to put the others in the same condition, I sold all seven on one Saturday afternoon.

One of the main functions of the middleman was to remodel properties and most retailers spent half of their time organizing tradesmen and inspecting their work. Conversion and remodeling were profitable during the early postwar years. For example, the purchase price of the Dolman row was $14,000 ($2,000 per unit) and approximately $7,000 ($1,000 per unit) was added for repairs. Other expenses included a 3 percent commission or $60 per unit service charge for the $2,000 first deeds of trust on each house, with a term of three years at 6 percent interest, no principal reduction, and miscellaneous expenses, including title search, tax and insurance adjustments, and carrying charges, of $60 per unit. The profit picture in this 1950 transaction looked as follows:

	Total	Per Unit
Expenses		
Purchase Price	$14,000	$2,000
Repairs	7,000	1,000
Loan Commission	420	60
Miscellaneous	420	60
Total	$21,840	$3,120
Income		
Down Payment (Sales Price $4,950/unit)	$ 3,500	$ 500
First Deed of Trust	14,000	2,000
Second Deed of Trust	17,150	2,450
Total	$34,650	$4,950

At first glance, a profit of $1,830 per unit ($4,950 - $3,120) seems fantastic, and appeared even more so to me 25 years ago when I was in my early 20s. However, the profit was not cash and money was received only when the second deed of trust was sold or repaid. From a cash flow standpoint, I had spent $3,120 on each unit and had received only the $500 down payment and the proceeds from the $2,000 first deed of trust in cash. In effect, $620 of my money was invested in the $2,450 second deed of trust.

Since many of the dealers were young men recently out of the armed forces or college and in business for a short time, cash was our primary concern. We had to dispose of the second deed of trust to make a profit at the time of sale. Several options were available because there was a ready market in the purchase and sale of second mortgages. One option was to sell the first 30 monthly payments at a discount. With the total payments on the two deeds of trust amounting to about $50 per month, about the same as rent, and with interest only, $10 per month, payable on the first deed of trust, the second deed of trust payment was about $30 per month principal plus interest. When the first 30 principal payments were sold at a 20 percent discount, $720 per unit in cash (30 months x $30/mo. x 20% discount) could be recovered. By this method, a cash profit of $100 ($720 - $620 cash investment) could be obtained along with a paper profit of $1,550 in the remainder of the second deed of trust, which was not payable until after the first 30 months. The balance of the second deed was also marketable at 35 cents on the dollar.

If it were sold, the cash profit could be $640 per unit, $100 from the sale of front notes plus $540 for the disposition of the balance.

Another option, depending upon the market, was to sell the entire second mortgage, usually at a discount of 50 percent. Cash received from the sale would be $1,225 ($2,450 x 50%) and net profit would be $605 per unit ($1,225 - $620 cash investment).

Trading in second deeds of trust continued when savings and loan associations became active in center-city neighborhoods in the 1950s, but there was a significant change. As the loan-to-purchase price ratio increased from about 50 percent to 70 or 80 percent with these new mortgages, the second deeds became less marketable. Before the savings and loans made first mortgages for us, the usual first deed of trust was payable interest only. They were called "straight" loans and retailers using them could allocate a much larger share of the purchaser's total monthly payment to principal reduction on the second deed of trust. In the second deed of trust market, the faster the principal amortization, the higher the price paid for the mortgage. When the savings and loan associations came into the market, their first mortgages were amortized with equal monthly payments until paid. The payments were considerably larger than the interest only or small principal reduction loans made by private parties. Principal payments on the second deeds declined appreciably because the total monthly amount that a purchaser could pay on a house or flat remained relatively constant. This pressure on the second deed of trust has increased even more in recent years, as savings and loans have followed the lead of government mortgage insurance by offering 90 percent loans insured through the private market.

Splitting rows and selling to individual purchasers declined in the early 1950s. Rents were decontrolled and many of the Chestnut Street real estate firms started buying property for investment. There was plenty of private mortgage money available, both from individuals and savings and loan associations. Dealers sometimes borrowed first, second, and even third mortgages on their properties. This money often cost the equivalent of 20 percent annual interest. They didn't care because the market was rising on both rents and equities and they could readily sell their investments to lawyers, physicians, and small business people wanting real estate as inflation hedges and for the future when their productive earning periods were over.

It didn't work out that way for the investors. They became disenchanted when they found that these properties were not blue chip investments. They required numerous repairs and services. Many of these investors and the small first deed of trust buyers lost their life's savings when buildings became vandalized and abandoned in later years.

As the outlook for long-term profits diminished in the early and mid-1960s, real estate companies and investors became reluctant to make permanent repairs that could be amortized over five or ten years. Blight often set in so quickly that repairs could only be justified on an annual basis. As dealers and professional landlords became fearful of improving their properties, deterioration set in. There was no long-term expectation of profit. Resident owners trying to maintain their homes in neighborhoods surrounded by investment property waged a losing battle.

Vandalism was one of the biggest problems. As structures became vacant, they would be stripped of their plumbing by thieves hoping to sell the metal, either copper or lead, for $10 or $20. Abandonment followed because owners would not spend $500 to $1,000 to install the fixtures again. I remember receiving a call that the water was shut off in a building where a tenant was living. I sent the plumber to investigate and he found that, although occupied, someone had entered the house and stolen all of the copper lines. I was furious; it was bad enough that this happened when units were vacant. The plumber was told to see if he could learn the identity of the thief. A few hours later, he called. "I found him; I caught him; I got the ringleader." That was great and I told the plumber that I was ready to prosecute. He cautioned me that "I don't know if you want to, he is 8 years old." It was very discouraging to see many years of work go down the drain.

Even the police department seemed unable to control vandalism. In the early 1960s, I talked to a colonel on the force in my office, but nothing seemed to come of it. Vandalism was ruining the city, but theft of materials seemed to have a low priority. Nobody was hurt, so it wasn't serious. Aside from that one visit by the colonel, policemen would never come to my office. They required a vandalism report be filled out at the site. This meant leaving my office and spending hours documenting the theft. I gave up reporting vandalism, because I felt my efforts ended up in the waste basket.

During the 1960s, when prices were falling on central-city properties, owners came out ahead if they did not pay real estate taxes. It was only in 1971 that the city of St. Louis enacted the Land Reutilization Act and began to take action on delinquent property taxes. By the time this legislation was enacted, the properties on which taxes were owed were worthless and the owners were glad the city took them over. They were thrilled to get the properties out of their names. Besides, tax delinquency was never a personal lien against the owner, and was treated as just another lien against the property that could be paid off with 12 percent annual interest. If you really wanted to pay the taxes, the interest and penalties were usually waived until the new act was passed.

By the late 1960s most of the real estate speculators had left
the business as a result of the collapse of both the rental investment
and sales market in many city neighborhoods. One went back to school
and became a professor of urban planning, specializing in housing and
redevelopment; another went to work for a large construction company
and later developed federally assisted apartment projects in renewal
areas; and a third became a director of a local FHA insuring office.
I became involved in urban renewal as a public employee. We were
the fortunate ones. Some of the others didn't know what to do or where
to go. They had spent their entire lives in the business since their
release from World War II service. A couple of them called me to see
if I had any idea about what they could do. They had gone broke and
were a pathetic lot.

Those few who retained their city real estate or managed
property for other owners became known as "slumlords." Some earned
this reputation, but most couldn't afford to provide the services expected by tenants, and others simply did not or could not leave the
sinking ship. Ironically, many unscrupulous speculators escaped the
heat that was put on the "slumlords." For example, those who hurt
the public by using the 36-month balloon note or those who falsified
FHA and VA documents escaped public vilification in the first instance
and imprisonment in the second. Many of them have been out of the
business for a long time.

Reputable dealers performed a service. They established a
cash market for property, were competent organizers of rehabilitation efforts, and managed troublesome investment property. Many
were able administrators and with their experience could have been
helpful to nonprofit groups or public agencies. However, they had
been labeled as villains by politicians and the press when, in reality,
they were often less dangerous than those making the charges. Intermediaries ceased to function in the central city when demand for that
housing declined. Those dealers who were opportunistic escaped; the
others were consumed by the problems with which they had to deal.

Speculation in Land

Although the decline of my business became evident about
1960, I remained in real estate. At the same time, I became increasingly concerned with finding enterprises other than those that were
drying up in St. Louis. How could I apply my St. Louis experience
to other ventures? I didn't feel confident competing as a builder, investor, or land speculator in the suburbs of St. Louis County. I didn't
know the county and I was fearful of trying to match my skills and

knowledge with those who had spent many years operating there. In retrospect, my fears were probably unwarranted. I could have stayed in this area, made money, and saved the time and expense of traveling. From 1960 to 1967, I conducted most of my business away from St. Louis and the surrounding counties, buying and selling land for specu- lation in Las Vegas and the Ozarks.

For some reason, making money seemed easier out-of-town. When we started in Las Vegas there were not many land speculators, but numbers grew dramatically as the population of the city and county expanded. I think Clark County, Nevada grew from 50,000 to 400,000 in 10 years. As more land speculators became involved in Las Vegas, the wholesale market in land grew stronger. It was like St. Louis all over again.

Our Las Vegas operation began when my brother went there on vacation. He saw a parcel of land next to the new convention center on Sierra Vista Drive and Paradise Road. It looked so cheap that we couldn't pass it up and we were able to apply our St. Louis part-pur- chase techniques, first and second deeds of trust, to the transaction. We put $5,000 down and the owner took back a $10,000 first mortgage for the remainder. Luck was with us; we caught the start of a rising market. Within two months, we sold it for $10,000 more than we paid, taking our profit in a St. Louis-style, amortized second deed of trust.

Then the same agent who sold us that first parcel came up with another one. This was much bigger—80 acres at $500 per acre. In 1960, it looked like big stuff, because we still didn't know the mar- ket. Although my father was inactive at the time, he wanted to accom- pany my brother and me to look at this land. The agent started driving into the desert and drove about a mile beyond the city limits. There were only a few houses and I asked him if we were almost there. When he said no, I cringed. He drove a little farther and I could hardly see any signs of life. Finally, he stopped the car. I thought he was crazy bringing us out there. Even more than that, I was embarrassed in front of my dad, who was a very smart guy. "Is this the land, Gordon?" "No, it's not on the road; it's up there, there isn't any road to it." I almost fainted when I heard my father say that it looked O.K. to him. We bought it and 30 days later sold it for a big profit. Then we rea- lized that the market was soaring and that we could make money on almost any land we bought.

We did not really capitalize on the strength of the market. If we had moved to Las Vegas for five years, we could have made many, many more deals than by operating out of St. Louis. Alternatively, we could have brought several bigger parcels and held them for the five year period and made huge capital gains. The 80-acre desert property went from $500 to $5,000 per acre and appreciation of 500, 600, or even 1,000 percent was not uncommon in relatively brief periods.

Speculation intensified after 1960. It was like the old pickle story. A fellow buys a jar for 20 cents, sells it for 30, and it is resold until it reaches a price of one dollar. The final purchaser opens the jar and tastes the pickle. It was terrible, so he complained to the person who sold it to him. The seller was shocked and reprimanded him for eating one of the pickles. "Those are trading pickles, you're not supposed to eat them." Trading has its own momentum. Some land out there had no value for building. It was 10 miles into the desert; yet, it was continually bought and sold.

Despite its dramatic increase in population, Las Vegas had slow periods when the town was overbuilt. Builders are notorious for jumping on a situation when it looks hot. They hear that a town needs housing and rush to enter the market in droves, supported by their partners, the lending institutions. Around 1960, Las Vegas had such a critical shortage that it was difficult to find a place to live. Within several years, the residential market was so flooded that there was a 20 percent vacancy ratio in apartments. They stopped building apartments for 10 years. During that time, if you went to talk to a savings and loan association about financing apartments, they would laugh at you because they had "eaten," or taken back from the developer by deed or foreclosure, so many projects. Ten years later there was another shortage. Instead of cautiously building a few units at a time, it was 1960 all over again. Builders and loan companies oversaturated the market with too many new units.

Developers only stop when the market is flooded. I remember one builder had a neat system. He would build only four-family apartment buildings that cost him $29,000 per building. He would obtain a $35,000 first mortgage on each. Every time a building was constructed it meant $6,000 in cash to him, so he built as many as he could. There was no personal liability on the mortgage to restrict his pace. When the market became overbuilt in the early and mid-1960s, the loan company took back all of his units. Inflation saved the savings and loan companies for now the same four-family buildings cost $50,000 to construct and the units can be rented at levels considerably below those of new construction.

Las Vegas had several factors in its favor. The population rose dramatically as it became a tourist and retirement center. In addition, fresh money was always available for land and building speculation and investment. Hotel owners made so much money that they continually invested in area real estate and Howard Hughes's purchases strengthened the market whe it tended to sag. Prices are very high now and there is less speculation. Smaller middlemen like me do not function nearly as well in this environment because it requires large-scale investments.

Housing and Urban Renewal Bureaucrat

By 1967, I had reached the point where my income was primarily from payments of principal and interest on deeds of trust on
land in Las Vegas and buildings in St. Louis, and from rents on St.
Louis properties. However, cash was short as I was always investing
in new ventures. There were no wholesale deals. Nobody bought and
sold second deeds of trust for cash.

Another opportunity appeared that would allow me to accumulate cash from my investments and become involved in what seemed
to be exciting and challenging new federal programs. There was an
article in the St. Louis Globe-Democrat describing the need for businessmen with management and organizational skills to work in government, so I made an unsolicited application for employment with the
St. Louis Redevelopment Authority. They hired me and, within a year,
I was the acting director of urban renewal for the city of St. Louis.
My three years at the Authority were stimulating, enjoyable, and
frustrating. I worked harder than I ever have worked in my life, including when I was in business for myself.

The inefficiency and confusion of both the local and federal
housing administrators was appalling. It was obvious that many political favors had been paid for with jobs at the Authority. About 10 of
the 120 employees actually did 80 percent of the work. This was my
first experience at public work and, being a loner anyway, I found it
easier to work with the 10 who wanted to work and let others worry
about those who didn't. I am not the type to follow up on people and
see if they are working. Instead of hounding people, I did much of
the work myself.

One of my early responsibilities was administration of the
Section 23 Leased Housing Program. This was during and shortly
after the riots and there was an intensive push by the Johnson administration to place people quickly into subsidized housing units. Section
23 was the only program that would do it because existing instead of
new housing could be used. The Department of Housing and Urban
Development (HUD) wanted quantity, not quality, and this attitude came
back to haunt the program.

Every month calls would come in from the HUD regional office
at Fort Worth asking how many units were leased. I would answer five
and they would tell me I should have leased 30. This went on and on.
In the first three months, I was able to obtain only seven leases. Real
estate owners neither trusted nor understood Section 23. To satisfy
HUD's statements that Johnson wanted "people in occupancy," we tried
to use the program in every possible way. In urban renewal areas,
leases were given to get structures repaired and remodeled and

incentives in the form of lease terms were also provided. Units in a newly constructed 221(d) (3) project were rented for the first time in this HUD region. Pressure mounted from HUD to increase the number of leased units. My work load was tremendous—I felt as if I had two full-time jobs in supervising the leased housing program and, at the same time, working on the thorny problems of the West End Urban Renewal Project.

Leasing of units finally reached 25 to 30 per month, at which time we were working with both real estate dealers and small private owners. Everyone was solicited to present his units for consideration in the leasing program. Actually, my major role in the leasing program was to get it under way; the majority of units were rented after I left the program. I used my contacts in the real estate business extensively and were it not for them, the leased housing program would have shown only meager results.

There was public criticism about the condition of some of the units that were leased. It was justified in part and landlords who would not respond to valid complaints were eliminated from the program. Eventually, most of these problems were resolved and many of the leases were renewed by the local housing authority long after I left. They must have been sufficiently satisfied with my original efforts to continue the relationship with the same landlords.

Other problems arose and HUD was one of them. An example of the bureaucracy was the unwillingness of the HUD regional office to provide the $10 fee that the city of St. Louis required to inspect all units in a building where we were leasing. This meant that if the Authority was renting one unit in a 24-family, all units had to be inspected at a cost of $240. After great tugging and pulling, it was worked out with HUD and the city. There were additional shortcomings in the leased program because new units could not be built in nice suburban areas and it was difficult to entice builders into risky core neighborhoods. However, I believe that leased housing in new construction is the best program that the federal government has devised. It requires fewer federal subsidy dollars, keeps property on the tax rolls, minimizes red tape, offers a reasonable return for the investor and allows private management rather than government to deal directly with tenants.

When I worked at the redevelopment authority, it was a very active and exciting place. Land sales were occurring in the Mill Creek and Kosciusko areas, the Busch Memorial Stadium project, which was private renewal, and Grandel Square. New programs were being created for DeSoto-Carr, LaSalle Park, Mill Creek North—which never happened—and other areas. Model Cities had started, and efforts were devoted to coordinating it with urban renewal. New ideas were being

formulated, such as having the Ralston-Purina Company donate the
city's share to start the LaSalle Park project because the city had no
funds.

One of the challenging, but frustrating, aspects of my job at
the Authority was a "loser" known as the West End project. The West
End project was ill-conceived from its origin in the early 1960s, and
should never have been attempted. As with many other renewal programs in the United States, the reason for the West End was that non-
cash credits were available to be used as matching local shares against
federal participation. New schools and other facilities built within
one mile of the project area qualified for the city's credits in lieu of
cash. At the time of the West End project, urban renewal legislation
called for the federal government to pay two-thirds of the project cost,
plus all of the relocation expenditures, and the city was to pay one-
third. Later, St. Louis was judged to be an area that was depressed
economically and its required participation dropped to one-fourth.
Project costs were figured so that the city would not have to use any
cash for its share and it would be paid for entirely by the federal government. So why not proceed?

However, there was a "slight" miscalculation in estimating
project feasibility—proceeds from land sales were overcalculated by
$8 million. Some of the loss in land disposition revenues was attribu-
table to falling value of city property, but not entirely. It was a poorly
conceived and managed project from the start. When federal money
ran out, the program wasn't nearly finished.

Urban renewal funds were made available in the late 1950s
for the West End because the federal government wanted large rehabilitation projects to counteract the bad reputation that urban renewal
was receiving because of clearance and inadequate provision for relocation. During the life of the West End project, every financing tool
available was employed as quickly as the feds could invent them. Some
rules were bent to use programs that had not been invented yet. It was
a workshop for federal ideas: Section 312 loans, 115 grants, 221 (d)
(3) new housing, 235 (new and rehabilitation), Turnkey I, II, and III
(new and rehabilitation), 221 (d) (4), 221 (d) (2), rehabilitation demonstration, and leased housing (new and rehabilitation). Yet, with all
of these programs concentrated on one project, there was only limited
success. Some residents had their homes repaired and some families
received new housing, but the neighborhood deteriorated faster than it
was rehabilitated. It is difficult to see it today and believe that it was
ever the site of urban renewal.

There never should have been a West End project. It was ir-
responsible fiscally; the area selected was much too large, one square
mile; and the houses were too big to be feasibly rehabilitated. Added
to these physical and financial constraints were social and economic

ones resulting from vastly different income backgrounds of the area's occupants.. Middle- and upper-middle income residents on the private streets wanted large homes,rehabilitated and new ones built that were like the structures they occupied and that were inhabited by people like themselves. Low-income residents demanded housing that poor people could afford. Both groups were on the project's Citizens' Committee and constantly fought each other and the Authority.

One example of the continuous conflict associated with the project centered on a vitally needed sales program that had been initiated by the Authority staff. I had drawn up a list of properties for sale for the first time since the project was begun over five years earlier. A program was devised whereby about 20 nonresident buyers would rehabilitate certain properties. Most of the prospective purchasers were private citizens who wanted to have homes in the West End. The others were real estate investors. We invented a gimmick for the home purchasers called the 312 loan sale. Originally HUD objected to it, but finally consented. The 312 loan program, Section 312 of the U.S. Housing Act, was devised for modernizing existing structures with loan funds at 3 percent interest. At that time, mortgages on residences could be refinanced in the program, but financing new purchases was not intended in the legislation. Our plan was to obtain temporary financing for purchasers through the Savings Service Corporation—a risk-pool of the savings and loan associations created for participation in the inner city—then process the buyer for a permanent mortgage under the 312 program. This action would then make purchasers eligible for a 312 loan because they could be considered as refinancing their existing mortgage. When the real estate section of the Fort Worth office of HUD cleared the scheme, it was also approved by the General Accounting Office despite objections that it did not meet original legislative guidelines. It was great for the purchaser who had an opportunity to convert a one-year temporary loan into a 20-year, 3 percent mortgage on a rehabilitated home.

The Citizens' Committee objected to the plan, demanding an exclusive 60-day option for residents of the area to buy the Authority-owned property. After the first 60-day period, they wanted more time. Ultimately, all the potential customers were lost because of the delays The buildings were vandalized and the Authority demolished them.

A powerful alderman was chairman of the Citizens' Committee and he played a political game by inciting the residents against the Authority as a means of maintaining his popularity. Even necessary new construction was blocked and it reached the point where the Authority staff could not do anything right. I tried to interest a developer of scattered-site Section 235 housing in constructing some of those units in the West End. By the late 1960s he had built more 235 housing

than anyone else in the St. Louis region. I knew of his competence
through the real estate business and felt fortunate to have him interested in working with us.

In line with citizen participation requirements, the developer
presented his plan before the Citizens' Committee. He was questioned
by the chairman. "Is the builder black?" "No, I'm white." "Is the
lawyer black?" "No." "Is the architect black?" "No." "We're going
to take a vote to determine whether we're going to accept your proposal." The developer told him that a vote wasn't necessary; he got
the message. The alderman insisted that he stay, but naturally, the
plan was rejected. About a year later, I heard that the developer was
asked to come back to the West End and was told there had been a mis-
understanding. He said that he wasn't the least bit interested.

It's amazing how most of the more vocal agitators in the
West End have disappeared since the late 1960s. I am told that many
received recognition and jobs. Today, everything seems quiet. The
money tap has been turned off and there isn't much left over which to
fight.

Congress passed new, innovative legislation, but the bureaucrats at HUD didn't care or weren't willing to implement the programs.
The Urban Renewal Manual was their Bible and the red tape was brutal.
Scattered-site new construction of large single-family units was des-
perately needed for relocation proposed in the West End. A developer
was found who was willing to build four-bedroom town houses on all
of the scattered-site lots and rent them for $175 a month under the
leased housing program. On one of those rare occasions, both the
staff and the residents wanted the project. This four-bedroom unit
was almost a duplicate of one in a housing proposal that had just been
approved by FHA for a 236 project in the same area with allowable
rents of $210 per month.

Our leasing project was turned down by HUD in an official
reply that justified the rejection by saing, "Had your developer been
able to accept a rent of $160 a month for the four-bedroom units,
there would be no question of approval, but the required $175 per
month would precipitate a gross rent of approximately $100 per month
for the tenant. This, we do not believe, can be accepted as 'low rent.'
It is $6 more per month than the newly remodeled units at Pruitt-
Igoe." Even today it is still hard for me to understand how one department of HUD could approve a market feasibility rent of $210 per month
in the West End and another department of HUD couldn't approve a
market rent of $175, a bargain, for a similar unit in the same area.
Objecting on the basis that the subsidy requirement would be $6 per
month more than a Pruitt-Igoe unit was ludicrous. I couldn't understand this inconsistency and I pleaded unsuccessfully with HUD to

change its decision. The entire process was bizarre. It was as if
I was dealing with two separate governments when, in fact, it was
the same governmental agency.

HUD bureaucrats continually drove us crazy. The Citizens'
Committee wanted to save as many buildings as possible from demolition, so we procured buyers who wanted to purchase structures for
the appraised value and rehabilitate them. HUD's real estate department determined from the Urban Renewal Manual that unless 20 percent of the final rehabilitated value was paid for the buildings "as is,"
they had to be demolished and sold as vacant land. This meant, of
course, that the federal government would have to pay additional funds
for demo-lition, that the citizens would be upset because another house
would be destroyed, and that nothing would be placed on the vacant lot.
When the resident group sent two of its toughest members to Fort Wort
to complain to the real estate department, I felt HUD would reverse its
decision. The manual prevailed, and our proposal was rejected.

At the present time, my only involvement in urban renewal
is as a housing consultant to the Project Area Committee, the residents, in the LaSalle Park Project. As originally planned, the project was 137 acres, contained mixed land uses, and adjoined the centra:
business district. While the LaSalle Park came under the standard
loan and grant program, the Authority's staff and the target-area
residents viewed it as different from previous projects. They believed
it would be implemented in its entirety despite division of the project
into three phases. HUD had only enough funds to finance one phase,
but the people didn't really understand staging or even urban renewal.
When the city fulfilled HUD's requirement by blighting the three-phase
area, the residents believed that the entire geographic and cultural
neighborhood of LaSalle Park would be redeveloped.

Because there was no guarantee that there would be money
for the second and third phases, the federal government felt that it
had lived up to its obligation when phase one was funded. However,
the residents who primarily rented and owned property in the second
and third phase areas were confused by the process and in spite of
horrendous crimes and vandalism in their neighborhood, they tried
to stay. They attended meeting after meeting in hope that some of
the generous benefits, up to $15,000 in replacement housing, provided
for by the Uniform Relocation Act would be received. Some of the luck
ones who had houses in the first area received payments, but many
people gave up and their homes became vandalized and abandoned.
There were those who missed receiving relocation benefits by only
three or four months because they couldn't hang on.

LaSalle Park held great promise for success. The first-phase
area contained the world headquarters of the Ralston-Purina Company
which donated more than $2 million in cash as the city's share of the

project. Expansion of this industrial giant meant help for the city's
tax base and possible employment opportunities. In addition, new
housing and commercial enterprises could be created. Currently,
funding of this program is dependent primarily on allocation of community development funds by the city and the availability of subsidies
for low- and moderate-income housing.

I worked long and hard when I was publicly employed and not
many others put forth comparable effort. Some were performing tasks
that were "make work" without any expectation of performance and
without any criteria for evaluation. At one point, I was accused of
conflict of interest, but it was a smoke screen. The regulations specified than an employee should not own real estate in urban renewal
areas. I didn't. My employed was cleared by Ralph Herod, who was
then director of urban renewal, and a complete list of all parcels
owned by me was furnished to HUD. Herod left St. Louis shortly after
my hiring to head renewal activities for the federal government.

My contacts with landlords were misconstrued to mean that
I was antiresident. Actually, I tried to use these relationships to obtain low- and moderate-income housing and make renewal projects
successful. Nothing can be accomplished by refusing to deal with the
owners of real estate.

Although there were some people who resented me as a
public official, most of the attacks on me resulted from the political
climate of the late 1960s. I was naive to think that I could be accepted
on the basis of competence, efficiency, hard work, or any similar
virtues. Some residents perceived me as an enemy because of my
involvement in real estate, and bureaucrats resented my entrepreneur-
ial approach to renewal. I spent 60 hours or more each week on the
job and I worried about the results. Every property in the West End
project was treated as if it were my own, all 2,400 structures. Somebody would ask me about Parcel 593 and, without referring to a list
or anything, I would tell them that it was a four-family flat with a bad
wall that could not be repaired, but if they were interested in rehabilitation, parcel 1012 was owned by the Authority and could be sold.
Every building in the project and the potential reuse was known. Although the work was exciting, I left discouraged because the city looked
worse to me than when I started.

Prospects for the Central City

My experiences at the Redevelopment Authority suggest some
of the difficulties encountered in efforts to renew older core areas.
Speaking about St. Louis, the city that I know best, there is no single

prescription for renewal. Some areas can be saved while others can only be treated through demolition, land banking, and new construction.

Neighborhoods that are attractive to middle- and upper-income groups can be conserved with very little encouragement. A few years ago, purchasers in this type of market might have been clients for my luxury suburban housing. During the gas crisis of 1973, I worried that gasoline restrictions would limit travel and deter potential clients from moving out to my subdivision. My fears at the time were probably exaggerated. Movement back to the inner ring by white middle-class suburbanites is, and will continue to be, limited. Aside from their negative perceptions of city living, most of this group considers housing in the city of St. Louis to be outmoded and impractical to rehabilitate.

Unfortunately, not many neighborhoods are feasible to rehabilitate. Those that are should receive concentrated municipal and educational services. Other neighborhoods might have to slide downward and become worse because there are insufficient local resources to do all things for all people. In severely deteriorated parts of St. Louis, the city may acquire almost all of the land through unpaid back taxes. When about 80 percent of the land is publicly owned in these deteriorated districts, a program should be formulated to take over the balance. After acquisition, it might be necessary to bank the land for a period of time until its image becomes favorable for development. Five years or five decades might be required.

The Mill Creek Project, a very large St. Louis urban renewal effort in the late 1950s, was undertaken in one of the city's worst physical environments. It required many years for industrial, commercial, residential, and institutional developers to invest in the area after it was cleared. Mill Creek is not a model of redevelopment, because too many poor people were injured by relocation policies that did not provide adequate compensation. However, if the city wants large suburban developers to build on deserted land, large sites must be available and developers must see the city as an opportunity and not as a slum. Sometimes this takes time.

Land aggregation is a major issue in the city of St. Louis because it is difficult to assemble acreage at a reasonable price— a price competitive with St. Louis County land, where the problems of assemblage are far less. In the county, a builder finds a vacant piece of land, lays out the site and plans the development within the restrictions of the zoning laws. In the city, however, many 25- or 50-foot parcels must be combined for a tract that is large enough to create its own environment and that will minimize decay and crime in adjoining neighborhoods. A reasonable tract of ground for redevelopment in the city is 10 acres, and it is difficult to obtain that much land.

The Land Reutilization Authority, an agency of St. Louis government, could play an important role in land aggregation because it can acquire parcels for taxes and has already taken many of them in St. Louis. Through tax foreclosures and through utilization of eminent domain under public and private urban renewal, it might be possible to accumulate enough land at a price sufficiently attractive to induce development. Still, it is a far more difficult process than in the county where there is vacant land.

When I was with the Redevelopment Authority, there was an area called Murphy Blair North that had been blighted for renewal years before, but no project had been started. The neighborhood association in that area wanted to build housing, and hoped to buy the land at a reasonable price. The association knew that in central-city development there always will be isolated parcels that cannot be bought. In this instance, the eminent domain powers of the Authority were used. Properties were condemned and sold to the citizens group for their fair market value. Those few scattered pieces where people either wanted exorbitant prices or wouldn't sell under any circumstances did not hold up the project.

St. Louis offers an attractive inducement to developers of "blighted" areas under Section 353 of the Missouri Statutes. For 10 years the property tax is the same as it was prior to construction, then for 15 years it is half the value of the land and improvements. It is only after 25 years that the total tax is paid on the land and new buildings. However, there is no write-down of the land under Section 353. It is privately financed urban renewal and the cost of land is very important to a developer. A square block of city property, even in abandoned areas, is expensive without public subsidy.

Developers have cited politics and red tape as deterrents to their involvement in the city. Although I haven't built extensively in the city, I have heard about the difficulties in going through City Hall. Rumors about the red tape involved in obtaining a permit are legendary. However, I can't imagine that the red tape is any worse than in the county or in small suburban municipalities. I recently completed the development of one-acre lots in a small, upper-income suburb where the land had already been zoned one acre. All that was needed was plat approval, yet the project took two-and-a-half years. We were told that we could go to court and fight, but we would not win. The suburb wanted to know about every detail and one delay followed another. Although there are published reports of builders claiming that they can't get permits, I can't imagine the city of St. Louis being any worse than that. Little suburban communities are like kingdoms unto themselves and they do whatever they want.

Today, red tape is not the basic reason for lack of development in the city of St. Louis. Whenever you build something, there's

red tape because of zoning, engineering, and planning requirements.
More importantly, suburban builders do not see the city as an opportunity. Most of them haven't thought seriously about the city for
15 years. They're afraid of getting hit on the head and of the vandalism and crime that take place on some city construction jobs. They
feel that if they build a project, 24-hour protection at the site will be
needed. With these fears, they avoid city projects even if there is a
potential for profit.

Unfortunately, prospects for rebirth of the city are not bright.
It is impossible to build without subsidies because most of the residents cannot afford privately constructed new residences. Large
amounts of public assistance for housing are not expected. Despite
the fact that the population of the metropolitan area is not increasing,
abandonment will persist in the city because construction in the county
will continue. Whether there's demand or not, builders have to make
a living, and they build and hope that their houses will rent or sell.
Despite the profit squeeze facing suburban developers, it is unlikely
that they will look to the city for alternative opportunities.

Turnkey Developer, Syndicator, and Luxury Home Builders

Since leaving the Redevelopment Authority in 1970, I have
played numerous roles in housing. Immediately after my departure,
I was appointed developer of a 100-unit turnkey public housing project
for the elderly in Henderson, Nevada, a small city located a few miles
from Las Vegas. The project was completed in May 1973, and has
been occupied fully since that time. Financially, the project was a
success for us, even though some money was wasted. If I had known
the aggravation that I was to endure with the executive director of the
housing authority, the stubborn inspecting architect, and the inefficient
general contractor, I doubt whether I would have undertaken the development.

In 1974, there was some unfinished business in connection
with the Henderson project and it seemed that my involvement would
never end. The executive director of the local authority claimed that
it was their finest, most attractive project, that the tenants were
thrilled with it, and that it was a candidate for a HUD award. Yet,
he wanted perfection, and the building trades in the Las Vegas area
are simply not capable, or interested, in being perfect.

In one instance, a leak developed in some sheet metal valley
flashing. This flashing was not part of our design and the roofing
subcontractor advised against the change. It was included at the insistence of the housing authority and an extra $1,000 was paid for it.

Soon after, the executive director and his architect claimed that it was installed improperly and we were responsible. We offered to take out all metal valleys and replace them with asphalt roofing, which was contained in our original plans. It would cost us $8,000, but we wanted to finish the job after four years and we were tired of arguing. Legally, we could have used a plastic spray costing $1,000 and plugged the leaks for a couple of years and said goodbye to the job.

The executive director was in a dilemma. Should he admit that he erred in putting in the flashing, or should he ask for return of the $1,000? Caught in the middle but interested in having the repairs made, he wrote us a three-page formal letter asking for an explanation and justification of our work. He wanted to avoid any criticism of his actions by his local commissioners or by HUD. To reply to his letter required considerable time and effort and shifted his responsibility to us, a classic bureaucratic maneuver. At that point, we were ready to tell him what to do with his flashing, his roof, and the entire project. Then an acceptable solution was found in which we retained the sheet metal valleys but applied roofing over it. As a result, there was no need to refund the $1,000.

Aside from the Henderson development, in recent years I have been involved in FHA-insured projects under Sections 221 (d) (4) and 236 of the national housing acts. Sometimes I have acted as a principal, the sponsor or developer, and, at other times, as a broker between a developer and a purchaser in an operation where profits are made on the sale of real estate equities to investors for tax purposes. Promoters or intermediaries like myself try to put together rental projects under federal or state programs with little or no money invested and with no responsibility for payment of the mortgage. We then sell the projects to wealthy people who can use accounting losses generated by the real estate to diminish their income tax liability.

Buyers of 221 (d) (4) and 236 developments pay varying prices for the equities over the mortgages. Usually, they command higher prices in November and December when investors know what losses they need to offset income and when there are more bidders. Equities are traded daily on the wholesale market, where they might sell for 13 to 15 percent of the mortgage. Payment from the equity buyers is usually on a staged basis; one-third at initial endorsement of the loan by FHA, one-third at final settlement on the loan, and one-third if and when the project is either 93 percent occupied or has no negative cash flow during a three-month period.

If the investor assumes ownership at initial endorsement of the mortgage he can, as first owner, deduct all interest during construction, some discount and mortgage fees, profit to the builder as salary, and rapid depreciation. Usually, an investor in a 50 percent bracket will have recovered his investment in four years through tax savings. Generally, the builder, sponsor or middleman in 221 (d) (4) and 236 programs has to be very knowledgeable because he is exposed to great risk. Profits can be considerable, but so can losses.

Trading equities is similar to investing in the stock market. There are wholesale prices and retail prices, higher prices for large groups of small investors and special prices for prestigious Wall Street firms who sell them to clients. I acted as a broker for (d) (4) projects in Reno and Carson City, Nevada, because the developers did not know how to market their equity. They only knew that they could build the project and obtain a federally insured loan. I took the feasibility letter, which FHA issues when it approves a project, and sold it to a company that purchases projects nationally. If I remember correctly, the builder received 12 or 13 percent of the mortgage and the seller paid 14 percent. I pocketed the difference.

Sponsoring one of these projects does not guarantee profit, and it is possible that obtaining a feasibility letter from FHA can result in losses. Conceivably, a project feasibility letter requires little, if any, cash outlay by the developer. There is no charge by FHA and if the land can be optioned inexpensively and the architect will work on an "if-come" basis, then only minimum advance money is needed. When an approved feasibility letter is received, however, the land must be purchased and the architect paid for working drawings. Caught in an upward spiral of rising construction costs and interest rates, the developer might find that he is unable to build the project for the allowable mortgage and that heavy expenses incurred prior to construction are not recoverable. I have been involved in projects that I wish had never been started.

This type of activity has a questionable future. It has been proposed that Congress not allow deductions by investors to offset outside income, but nothing has happened and projects are still being sold. One especially obvious danger to investors is that projects have proved to be unrentable and were foreclosed. When this occurs, recapture of depreciation deductions is required. A number of foreclosures have already taken place in inner-city developments, and equities in those projects are considerably less valuable than those built in small towns or suburbs.

After pursuing many phases of housing for 25 years, I now concentrate on the construction of luxury and semiluxury homes in the western part of St. Louis County. In 1970, I became a partner with a talented builder, Richard Manlin, by buying out his previous partners. Besides the money, I added organization and management skills to his creativity and experience in single-family building, and our partnership has resulted in successful developments. Much of our time is spent in designing and constructing custom homes for specific owners, but we also have speculative houses that sell for $150,000 to $180,000

These homes feature antiques and fine finishes that are reminiscent of the homes built in Europe or early St. Louis. Building homes that are not presold in this price range is very risky, but none of our houses has been on the market for more than a few months. It is exciting to create expensive homes and it enhances our reputation for the sale of those that are less costly.

It is not an easy business. Purchasers, city engineers, and subcontractors hassle you, but there is the advantage of freedom from government restrictions. Luxury home construction is highly competitive and special inducements must be included if houses are to sell quickly and not have profits eroded by costly interest payments. One of our projects is on a heavily wooded tract and we are trying to conserve every 100-foot oak tree even if costs run higher by shifting roads and adding sewer line manholes.

Costs are escalating at the rate of 5 to 10 percent annually and it seems that more people are being excluded from the new home market. A 1974 construction strike in the St. Louis area included the carpenters who, in my memory, have never struck. For three successive years, the carpenters had not asked for an increase, but in 1974 the union insisted that they ask for $1.25 per hour more. Many ran rank and file carpenters were fearful of a construction shutdown because there was already a 30-50 percent unemployment rate among carpenters. I still receive calls every week from carpenters looking for work.

The entire industry is crippled by these often lengthy strikes. Meantime, you have to pay interest on uncompleted buildings. If you have 15 or 20 houses underway, it can break you. Construction loan interest is no longer 6 or 7 percent. It is closer to 12 percent. Banks charge me 2 percent over prime and I know they can't make any money when they are paying 11 percent and over for their money. The whole process seems insane.

St. Louis's reputation as a tough union town is deserved. Other cities like Atlanta and Tampa have open shops and only the good workers have jobs. That isn't true in St. Louis and we have to hire union labor at prices that are hard to bear. For example, we have to pay our St. Louis carpenter contractor $14.50 an hour, while in Florida the scale is about one-third that amount, union or nonunion.

In May and June 1974, there was a construction strike in the St. Louis area. Strike mediators acknowledged that a central issue was the laborers' pursuit of greater power. The laborers prevailed on four other unions, including the carpenters, cement masons, operating engineers, and teamsters, to join in the negotiations, and they called themselves the Five Pact. The laborers' union demanded that they retain the right to appoint a shop steward on every job. This meant that the steward would be sent from the union hall instead of being appointed from the builder's work force. Builders were afraid

that if the laborers got the power to send anybody they wanted, their
choice might be loafers, crooks, or musclemen who would enforce
inane union rules that are on the books. At stake were rules like the
one that would require a carpenter wanting a drink of water to have a
laborer bring it to him. The union backed off finally on the shop steward
issue in return for other concessions, but the fact remains that St.
Louis is a rough union town.

Zoning regulations also make it difficult to hold down project
costs, especially in wealthy suburban communities that are protective
of low density. One-acre development is prohibitive in cost except for
those with very large incomes. My firm has been trying for three to
four years to build luxury condominiums in high-priced residential
neighborhoods. These are single-family condominiums, cluster-type,
attached only at the garages and designed to sell for between $75,000
and $100,000. After being turned down by several planning commis-
sions, we found a "sleeper" and purchased under option an abandoned
tree nursery in the village of Westwood, a luxury suburban area in St.
Louis County. It was 9.5 acres and only needed the approval of the
village trustees for rezoning. We were optimistic because three of the
five trustees wanted to move into our development. The site contained
a series of old storage sheds, deserted cars and buses, and outside
storage for about 100 golf carts. It was a nonconforming commercial
use under a grandfather clause. Our proposal was to build 36 unattach-
ed luxury condominiums, selling for $80,000 and up. The trustees
felt that a public hearing for the 100 families in Westwood was desirable. At the meeting our proposal was overwhelmingly rejected because residents a mile or two away from the site felt that their one-
acre community was being threatened. Others said they knew the nursery was ugly, but it was there when they moved in and they were
accustomed to it. The powerful always protect their interests, even
when the interests are questionable.

Functioning in the land of the wealthy is like walking on egg-
shells. Land-use plans drawn up by public agencies are ignored because the residents fight everything zoned under one acre. Higher
density projects can only occur in moderate-income areas where opposition is weaker. As a result, expensive and inefficient utility extensions are continually needed.

Conclusions

After 25 years, a housing intermediary like myself, who has
played so many different roles in the system, should be filled with
sage advice for the future. This isn't the case at all. Perhaps after

living so intensely in the present—jumping from one opportunity to
the next—my capacity for looking ahead has been underutilized.

I don't find it as difficult to reflect on the past, and one of my
observations is that much undeserved blame has been heaped on middlemen. After all, they don't devise programs, but operate squarely within the system created and established by others. Once limits of the
game are set, the competent intermediary is opportunistic and enterprising in achieving maximum rewards. In the case of the failure of
some FHA high-rise programs in the inner city during the late 1960s
and early 1970s, the responsibility rests to a far greater degree on national politics and the programs of Congress than on the speculator. He
was merely a front man for others who were less visible. In fact, the
intermediary makes an excellent scapegoat because of his visibility.
This type of vilification leads to ridiculous charges that landlords were
the major reason for central-city decline when reality tells us that industry, commerce, and people have been leaving the urban core for
decades with federal help.

I have also learned that there is nothing holy or sacred about
public agencies and nonprofit corporations. Often, only a few people
actually do the work in these institutions, while others are engaged in
meaningless activity. Many do not take responsibility for their actions,
do not complete work assigned to them, and do not understand the mis-
sion of the agency in which they are employed. Public and quasi-public
intermediaries provide services frequently at much higher cost and
with less success than capable private entrepreneurs. Working with
bureaucrats at all levels of government has convinced me that many
are so fearful of losing their jobs that they do not respond quickly or
creatively without pressure from someone over them. The same is
probably true in large corporations, but I do not have firsthand knowledge of these enterprises and I am basically a small entrepreneur.

It is unfortunate that no one wants to use the housing experience of inner-city landlords and dealers for public purposes. Many
of us who were involved in real estate between 1948 and 1960 have
skills for organizing rehabilitation projects and managing difficult
rental properties. But public policy is so anxious that it does not
consider these resources. At any rate, I have learned that it is much
easier to provide housing for the wealthy than it is for the poor.

6

FANNIE MAE-GINNIE MAE:
HOW THE SECONDARY
MORTGAGE MARKET WORKS
James E. Murray

During periods of tight mortgage money, the secondary mortgage market takes on increased importance. When money is easy to
obtain, most of us go to a savings and loan association or a commercial bank where we have conducted business and apply for a home loan.
If the loan is made, it becomes a mortgage on our house. The funds
for that mortgage are ordinarily provided by the depositors of the financial institution. Savings and loan associations and commercial
banks have become the major sources of home financing since World
War II. Prior to that time money was available primarily on a short-
term basis of three to five years from private investors.

In the primary market, the borrower approaches the lender
and negotiates financing for his residence. Lenders use the savings
of their depositors to make these mortgages. Everything works fairly
well as long as the savings are coming in steadily. However, this is
not always the case. There is no way that lenders can count on the
use of depositors' funds for the duration of the mortgage. Money is
lent for long periods, 25-30 years, while it is only kept on deposit
for a short time, six months to one year or for extended periods at
the discretion of the depositor.

The views and opinions stated herein are those of the author
alone and not of the Federal National Mortgage Association. The author
gratefully acknowledges the assistance of John T. Mansfield, Senior
Counsel in the Office of General Counsel, FNMA, in the preparation
of this paper.

Uncertainty in having funds available for a long duration is intensified by restrictions placed on the return that financial institutions can pay to savers. One of the devices that has enabled interest rates on home mortgages in the United States to be low in relation to rates in other countries is called Regulation Q. It is a federal regulation that keeps the interest paid by savings and loan associations and commercial banks unrealistically below what borrowers pay in the capital markets. It means that while small depositors receive lower returns on their investments, home financing charges are also considerably less than charges to industry for financing plant expansion.

Because rates are held relatively constant by Regulation Q, deposits increase when the interest rates paid by mortgage institutions are high compared to interest rates paid on treasury bills, corporate bonds, and other competing financial mechanisms. In periods when money is loose and available, funds flow to home lenders. The opposite is true in periods of tight money, which are characterized by a phenomenon called disintermediation, in which people take their money out of savings institutions and place it elsewhere. Even the "little old ladies in sneakers" look favorably toward treasury bonds and notes when they pay several percentage points more than passbook interest.

During the first half of 1974, for example, a bank depositor could withdraw all of his savings from one window and go to another and buy treasury bills. His savings account was paying 5.5 percent annual interest, while his new investment, backed by the full faith and credit of the U.S. government, would pay 8.5 percent. Imagine what happens to the savings flow as this information becomes widespread. Funds flee the savings and loan associations and banks.

A major function of the secondary market is to provide funds for home mortgages when a shortage exists in the primary market. Mortgages do not originate in the secondary market; they are bought from others. Dating from World War I, this secondary function was initiated by life insurance companies interested in investing their premiums. Sufficient mortgages were not available in areas where their home offices were located—Des Moines, Omaha, Hartford, or Newark—so relationships were established with those who would initiate mortgages for them around the country. In this way, a network of correspondents was established for the insurance companies. Funds could flow throughout the country from areas where mortgage money was overly abundant to areas where growth was so rapid that funds were scarce. Life insurance companies remained a major participant in the secondary market until after World War II.

Government Involvement in the Secondary Market

Contemporary federal involvement in mortgage financing
dates back to the early 1930s when the liquidity and solvency of financial institutions were under great pressure because of the Depression. A stable system of home financing was needed and ways had to
be found to circumvent lenders' traditional distaste for the long-term
fixed investments in home mortgages.

The Federal Home Loan Bank Act in 1932 and the Home Owner's Loan Act in 1933 began the flow of New Deal housing legislation.
In 1934, the Federal Housing Administration (FHA) was created and
the structure of mortgage financing was altered dramatically. This
new agency insured the repayment of principal and interest to lenders.
Low down payments were provided along with smaller monthly payments. Mortgage lengths were dramatically extended and notes were
fully amortized. FHA pioneered the 20, 25, and 30-year mortgage,
which was probably its greatest achievement. Prior to the creation
of FHA, mortgages were for very short duration with renewal fees
continually charged by lenders.[1] Even with the government's support
of FHA insurance, it was feared that no one would buy the mortgages.
To encourage lenders, national mortgage associations were authorized
in the same 1934 Housing Act. These were to be private organizations,
like savings and loan associations, mutually owned by the depositors,
but investing only in FHA mortgages. Responsibility for the charter
and supervision of these mortgage associations was given to the federal
housing administrator. Their operations were to be financed through
the public sale of bonds and notes.[2]

It was hoped that investor confidence would be generated for
FHA mortgages and that funds would flow smoothly from rich capital
to poor capital regions of the country. As often happens in federal
legislation, expectations exceeded reality. The atmosphere of the
1930s was so pessimistic that even those financial institutions that
were liquid didn't want long-term mortgages signed by purchasers
with minimum down payments. As a result, no private mortgage associations were formed, despite an awareness of the need to support
primary lenders through a secondary market.

Awareness of this problem was translated into legislation in
1935, when the Reconstruction Finance Corporation (RFC) established
a subsidiary agency to assist the mortgage market. Although not
originally devised as a secondary market for FHA-insured mortgages,
it made limited purchases of FHA and later VA loans until 1948 when
the subsidiary was dissolved. Since the RFC was not handling a large
volume of FHA loans and because no national mortgage associations
had been formed, the president pushed the chairman of the RFC to form

one in 1938. It was called the Federal National Mortgage Association
(FNMA) and promptly labeled "Fannie Mae."[3] Operations were begun
with initial capital of $10 million, increased to $20 million in 1948, and
paid-in surplus of $1 million provided by the RFC. FNMA remained a
subsidiary of RFC until 1950, when it was transferred to the Housing
and Home Finance Agency, which later became the Department of
Housing and Urban Development.[4]

The original goal of developing a market in FHA mortgages
was achieved and investors around the country began to accept the
FHA insurance. Mortgage bankers would initiate the mortgage, but
since they were not portfolio lenders or deposit institutions, they
would sell them to FNMA, to the insurance companies, or to commercial banks. Liquidity of these mortgages was obtained by FNMA's entrance into the market.

From 1938 to 1954, FNMA was a wholly owned government
corporation. In the early 1950s, a strong constituency developed to
make the secondary market privately operated and financed. Included
in the coalition were such groups as the National Association of Home
Builders, the Mortgage Bankers Association, the National Association
of Real Estate Boards, and the United States Savings and Loan League.[5]
Movement toward private ownership was enacted into law in the Housing
Act of 1954. Like most of our housing legislation, the private role was
to be enhanced, with the progressive, phased withdrawal of government
participation in Fannie Mae and the secondary market.

Three functions were ascribed to Fannie Mae in 1954 and separate accounting systems were established for each. They were:

●   Maintenance of a secondary mortgage market to insure
        liquidity in residential loans.
●   Special assistance to certain kinds of mortgages as designated
        by the President or Congress with funds provided by the
        Treasury.
●   Managing and selling mortgages bought prior to 1954.

Secondary market operations were to be self-supporting and the enterprise was intended to be placed eventually in private hands. Fannie
Mae had a mandate—purchase mortgages in the market and don't lose
money in acquiring a portfolio of residential loans.

The 1954 legislation created a new charter changing FNMA
into a mixed-ownership government corporation.[6] One part of the new
organization, capitalized by preferred stock issued to the government
and common stock to private investors, was authorized to operate in
the national mortgage market much as a private corporation, with most
of the funds borrowed from private sources. The other part was to
continue to operate as a government agency, financed almost entirely

by the Federal Treasury. Though it continued to be one organization, it conducted these functions separately. Upon retirement of the preferred stock held by the government, assets, liabilities and control of FNMA were to pass to the holders of the common. At that point, the secondary market was to be entirely a private responsibility.

In 1968, Congress formally divided the three functions performed previously by Fannie Mae. Another organization was created, the Government National Mortgage Association (GNMA), which came to be known as "Ginnie Mae." It was made a part of the U.S. Department of Housing and Urban Development. [7] The "new" FNMA bought out the government's preferred stock investment in the private-type "Secondary Market Operations" and operated with completely private ownership. GNMA assumed the Treasury-financed functions of the old FNMA, known as the "Special Assistance Function" and the "Management and Liquidation Function."

By the time FNMA left the government, its portfolio of mortgages amounted to $6 billion. Removing these loans from federal control caused the only surplus in the U.S. budget during the Johnson administration. One of the reasons for taking FNMA out of the government was to release it from federal budget constraints. Fannie Mae had been unable to provide more funds and greater support to the mortgage market because of a prevailing practice of federal accounting. When mortgages were acquired by FNMA prior to 1968, they were carried in the budget as a debt. This was because FNMA had to borrow money to acquire these mortgages. However, a corresponding credit was not made to include them as assets of the federal government. When FNMA left the government, expansion of its investment portfolio was no longer severely limited.

The "New" FNMA

Two years, 1968 to 1970, were needed to complete the transition of FNMA to a private corporation. In 1968, Fannie Mae was turned over to the stockholders, of which approximately one-third were mortgage bankers. Until that time equity capital was raised through a requirement that those who sold mortgages to FNMA, usually mortgage bankers, had to purchase stock in the corporation amounting to a small percentage of the face value of the residential loans they sold to the government. After 1968, this means of obtaining equity capital was correctly recognized as an extra cost passed on to the home buyer. New sources of ownership funds needed to be tapped. This was done through two public offerings of stock and debt convertible into stock that raised over $300 million of the $800 million total in

equity capital held by the corporation. Of the 45 million shares of
stock presently outstanding, only 27 percent are owned by mortgage
bankers.

Today, FNMA is a publicly owned corporation in the sense
that it is owned entirely by its approximately 50,000 stockholders,
to whom it pays dividends out of profits from its operations. Its stock
is traded on the New York Stock Exchange and the Midwest and Pacific
Stock Exchanges and in terms of assets, it is one of the largest corporations in the country, with assets of approximately $29.7 billion as of
December 31, 1974.[8] FNMA is also the country's largest borrower in
the private sector, with about $28.3 billion in debt outstanding as of
December 31, 1974.[9]

FNMA's corporate purpose, as stated in its Charter Act, is
to "provide supplementary assistance to the secondary market for
home mortgages by providing a degree of liquidity for mortgage investments, thereby improving the distribution of investment capital available for home mortgage financing."[10] To accomplish this purpose, it
is specifically authorized to purchase FHA and VA mortgages and
certain mortgages insured by the Farmers Home Administration.[11]
In addition, legislation enacted in 1970 authorized FNMA to deal in
conventional mortgages that are not insured or guaranteed by the
federal government.

While FNMA is privately owned, and must therefore earn
profits to be distributed to its stockholders, it nevertheless has close
ties to the government. Until the 1970 Act, its purchasing activity was
limited to government-underwritten mortgages.[12] FNMA's debt obligations have enough characteristics of government bonds to enjoy
the status of "Federal Agency Securities." This means that private
financial institutions, banks and savings and loan associations, and
state and local governments can buy the debentures and notes. Because of the federal agency status that FNMA's debt obligations enjoy, the interest rates paid in the money market are generally lower
than those for the highest rated, Triple A, corporate bonds. Approximately $24.7 billion is outstanding in debentures that have an average
maturity of four to five years and another $3.6 billion in short-term
discount notes of one to nine months. The notes are sold like commercial paper. They are "rolled over" frequently and are especially
attractive to banks, municipalities, and other investors desiring to
invest idle funds for interim periods between receipt of revenues and
expenditures.[13] As previously stated, FNMA is the largest borrower
outside of the federal government, coming to the market at least every
three months for amounts as large as $1 billion, depending on FNMA's
needs and those of the mortgage market.

Fannie Mae has an avowed public purpose to improve the
national secondary mortgage market, especially when tight money

threatens to destroy that market. To show an expression of public
interest, Congress has authorized the secretary of the treasury to
purchase $2.25 billion of FNMA's debt obligations when he considers
it an emergency. Other examples of FNMA's relationship with the
government are the Charter Act provisions that one-third of the members of the FNMA Board of Directors be appointed by the president
of the United States and that certain regulatory authority rest with
the secretary of housing and urban development. [14] This is a unique
partnership between government and the private sector, a character-
istically American improvisation that defies tidy categorization but
seems to work well.

Private investors have not fared poorly by purchasing FNMA
stock. Dividends, which have steadily increased, have been paid on
the stock since the company's departure from government. Profits
have been earned every year and the stock has split 16 to 1. FNMA
has become a successful private operation, and federal sponsorship
has played a major role in its success.

Fannie Mae stock has been described as an "interest rate
play," which means that profits escalate rapidly when interest rates
drop. Since FNMA invests in long-term securities and borrows on a
much shorter basis, changes in the cost of money tend to have an immediate impact on the company's earnings and, therefore, on the performance of the stock. [15] When the interest rate on the money that
FNMA borrows is greater than what it receives on investments, profit
possibilities are erased. As the size of the loan portfolio has grown,
however, and the maturity of the outstanding debt has been extended
to over four years, FNMA has become much less vulnerable to short-
term interest rate fluctuations.

FNMA holds billions of dollars in mortgages, but few homeowners realize that the mortgage lender who originated their loan is
not the mortgagee. Although Fannie Mae is more visible now that its
stock, the most active in 1972, is traded on the New York Stock Exchange, the company previously operated in relative obscurity. This
lack of visibility was not intentional; rather, it resulted from the
origin and growth of FNMA.

Formed as an agency of the federal government, it was one
of a group of agencies created to provide liquidity in lending. There
was the Farm Credit Administration, which was patterned along the
lines of the Federal Reserve Board, that had been designed to assist
commercial banks. The savings and loan associations had the Home
Loan Bank Board and FNMA was chartered to encourage the acceptance of FHA mortgages. All of these agencies were essentially supporting other institutions which dealt with the public. As a result,
they were not widely known.

In the money markets, FNMA acts as a converter transforming illiquid FHA, VA, and conventional mortgages into debentures that can change hands freely on the capital markets. "Thus enjoying the benefits of federal sponsorship, Fannie Mae has become a gigantic money-transfer machine, using its government credit rating to borrow billions on Wall Street, and relending funds at higher interest rates to finance homes and apartments."[16]

For many years, Fannie Mae purchased primarily single-family mortgages. This practice changed with passage of the National Housing Act in 1968. Under Section 236 of this legislation, FHA insurance and subsidies reducing interest rates were made available for rental project mortgages—most of which were purchased ultimately by FNMA. Unless there is a change in federal policy, future activity will decline substantially in subsidized multi-family commitments with FHA insurance. In fact, Section 236 is being phased out with the passage of recent housing legislation in August 1974. FHA and VA mortgages generally seem to be playing an increasingly smaller role in home financing. In 1971, FHA-insured housing starts were 527,900, or 25.3 percent of all starts, while in the first quarter of 1974 there were only 24,400 FHA-inspected starts, or 7.6 percent of the total.[17] Perhaps the most dramatic change in FNMA's operations has been the purchase of conventional mortgages. Authority to acquire conventional loans was granted in 1970 and initial purchase began with about $50 million in 1972. In 1973, purchases soared to $1 billion with the issuance of $2 billion in commitments. FNMA bought about $1.2 billion in conventional mortgages in 1974. However, the existing portfolio of Fannie Mae still consists of 92.7 percent FHA-VA loans.

When FNMA purchases conventional mortgages, sound underwriting requirements are followed. The statutory limits are now $55,000 on the amount of the mortgage with an 80 percent loan-to-value ratio that can be increased to 95 percent with private mortgage insurance. With respect to FHA-VA loans, FNMA does not do any underwriting at all, relying instead on the federal insurance or guaranty.

This detachment from underwriting was a major factor behind FNMA's involvement in America's inner cities in the mid-1960s. At one time, FNMA was underwriting FHA mortgages and reviewing the credit of prospective borrowers. The result was that there was considerable criticism of FNMA's undercutting the FHA insurance. When FHA agreed to insure loans in the inner cities after the riots, FNMA pledged that it would not second-guess FHA insurance on any loan. This put mortgage money into core areas such as Brooklyn, Detroit, and St. Louis.

FNMA faces a potential dilemma in attempting to serve a public purpose and at the same time operating profitably for its stockholders. This is particularly apparent when interest rates reach

dramatically high levels. Should FNMA invest at yields below the
market or should that kind of support come from the federal government? It has been established that subsidies must be the government's
responsibility and this has been met in part through the FNMA-GNMA
Tandem Plan, which will be explained later. Our purchases must reflect the market for the company to be self-sustaining. If FNMA has
a negative differential in the cost of its debt as against its yield from
the portfolio, then before long no funds will be available to the market.
FNMA should be counter-cyclical, entering the mortgage market when
others are leaving it and withdrawing when other lenders, such as the
savings and loan associations and commercial banks reenter.

The public-private quandary is also reflected in FNMA's inability to operate nationally in the current market. Conventional mortgages tend to be bought mostly in the southeast, southwest, and west,
because usury laws block entry into many other areas. These outmoded
restrictions are frustrating to FNMA because it is chartered by Congress to provide liquidity for the entire country. Funds are invested
in states that traditionally have been capital poor because the financial
institutions on those states do not have the funds to finance the growth.
Therefore, the demand and price of money are high.

Although usury laws keep FNMA out of much of the midwest
and east, consumer legislation also limits FNMA's lending capacity
even where it has been a major source of real estate funds. Many
buildings in Bedford-Stuyvesant and Harlem in New York City are financed by FNMA. It is not the best portfolio, but few New York banks,
or any other banks, will lend there even with FHA insurance. FNMA
is there because, as noted, it is not our policy to underwrite FHA or
VA loans. Although FNMA has been criticized for not evaluating the
quality of the loans, we do not second-guess FHA or VA. These are
government programs and reflect priorities determined by the government. If there is insurance against loss, then that should be sufficient.
FNMA is only the investor. Concerning consumer legislation, the
legislature of the state of New York unanimously passed a law requiring that interest be paid on escrow accounts for the taxes and insurance
collected on mortgage payments. Passage of this legislation is of doubtful benefit to homeowners and it gives little recognition to the effect on
the flow of mortgage funds into that state. This law directly affects
FNMA's yield in New York, which is already below what can be obtained in other jurisdictions. In the future, FNMA will have even greater
difficulty purchasing mortgages there because the New York rates will
not be competitive with other regions of the nation.

FNMA Operations

FNMA purchases mortgages from approved sellers. There
are about 1500 institutions approved by FNMA as qualified to sell
mortgages to it. Eighty percent are mortgage banking companies.
Others are commercial banks, savings and loan associations, mutual
savings banks, life insurance companies, state housing finance agencies,and pension funds.

At one time, FNMA carried out all its mortgage purchase
operations by posting prices at which it would buy mortgages. The
prices, which varied by geographical areas, were determined by
frequent surveys of area markets to enable FNMA to fix prices based
on market values. This system had several disadvantages.

Despite the frequency and the care with which prices were
fixed, it was difficult to reflect accurately all the price fluctuations
that take place in the mortgage market. It was especially difficult
to make realistic distinctions regarding mortgage prices in different
geographical areas, particularly because the very activities under
which they were being purchased were helping to create a more nearly
uniform national market for the entire FNMA portfolio. Thus, the
regional price distinctions tended to be discriminatory at times. A
more basic defect of this system of buying mortgages over-the-counter
and at prices fixed at the time of purchase was that it didn't enable the
home building and mortgage lending industries to plan ahead. While
new homes in a large development were being prepared for sale,
neither the builder nor the lender had any way of knowing whether the
mortgage funds were going to be available from FNMA at the time they
were needed or what interest rate would be charged.

A new operating method for the purchase of mortgages was
developed to avoid these three defects of the posted-price purchase
system. Known as the Free Market System Auction, it was used first
in 1968. It is now FNMA's principal method for purchasing mortgages
on one-to-four family homes and also for determining the precise
amount of these mortgages that it will purchase at any one time and
the prices it will pay for them. As the name indicates, the system
involves competitive bidding by those who wish to sell mortgages to
FNMA. Bidders specify a yield to FNMA that, in effect, indicates how
large a discount, if any, from the face amount of the mortgage they
are willing to offer FNMA. Since bidders are in constant touch with
the mortgage market, their bids collectively reflect that market far
more accurately than could be done under the posted-price system.
FNMA, of course, buys those acceptable mortgages that are offered

to it at the range of prices that yields the highest return. Funds naturally tend to gravitate to those parts of the country with the greatest growth, because the shortage of capital in these areas bids up the price of money beyond the point at which other regions can compete.

The bid system permits FNMA to buy mortgages at the lowest possible price and facilitates control over the volume of mortgages to be bought at any one time. At each auction, FNMA will commit itself to buying varying quantities of mortgages, depending on how many bids are received at or below a price that permits it to maintain a profitable spread between the yield on the mortgages being purchased and the cost of borrowing money.

The Free Market System Auctions are announced at frequent intervals, typically two weeks apart, with separate auctions being held for government-insured or guaranteed mortgages and conventional mortgages. The notice announcing the auction for the government-backed mortgages usually specifies that the mortgages being offered must bear the currently prevailing interest rate. FNMA may agree to purchase mortgages bearing different rates of interest, in which case the purchase price is adjusted accordingly. The seller of a mortgage that bears a lower interest rate would be required to sell it to the FNMA at a larger discount than the seller of a mortgage that bears a higher interest rate. FNMA utilizes a set of tables that enables it readily to determine the yields on mortgages that bear interest at different rates and that are acquired at different discounts. For example, a 30-year mortgage bearing a 7.5 percent interest rate that is prepaid, as is common, at the end of 12 years, will have yielded an annual return of 8.5 percent if the sales price of the mortgage had originally been discounted down to 92.94 percent of its face amount. A comparable mortgage that bears an 8 percent interest rate would only have to be discounted to a sales price of 96.45 percent to return the same 8.5 percent yield.

The principle underlying the preparation of FNMA's tables can best be understood if it is recognized that when a mortgage loan or any other loan is sold at a discounted price there are several factors that contribute toward determining the yield received by the buyer. By way of a simplified example, if someone were to borrow $1,000 and agree to pay $50, or 5 percent, each year as interest and to return the $1,000 at the end of the five years, the annual rate of interest and the yield would each be 5 percent. If the maker of the loan were to sell it immediately to someone else for $900, the buyer would be receiving $50 in interest each year on his $900 investment, representing an interest rate of over 5 1/2 percent. He would also, at the end of the five years, receive the full $1,000, which is $100 more than he paid for the loan, thereby returning to him $20 for each of the five years he held the loan, about 2 percent additional, making the total annual yield about 7.5 percent. If the loan were to be paid off fully after only one year, the additional $100 would represent an annual return of about 11 percent additional on the $900, or a total yield of about 16.5 percent to the buyer of the loan. Calculations have been made converting mortgage interest rates to mortgage yields under varying assumptions as to the interest rate of the mortgage, the mortgage term, and the discounted price at which it is sold. Because not all long-term mortgages run to maturity but often are paid off before they are due, as when homes are sold, the conversion tables assume that the mortgage will be repaid in 12 years.

FNMA permits prospective sellers to submit two kinds of bids in the Free Market System Auction. The basic "competitive" bid is submitted for the sale of a stated volume of mortgages at a specified yield. Sellers are also permitted to submit a "noncompetitive" offer to sell a specified volume of mortgages at the average yield—whatever that may prove to be—of all accepted competitive offers. No bidder is permitted to submit both types of bids at the same auction. Bidders telephone either type of bid to FNMA's Washington, D.C. office during specified hours on the announced auction date. FNMA retains the right to accept or decline any offer, in whole or in part, and it notifies the bidder in writing whether his bid has been accepted or declined.

The notice announcing the auction normally specifies the maximum dollar amount of mortgages that may be submitted for sale by any one seller and this maximum has been has been set at a lower amount for noncompetitive bids than for competitive bids. The competitive bid limit has recently been set at $3 million for auctions of both government-aided and conventional mortgages. The noncompetitive limits are $200,000 and $100,000, respectively.

Announcement of the auction also specifies the commitment period during which FNMA is obligated to purchase the mortgages from the successful bidders. It has been set by FNMA at four months since 1972. This permits builders and lenders to plan ahead with the knowledge that funds will be available at an agreed-upon yield when the time comes to finance the sale of new homes. FNMA collects fees, now set at .5 percent, in return for these commitments. The fees are intended to compensate FNMA partially for the risk that interest rates will rise during the commitment period. The successful bidders do not bear an equivalent risk, being free to sell the mortgages elsewhere if at any time during the commitment period interest rates drop and they can obtain better terms. FNMA is thus providing a three fold service—it is not only a source of additional mortgage funds as a long-term investor and a source of liquidity to the successful bidders, but it also provides a hedge against unexpected interest cost increases during the commitment period. The commitment fee, which is normally collected by the original lender from the builder, represents a relatively

small price for builders to pay for this hedge because sudden changes
in the money market represent a high risk to them. FNMA, however,
with its far greater resources than either builders or primary lenders,
generally can, like an insurance company, afford to assume this risk
in return for a reasonable commitment fee geared to the length of the
commitment.

The Free Market System Auction has not been extended to
the purchase of mortgages on "projects"—that is, on apartment houses,
nursing homes, and hospitals. Also, the auction system does not apply
to the purchase of mortgages on single-family properties involving pro
posed construction. There are several reasons why the auction system
does not readily lend itself to these purchases. One reason is that the
commitment period needed by the builder and lender is much longer.
FNMA offers so-called "standby" commitments of 12 months, duration
on both government-aided and conventional home mortgages involving
proposed construction, and it offers 24-month commitments for the
purchase of project mortgages. Accordingly, standby commitments
continue to be offered on the basis of prices posted by FNMA, and
project mortgages are purchased on a project-by-project basis. Neve
theless, advantages of the Free Market System Auction instituted in
1968 have spilled over to these transactions simply because the pricir
information gained by FNMA from the auction is used to help determir
acceptable prices and yields for purchases made outside the auction
system. For example, a standby commitment will be issued by FNMA
at a purchase price producing a higher yield to it than the current auction yield in order to compensate it for the additional risk of increase
interest rates assumed by FNMA during the longer period of coverage
However, at any time during the 12-month commitment period, the
standby commitment can be converted by the holder to a four-month
commitment at the then current auction yield upon payment of an additional fee.

FNMA's assistance to the secondary mortgage market is not
confined to mortgage purchases, but also includes the sale of mortgages, loans on the security of mortgages, and participation with primary lenders in making loans to finance the construction of FHA-insu
ed multi-family, apartment house, projects. Most recently, Fannie
Mae has also announced a program to purchase GNMA-guaranteed
securities backed by a pool of loans on mobile homes.

Under the "participation" loan option, FNMA and the primar
lender make the loan jointly, with the FNMA portion of the loan being
restricted to a maximum of 95 percent. These loans are limited to
FHA-insured multi-family projects because FHA mortgage insurance
during construction is similarly limited, and FNMA wishes to have th
protection of that insurance. Without such insurance, a construction
loan is riskier than a permanent loan, partly because the unfinished

property securing the loan is not yet producing income. Participation loans are also limited to properties for which FNMA or GNMA has already issued commitments to purchase the permanent mortgages on completion of construction. Along with careful individual review of each participation loan, these multiple safeguards—shared risk, FHA mortgage insurance, and commitment for permanent financing—assure the safety of the investment. At the same time, FNMA benefits from a yield which is generally higher for construction loans than for permanent mortgage loans.

Throughout Fannie Mae's history, the volume of its mortgage purchases has far exceeded the volume of its sales operations. Since 1954, when FNMA undertook its "Secondary Market Operations," there have been only two years, 1958 and 1963, in which the corporation sold more mortgages than it purchased. The highest volume of sales was reached in 1963 when about $790 million in mortgages were sold and only about $181 million were purchased. More recently, purchases have far exceeded sales as shown by the following:

Year	Total Purchases	Total Sales
1969	$4,120.0 million	None
1970	5,078.8 million	$ 20.3 million
1971	3,573.9 million	335.5 million
1972	3,699.3 million	207.6 million
1973	6,127.0 million	70.0 million
1974 (estimated)	7,010.0 million	4.3 million

Because of the sharp fluctuations in the volume of sales and the relatively low volume, it has not been considered advantageous so far to establish a system of periodic auctions for the sale of mortgages similar to the system established for their purchase.

There are other disadvantages in conducting a routine national sales auction as compared with a national purchase auction. These disadvantages flow from the fact that the mortgages that FNMA sells are more varied than the mortgages it buys. The mortgages that it buys are normally new and normally have the same interest rate and relatively long terms. But the mortgages that FNMA sells may have been written five years ago or 25 years ago. Their interest rates may vary from 4.5 percent on those written a generation ago to about double the rate on some more recent mortgages, and their maturity dates may be a few years away or many years in the future. The demand to buy mortgages not only varies from time to time, but it also varies on the basis of these differing characteristics and according to location. For example, prospective buyers who happen to have surplus funds to invest at a particular time may wish to buy only mortgages on properties in the geographical areas of their operations. For these many reasons,

FNMA has avoided routine or periodic sales auctions, but stands ready to sell whenever there is a demand. In setting the prices at which it sells, FNMA takes into consideration the yields currently demanded by the mortgage market as revealed in the Free Market System Auctions that it utilizes in its purchasing program. FNMA may also insist that a certain volume of older mortgages nearing its maturity dates be purchased along with the more recent, although seasoned, mortgages that buyers often prefer to purchase.

FNMA and the Mortgage Banker

Mortgages that are purchased by FNMA through the auction system are originated when a real estate broker needing financing to complete a purchase or sale calls a mortgage lender eligible to sell mortgages to FNMA to find out how many points or what percent of the mortgage will have to be discounted, if any. A discount, as explained earlier, may be necessary to increase the rate of interest specified in the mortgage to that of the market rate. To illustrate, if the rate specified on a mortgage is 8.75 percent and the market rate 9.75 percent, then the mortgage will have to be discounted about five or six points.

The mortgage lender, or banker, watches FNMA purchases very closely and provides the broker with a price at which he will make the loan to the borrower, say, at 95 cents on the dollar. At the next auction, the lender obtains a FNMA commitment to purchase this mortgage along with others. Commitments are issued in minimum amounts of $100,000. When the broker completes the transactions and the borrower signs the appropriate papers, the loan is delivered to the mortgage lender, who then sells it to FNMA.

That is a thumbnail sketch of the process. In reality, it is far more complex. Mortgage bankers, for example, use borrowed money to finance their operations, engaging in a relationship with commercial banks called "warehousing." Their operations are usually financed thinly, with a balance sheet capitalization of only $100,000 required. Because mortgage bankers do not hold mortgages for investment, they need short-term loans to enable them to enter into mortgages arranged by real estate brokers and keep them until final purchase by permanent investors such as savings and loan associations or FNMA. Mortgage bankers "warehouse" or place mortgages with commercial banks until they accumulate a number large enough to meet the purchasing requirements of the particular lending institution such as FNMA. This is done with a line of credit from a commercial bank, which may run to $10 million for a medium-size mortgage banker. Profits can be derived from warehousing by the mortgage banker if the interest that he pays to the commercial bank is less than the interest that he receives on the mortgages that are in his possession. Conversely, when money is very tight, the interest that commercial banks charge the mortgage banker, often one or two points over the prime rate, may be considerably higher than that earned from the mortgages. Under these conditions, the longer the mortgages are held in "warehouse," the greater the loss to the mortgage bankers.

Warehousing can be a profitable operation for the mortgage banker. It is dependent entirely on what interest rate he pays on his short-term loans at commercial banks and what the market interest rate is on his long-term mortgages. The ideal situation for the mortgage banker is to pay considerably less in short-term than long-term interest and to have market interest rates drop on mortgages. Although he may have a FNMA commitment, he does not have to sell the mortgage to FNMA if he can obtain a better price from a savings and loan or a commercial bank on the open market. When interest rates on mortgages are rising, however, the mortgage banker will take advantage of his commitment from Fannie Mae. In this way, FNMA commitments are played against the market. Mortgage lenders can also make more than the one point they receive from the mortgagor for originating the loan if they can earn additional points in the warehousing process.

Mortgage lenders dealing with FNMA make money in other ways. When they sell a mortgage to FNMA, they retain the servicing and receive a regular fee for collecting the payments and sending them to FNMA.

GNMA and the Tandem Plans

The Government National Mortgage Association (GNMA) was established in 1968 as a separate, wholly owned government corporation which took over the U.S. Treasury-financed functions performed by FNMA prior to that date. [18] In addition to managing the substantial U.S. Treasury-financed portfolios existing in 1968, [19] GNMA continues to purchase mortgages that are not generally acceptable to the private mortgage market, but for which the Congress or the president has decided the government should offer special assistance. [20] GNMA also performs a new function given it at the time of the 1968 reorganization—the guarantee of mortgage-backed securities issued by FNMA and other private holders of FHA and VA mortgages. [21]

GNMA is organized as a corporation without capital stock within the Department of Housing and Urban Development, directly under the control of the secretary. Even though GNMA's operations are

integrated with those of the department, the similarity of many of
FNMA's and GNMA's functions, together with the circumstances of
their separation, dictate that they continue to maintain a close relationship with each other. One measure of this closeness is that GNMA's
mortgage portfolio is managed under contract by FNMA. The contract,
authorized specifically by the 1968 legislation, [22] provides that FNMA
will supply those services for GNMA at a mutually agreeable rate of
compensation. GNMA is thereby able to operate with a small headquarters staff and does not maintain regional offices around the country.

FNMA and GNMA also work together under the so-called
"Tandem Plan" arrangement, designed to make several of GNMA's
Special Assistance Programs more effective. Because GNMA is financed directly from the federal treasury, its mortgage purchases
affect the federal budget. Under the federal budget system, such
investments are counted as spending, and, for this reason, the effectiveness of GNMA's Special Assistance Programs can be severely
limited by overall limits imposed on the federal budget.

The Tandem Plan program is based on GNMA's issuance of
commitments to purchase eligible mortgages at above-market prices.
Because GNMA sales of mortgages are treated for federal budget purposes as reductions in spending, GNMA can issue a commitment at a
supported price and sell it to FNMA or another investor at the market
price, with only the resulting discount, if any, amounting to a subsidy
and appearing as a charge against GNMA's funding authority. The
budgetary impact of the transaction is only the relatively small discount instead of the amount of the entire loan. To illustrate, if GNMA
purchases a $20,000 mortgage at par, or 100 percent of value, that
has a market value to FNMA or another investor of $19,000, the mar-
ket discount is $1,000 or five points, 5 percent of $20,000. When this
mortgage is sold by GNMA, the only impact on the budget is the $1,000
price difference.

The foregoing Tandem Plan put into operation was in support
of GNMA Special Assistance Programs 17 and 18, involving the purchase of subsidized multi-family and home mortgages. This began as
a comparatively simple Tandem Plan, with GNMA buying the mortgages
at support prices and selling them immediately to FNMA at market
prices. Special Assistance Program No. 17 authorizes the issuance
of commitments covering the purchase of FHA multi-family mortgages
insured under Section 221 (d) (3) (Rent Supplement) and Section 236
of the National Housing Act. As of December 31, 1973, GNMA had
issued $5.1 billion of commitment contracts since the inception of Pro-
gram No. 17. Special Assistance Program No. 18 authorizes the issuance of commitments covering the purchase of FHA single-family mortgages insured under Sections 235(i) or 237 of the National Housing Act.

Approximately $3.6 billion of commitments had been issued by GNMA under this program as of the same date.

The largest and most ambitious of the Tandem programs was launched in August 1971, when GNMA instituted its Programs 21 and 22. Under these programs, Ginnie Mae issues commitments to purchase a broad range of nonsubsidized, FHA-insured and VA-guaranteed mortgages at support prices, the purpose being to support a desired FHA-VA interest rate and thereby maintain a high level of residential home building activity. As of April 30, 1974, GNMA had issued $1.7 billion of commitments under Program 21, multi-family, and $4.25 billion under Program 22, single-family. Under the Tandem Plan agreed to for these GNMA programs, instead of purchasing the mortgages and then selling them to FNMA, GNMA immediately assigns the commitment to purchase the mortgage to FNMA. FNMA holds the commitment and, acting on behalf of GNMA, makes the commitment available at any time for assumption of "purchase" by other mortgage investors at a supported price established by GNMA from time to time. FNMA also conducts auctions of these commitments on behalf of GNMA at which investors, including FNMA, make bids to acquire the commitments and thus, the right to buy the mortgages.

In addition to those mentioned, other Tandem Plan agreements have been concluded between Ginnie Mae and Fannie Mae. Program 16 authorizes commitments to purchase mortgages insured by FHA under Section 235 (j) or 237 of the National Housing Act. Entered into in October 1971, $37 million of commitments were issued as of December 31, 1973 under this particular Tandem Plan agreement. Program 19, initiated in January 1971, with $14 million committed as of the end of 1973, authorizes commitments to purchase FHA-insured mortgages relating to the Operation Breakthrough program of the Department of Housing and Urban Development. Finally, Program No. 20 authorizes commitments to purchase mortgages covering properties on the island of Guam that carry FHA or VA mortgage insurance under Section 1810, Chapter 37, Title 38 of the U.S. Code. Under this agreement, approximately $77 million in commitments had been issued at the close of 1973.

To illustrate how the Tandem Plans are operated by FNMA and GNMA, let us take the case of the origination and sale of a subsidized FHA Section 236 mortgage on a rental project. After the project sponsor, in many cases nonprofit, and lender have obtained FHA's commitment to insure the mortgage, the lender makes application to GNMA under Program 17 for a commitment to purchase the insured mortgage at par upon completion of project construction, thereby ensuring long-term financing for the loan that many originating lenders are unable to provide. If the documentation of the loan meets the applicable requirements, GNMA issues its commitment to the originating lender, who pays a commitment fee in the amount of 1 percent of the principal amount of the mortgage. By the terms of the Tandem Plan contract between FNMA and GNMA, the commitment is assigned automatically to FNMA. FNMA temporarily assumes GNMA's obligation to purchase the mortgage at par, in consideration of which FNMA earns a portion of the commitment fee GNMA collected from the originating lender, the amount earned depending on the period of time FNMA holds the commitment.

During the commitment period for project mortgages eligible under Program 17, normally 24 months, several events may occur. GNMA may assign or "sell" the commitment contract permanently to FNMA, to another private investor, or even back to the originating lender for placement with an investor with whom the lender has made an agreement. A commitment to purchase a mortgage is an obligation, not an asset, and one ordinarily does not sell an obligation. When GNMA "sells" the contract, it is actually subsidizing the "buyer's" assumption of the commitment obligation. The commitment is to purchase the mortgage at par, but the value of the mortgage money market may be, for example, 97 percent of par. This situation occurs because the FHA-VA maximum mortgage interest rate may be below the market rate, requiring a lender to obtain discounts or points to make effective yield of the mortgage equal the market rate at the time. Therefore, to attract another investor to assume the commitment, GNMA must promise to pay the 3 percent difference.

When the mortgage is ready for delivery, ordinarily upon completion of construction, it is delivered to whoever at that time is obligated to purchase. If GNMA has not exercised any of its options, GNMA automatically reassumes the commitment from FNMA and makes the purchase of the mortgage at par. If FNMA has made a permanent assumption of the commitment, then FNMA buys the mortgage at par and immediately collects the 3 percent difference from GNMA. The net result is that FNMA has purchased at the market price of 97 percent, the mortgagor has received the benefit of financing at par, and the impact on the federal budget has been reduced from 100 percent to 3 percent of the amount of the mortgage.

Conclusion

In closing, it should be stressed that the secondary market functions accorded to Fannie Mae under the Charter Act make it possible for the corporation to bring a measure of liquidity to an investment that has been historically illiquid. The specific and detailed provisions contained in the Act provide the means for performing this

service, largely through the issuance of FNMA debt obligations, which
are highly marketable investments. Essentially, FNMA is a conduit
between the mortgage market and the money market. The degree of
liquidity provided to the mortgage market may, of course, be distinguished from support of the mortgage market by the purchase of
mortgages at a premium over the going market rate. This direct
subsidy support is one of Ginnie Mae's statutory functions, one that
costs the U.S. Treasury about $300 million annually. As long as this
division of statutory functions is recognized, it might be said that
Fannie Mae has indeed "supported" the mortgage market to the extent
that it has succeeded with its liquidity-providing function. The special
assistance functions of Ginnie Mae and the liquidity-providing role
performed by Fannie Mae have been blended effectively in the Tandem
Plans, which involve the close cooperation of both agencies in the
secondary mortgage market.

NOTES

1. For an interesting discussion of the private mortgage
market prior to World War II, see the essay in this work by Charles
Liebert.
2. Federal National Mortgage Association, Background and
History, 1973 (Washington, D.C.: Federal National Mortgage Association, November 1973), p. 2.
3. Title III of the National Housing Act, Pub. L. 479, 73d
Congress, approved June 27, 1934, provided for the establishment
of national mortgage associations. On February 10, 1938, pursuant
to Title III of the National Housing Act, as then amended (P.L. 424,
75th Congress, approved February 3, 1938), the organization known
today as the Federal National Mortgage Association was chartered by
the Federal Housing Administrator as the National Mortgage Association of Washington. The name of the Association was changed to
Federal National Mortgage Association in April 1938.
4. Fannie Mae was transferred to the HHFA pursuant to
Reorganization Plan No. 22 of 1950, effective July 9, 1950, 15 F.R.
4365, 65 Stat. 1277. See FNMA, Background and History, 1973, p. 3.
5. Ibid., p. 4.
6. Title II of the Housing Act of 1954, Pub. L. 560, 83d
Congress, approved August 2, 1954, 68 Stat. 612 originated the existing Federal National Mortgage Association Charter Act, 12 U.S.
C.A. Sec. 1716-1723d (Supp. 1973), hereinafter cited as the Charter
Act. This 1954 legislation rewrote Title III of the National Housing
Act.

7. Section 802 (c) (3), Pub. L. 90-448, approved August 1, 1968, 82 Stat. 536, amending 12 U.S.C.A. Sec. 1717 (2) (1969).

8. Source: Office of Corporate Planning, FNMA.

9. Ibid.

10. Section 301 of the Charter Act, 12 U.S.C.A. Sec. 1716 (a) (1969).

11. Section 302 (b) (1) of the Charter Act, 12 U.S.C.A. Sec. 1717 (b) (1969).

12. Emergency Home Finance Act of 1970, Section 201, Pub. L. 91-351, approved July 24, 1970, 84 Stat. 450 as amended 12 U.S.C.A. 1717 (b) (2) (Supp. 1973).

13. "Rollover" is an expression used in financial circles. It means that when the maturity date of the security is reached, it is automatically exchanged for a new note or debenture by the investor and the obligation is in effect refinanced.

14. Section 308 of the Charter Act, 12 U.S.C.A. Sec. 1723 (b) (1969), and Section 309 (d) (2) of the Charter Act, 12 U.S.C.A. Sec. 1723 (h) (1969).

15. Gurney Breckenfeld, "Nobody Pours It Like Fannie Mae," Fortune, vol. 85, no. 6 (June 1972), p. 89.

16. Ibid., p. 88.

17. "Housing Hit By Shortages of Supplies and Money," St. Louis Post-Dispatch, July 17, 1974, p. 20D.

18. Section 302 (a) (2) (A) of the Charter Act, 12 U.S.C.A. Sec. 1717 (a) (2) (A) (1969).

19. Special Assistance and Management and Liquidation Functions, Sections 305 and 306 of the Charter Act, 12 U.S.C.A. Sec. 1720, 1721 (1969).

20. Section 305 (a) of the Charter Act, 12 U.S.C.A. Sec. 1720 (a) (1969).

21. Section 306 (g) of the Charter Act, 12 U.S.C.A. Sec. 1721 (g) 1969).

22. Section 810 (d), Pub. L. 90-448, approved August 1, 1968, 82 Stat. 546 as amended 12 U.S.C.A. Sec. 1716 (b) (1969).

7

THE POLITICS OF
THE SECONDARY MARKET
Editors' Note

The secondary mortgage market came into existence to stabilize the residential construction industry, to promote the liquidity of
housing investments during periods of tight money, and to provide a
market for federally insured mortgages.[1] As with most federal housing
programs, the accomplishments have fallen short of original expectations, but the results have not been completely negative. Although
upper- and upper-middle-income groups appear to have been favored
overall, benefits have not been narrowly confined. Many U.S. homeowners and, to a lesser degree, renters have also received substantial
advantages from the operation of the secondary market. Critics of
this market argue, however, that instead of helping the clients of housing, especially low- and moderate-income owners and tenants, the
real beneficiaries have been the middlemen—the mortgage bankers,
Fannie Mae stockholders, builders, bureaucrats, and speculators.

Middlemen have been accused of acting irresponsibly, im-
morally, and illegally. A particularly strong attack on the intermediaries was made by one of the seminar participants, journalist Brian
D. Boyer, who contended that mortgage bankers made excessive profits on inner-city programs because the Federal National Mortgage
Association (FNMA, or Fannie Mae) failed to review critically FHA
mortgages which were destined for foreclosure from the start. In his
expose, Cities Destroyed for Cash, Boyer argues that

> The actual fact of the matter is that banks and others
> who buy FHA mortgages from mortgage bankers are
> extremely careful about the ones they accept. Because
> mortgage bankers rely on these institutions for the money
> they use to make mortgage loans, it would be a rash in-
> dividual who would try to pull a fast one on his capital
> source....

> But mortgage bankers sell most of their mortgages to
> Fannie Mae, and the good old lady is much less choosy.
> FNMA does protest when delinquencies and foreclosures
> rise too high, sometimes two or three years running.
> But nobody is overly concerned about delinquencies be-
> cause the mortgages are insured and once the govern-
> ment pays them off they are no longer on the record
> books . . .
>
> FNMA, by the way, accepts FHA mortgages as good
> on face value. After the mortgage banker writes his
> application, nobody—not FHA, FNMA, or anybody
> else—goes beyond the figures on the form. Sometimes,
> FNMA suspends a mortgage banker in disciplinary
> action. But its audits are not sent to FHA, even
> though FHA pays off the bad mortgages; the commer-
> cial reports are used for FNMA purposes alone.
> FNMA does audit mortgage bankers—one every three
> years. It does not audit the credit underwriting.[2]

These charges cannot be refuted on moral grounds. Certainly,
the world would be a better place if self-seeking tendencies could be
minimized. Even the most cynical would find it difficult to support
the selling of houses in declining neighborhoods to people with insufficient income to maintain them. Still, Boyer's treatise does not
provide a balanced appraisal of the secondary mortgage market. First,
he fails to consider the reasons for Fannie Mae's formation. No one,
including savings and loan associations and commercial banks, wanted
to buy FHA loans during the Depression. Fannie Mae performed an
important service by stepping into the vacuum. Boyer is also naive
in another way—to expect mortgage bankers to perform their middleman role at reduced profit levels is contrary to the history and evolution of all professional groups, including journalists. Although correct
in charging that many mortgages written on inner-city properties durin
the late 1960s and early 1970s were of poor quality and should never
have been made, and that neither FNMA nor FHA assumed responsibility for sound underwriting practices or reasonable credit standards
for purchasers, he gives little weight to the fact that political pressures were mounting to make FHA-insured mortgages available for
projects and single-family units in areas where civil disorders had
occurred.

Congress gave ultimate responsibility for the inner-city foreclosures to FHA when it sent that agency into blighted city neighborhoods. Prudent mortgage insurance practices were dropped to compensate blacks who had suffered a history of exclusion from the

program. Sound underwriting was replaced by extreme laxity and
middlemen flocked to get on the gravy train. The numerous abuses
that resulted were summarized in the following way by the St. Louis
Post-Dispatch:

> In the case of single-family dwellings, the scheme
> commonly works this way:
>
> A real estate speculator buys up dilapidated houses
> for a pittance, makes cosmetic repairs to conceal
> the extent of the ruin, and often persuades or bribes
> an FHA appraiser to jack up the appraised value.
>
> The speculator then peddles the heap to a trusting
> and inexperienced buyer who obtains a mortgage
> guaranteed by FHA at the inflated price. The
> schemes sometimes involve false statements
> about the buyer's financial status and ability to
> meet even the low payments made possible by
> the federal subsidy.
>
> The disillusioned buyer soon finds the house crumbl-
> ing around him. He does not have enough money to
> pay for repairs and to continue to meet mortgage
> payments. The mortgage holder forecloses and
> demands that the Government pick up the mortgage.
>
> The speculator has reaped a fat profit on the sale
> and the mortgage holder has shared in the bonanza.
> The buyer has been cheated out of his nest egg. And
> the Government has been bilked for the inflated sale
> price and has become the custodian of still another
> ramshackle dwelling.
>
> . . . . in the case of multi-family developments,
> scheming contractors jacked up construction costs
> and developers persuaded the FHA to guarantee
> vastly inflated mortgages. [3]

If FHA insurance had not been extended on an almost unconditional
basis to poorly qualified purchasers and project sponsors, in the most
marginal neighborhoods, both the speculative profits and the number
of defaults would have been considerably less.

It doesn't seem logical to assume that congressmen passed
laws and FHA officials administered them solely to profit evil

mortgage bankers and speculators. They acted because of pressure put on them by a strong coalition, with support in both political parties, that wanted FHA to change its suburban image and cool the flames in areas where blacks were rioting. Many acted out of a sincere concern for social justice. For others, the primary concern was simply to placate the rioters and thereby prevent a long-run change in the status quo.

In effect, passage of the National Housing Act of 1968 gave Fannie Mae a confusing mandate—it was to maintain quality in its investment portfolio and, at the same time, participate in the financing of high-risk low- and moderate-income housing carrying FHA and VA mortgage guarantees. FNMA was a key element in the game plan. Few lenders wanted mortgages of questionable quality, even with FHA or VA insurance. "So Fannie Mae has provided 60 percent of the capital to build homes under the controversial Section 235 program and 90 percent of the money for Section 236 apartment projects."[4]

FNMA came out of the government in 1968 without clearly understanding whether the company was to assume responsibility for underwriting mortgages. It originally decided to review FHA loans carefully and, as a consequence, it considered many inner-city mortgages poor risks, to be avoided. Someone at the seminar mentioned that this reluctance brought an uproar from senators, congressmen, and HUD administrators. Arguments were advanced that FNMA should withdraw from underwriting. FHA insurance was sufficient to protect Fannie Mae against loss, and a private corporation supported with government powers should not counter priorities established by the legislature and administration. So when FHA rushed into the cities, they had obtained assurances that FNMA would buy the mortgages without questioning appraisals, mortgage terms, or credit information. Without Fannie Mae, the mortgages would never have been made.

The racial conflicts of the 1960s also stimulated public and private efforts to alter the composition of the mortgage banking business. After his formal seminar presentation, James E. Murray discussed attempts to encourage minority participation in the industry, which could count only five blacks and several Chicanos among its 1,500 members. FNMA had a program, in conjunction with the Ford Foundation, to bring blacks into the industry. It was a near-failure and only a few survived. There were many problems: delinquency rates were high, defaults were excessive, banks would not give them a line of credit large enough to keep them going, and their capital was insufficient. They were doing business in inner cities, and it is very difficult to make that type of operation profitable.

Another issue raised by Boyer and others is whether middlemen in the secondary market took all the benefits and left little for the clients of housing, the intended beneficiaries. In this regard, the

verdict is not clear. For example, did FNMA contribute to excessive
central-city foreclosures and abandonments? The answer must be a
tentative yes, to the extent that it agreed to unqualified support of
FHA's entry into extensively blighted neighborhoods. This demon-
strates the confusion over public and private roles of the corporation.
One questioner at the seminar even alleged that FNMA contributed to
red-lining—the practice of withholding mortgage funds from certain
neighborhoods. Because Fannie Mae did not evaluate the quality of
FHA loans, losses were high in the inner city and ultimately Fannie
Mae withdrew from those areas. However, without FNMA's initial
participation many marginal neighborhoods would have been devoid
of any source of residential financing. The record, if anything, indicates the opposite of red-lining, often to Fannie Mae's chagrin.

　　Without question, powerful economic groups have benefited
from the secondary market operations of Fannie Mae and her government counterpart, the Government National Mortgage Association
(GNMA or Ginnie Mae). For this reason, both agencies have enjoyed
the more or less continuous support from groups like the National
Association of Home Builders (NAHB), among others. [5] A strong
secondary market provides funds for builders' operations at low interest. According to a recent book on housing, the NAHB assisted in
the preparation of the Emergency Home Finance Act of 1970, whereby
Congress devised a publicly assisted secondary market for conventional mortgages—a major NAHB goal since 1954. [6]

　　As a private corporation in the housing market, Fannie Mae
also benefits stockholders. People must be attracted to purchase stock
and earnings and dividends are the inducements. In the case of FNMA,
the amount of stock determines the size of the company's debt which,
although enormous, is essential to the corporation's operations; without equity capital, FNMA cannot borrow and, ultimately, cannot lend.
Federal regulations state explicitly that general obligations of the
company may not exceed 25 times stockholders' equity and subordinated obligations. Under the present system, then, some of the benefits
from secondary market operations must go to the company's stockholders.

　　Are there alternatives to this system that can eliminate middlemen? Probably not, in entirety, for even when attempts were made
to minimize the involvement of intermediaries, as in Section 202,
housing for the elderly, and turnkey programs, there are still project
consultants' fees, contractors' profits, and bureaucrats' salaries. If
the intention is to avoid private middlemen by substituting public or
nonprofit participation, the proposed cure may be worse than the
disease. Bureaucracies are rarely noted for their effectiveness, efficiency, and nonprofit housing groups have often suffered from lack
of competence and money.

Perhaps the issue should not be whether intermediaries benefit, but whether programs also help the intended clients. Programs must be regulated to insure that major benefits accrue to the clients, because middlemen cannot be entrusted to perform this function. Boyer claims that mortgage banking operations are not supervised externally and that bankers are incapable of policing themselves. In reply to an article written by an industry spokesman pleading that "[t]he burden of proof is not on the mortgage banking industry," Boyer retorted, "[b]ut the burden of proof has been taken up by federal grand juries in half a dozen cities, and half a dozen congressional investigatory committees and they have all proved the mortgage banking industry rife with corruption."[7]

Corruption came only because nobody cared where FHA-insured mortgages were located as long as they weren't in areas where the wealthy and the middle class lived. As long as those with money and power were not affected personally, there was little concern over whether homes were foreclosed and returned to HUD. Responsibility for these programs was diffused and foreclosures resulted in profits to FNMA and other portfolio lenders. Since the FHA interest rate has never been right on the market, but usually below, mortgages with FHA insurance are sold at a discount. However, when the property is foreclosed the holder of the mortgage receives full value from the insuring agency.

After his prepared talk, Murray discussed regulation of mortgage bankers, saying that FNMA auditors look closely at those with high rates of foreclosure and defaults on the loans they service. Portfolios have been taken away from some servicers and given to others.

When Fannie Mae forecloses, procedures vary from state to state. If the mortgage has FHA insurance, then FHA's regulations are followed. When loans go into default, efforts are made to reinstate them. Should this action fail, the mortgages are referred to an attorney for foreclosure. In some states, procedures are so lengthy that buildings become abandoned. According to Murray, FNMA makes every possible effort to continue project mortgages, but where they don't work out, the mortgages are assigned generally to FHA and Fannie Mae receives the full market value on the mortgages less a one percent assignment fee.

One final criticism often leveled at secondary market operations is that they discriminate against small investors. In the process of converting mortgages into financial instruments that are readily salable in the capital markets, high-yield debentures and notes are created that can only be purchased by those with greater wealth than the average depositor in a bank or savings and loan association. This discrimination is no different from what is found in other parts of the banking system. For example, holders of $100,000 certificates of deposit in June 1974 received 12 percent, while those with $1,000 certificates were paid 7 percent. In the case of FNMA debentures, GNMA pass-throughs, and even U.S. Treasury notes, the minimum amount that can be invested is $10,000.

This discriminatory practice is not without benefits to owners and renters. Retention of small savers as accounts in savings and loan associations and banks results in lower interest rates for home and apartment borrowers. For example, when the U.S. Treasury issued 9 percent notes, in $1,000 amounts, in August 1974, funds flowed rapidly out of mortgage institutions. In the case of FNMA debentures, the money at least goes back into the mortgage market. Without FNMA, interest rates undoubtedly would be higher, mortgage lengths would be shortened, and loan-to-value ratios would decline. Despite the criticism that "artificial stratification of capital markets means less return for small investors,"[8] there are distinct benefits to low- and moderate-income homeowners and tenants from Fannie Mae's operations in the mortgage market.

In conclusion, a balanced appraisal of the secondary market is provided by Henry J. Aaron, who describes Fannie Mae as an institutional formation as opposed to a subsidy or tax provision. While all of these devices provide benefits, it is more difficult to determine those that arise from the creation of new institutions. In the case of FNMA, there are benefits to middlemen, but there are also benefits to householders and, to a lesser degree, to tenants. Borrowing is cheaper and more mortgage money is available because of the existence of FHA and the secondary market. Lenders probably accept lower interest rates because their mortgages are more marketable. Aaron's analysis is certainly not conclusive. "The need to estimate accurately the impact of FNMA operations on residential construction, or, one step removed, on the price of housing services has grown sharply in recent years . . . Unfortunately, existing data can only support the conclusion that FNMA probably generates some benefits for home buyers and homeowners and may also help stockholders of financial intermediaries."[9]

It is worth noting here that it is the difficulty in determining who gets what that gives the politics of the secondary market its highly charged atmosphere. Given the complex nature of the subject, actors in the process who are pushing their interests must simplify the situation to make it comprehensible to the public. Shallow accusations and countercharges often result, and the complexities are ignored.

NOTES

1. See Henry J. Aaron, Shelter and Subsidies: Who Benefits from Federal Housing Policies (Washington, D.C.: Brookings Institution, 1972).

2. Brian D. Boyer, Cities Destroyed for Cash: The FHA Scandal at HUD (Chicago: Follett Publishing Company, 1973), pp. 109-110.

3. "Finding of New Frauds Expected in Housing for Poor," St. Louis Post-Dispatch, December 12, 1973, p. 6E.

4. Gurney Breckenfeld, "Nobody Pours It Like Fannie Mae," Fortune, vol. 85, no. 6 (June 1972), p. 145.

5. "Housing and Urban Development Legislation of 1968," Hearings Before the Subcommittee on Housing and Urban Affairs of the Committee on Banking and Currency, U.S. Senate, 90th. Congr., 2d Session. (Washington, D.C.: Government Printing Office, 1968), part 1, pp. 296-297.

6. William Lilley, 3d, "The Homebuilders' Lobby," in Housing Urban America, Jon Pynoos, Robert Schafer, and Chester W. Hartman, eds. (Chicago: Aldine Publishing Company, 1973), p. 38.

7. Boyer, op. cit., pp. 108-109.

8. Aaron, op. cit., p. 101.

9. Ibid., p. 96.

The American housing delivery system has done a fairly good
job of providing decent, comfortable shelter for the affluent and many
middle-income people. Since the end of World War II, the Bureau of
the Census reports a steady decline in the proportion of substandard
dwelling units throughout the nation, from 35 percent in 1950 to 8 percent 20 years later. Rising incomes, widespread automobile ownership, federal highway and housing subsidy programs and a generally
high level of home building activity have made it possible for many to
fulfill a dream by moving to new homes in the suburbs.

At the same time, some groups have yet to participate in the
fulfillment of that dream. Blacks and the elderly are two such groups
that are particularly visible in our older cities and suburbs. Beyond
the confining effects of racial discrimination and old age, both groups
currently are suffering from the disability of limited income. While
black family income is only three-fifths that of the white family, the
income of the family headed by a person 65 years old and over falls
to about half of the median for all families.

The economic constraints apparent in these figures have been
an important factor holding both groups in older core areas, while
others have moved to newer housing on the fringes of urban development. Central-city populations in the Northeast and Midwest are
"blackening" with the flight of younger, relatively affluent whites to
the suburbs; those whites who stay behind tend to be older persons
without young children. At present, 60 percent of all blacks and nearly
one-third of all persons 65 years of age and over live in the central-
city portions of the 243 standard metropolitan statistical areas. These
considerations suggest that blacks and the elderly are strategic client
groups whose problems deserve special attention in any discussion
of the performance of housing markets in older urban areas.

In the first essay in this section, Phillip Thigpen brings more
than a decade of practical experience to bear on the problems of low-
and moderate-income blacks in their continuing search for decent
urban housing. He recounts graphically how the politics of site
selection have turned public housing into storage bins for " . . . the
poor, the black, and the troubled." In the absence of a change in
policies to allow for geographic dispersal and diversification of clients,
Thigpen concludes that public subsidies for housing will continue to
perpetuate the very problems they are intended to solve.

Thigpen also casts some much needed light on the role of
the black developer in the housing process. Excluded from most

151

market by racial bigotry and a variety of performance-related constraints imposed on him in what is essentially a white man's game,
the black developer and building contractor is limited to participation
in public projects that carry affirmative action requirements.

Finally, Thigpen concludes with some thoughts on how blacks
will fare in urban housing markets in the foreseeable future. He sees
little chance for significant improvement, except for the comparatively
well-to-do. Neither the recently enacted Section 8 program nor the
possibility of direct cash allowances is likely to alter appreciably
the housing conditions of the poorest black families.

In the second offering in this section, Ira F. Ehrlich argues
that the aged also have had serious problems in urban housing. He
debunks systematically the myth that the elderly receive special consideration from housing policymakers. After developing several basic
concepts necessary for understanding senior citizens' needs for decent
housing and what he calls "good life space," Ehrlich shows how little
public policy has done to meet these fundamental needs.

The inadequacy of government response to the housing requirements of the aged follows directly from the comparative weakness of
their power base in the political arena. Although they have made significant gains in recent years, the elderly still have a long way to go
if they are to move beyond public relations and improve their performance in the practical arts of political organization and legislative
lobbying. Ehrlich's handling of this topic will be of interest to all
who seek an understanding of the politics of housing the elderly.

Both of the contributions presented in this section point to
certain problems which underprivileged minorities are likely to encounter in the political arena. Significantly, blacks and persons 65
years of age and over are simply outnumbered in the competition for
scarce public resources at the national level, accounting for roughly
11 and 10 percent of the total population respectively. Although it is
true that, separately, they may constitute a majority in some older
cities and neighborhoods, there are serious problems which prevent
them from capitalizing on their potential numerical advantage in these
areas.

One such difficulty is discussed by both Thigpen and Ehrlich—
factionalism within the ranks of each minority concerning the appro-
priateness of given courses of action for improving group conditions.
Thigpen describes the conflict within the black community over the
desirability of geographic dispersal, the strategy that Anthony Downs
refers to as "opening up the suburbs." In his presentation, Ehrlich
mentions the problem of securing cooperation among the various
national organizations advocating for the elderly. The problem in
both instances is that the practical interests of organizations within

each minority are not perfectly aligned. There are even groups within the respective minorities that actually benefit from maintenance of the status quo in housing.

Another important dimension of the problem of political action by minorities concerns the feasibility of joint efforts to enhance their strength in relation to the larger society. Although they have provided ad hoc support to one another at various times in the past, there are numerous pressures that prevent blacks and the aged from forging a stable coalition. At the most basic level, it is clear that the interests of the two groups are not identical and that organizations on each side have maintenance needs that introduce an obvious element of competition into any possible relationship between them. In addition, the scarcity of public resources available for socially worthy causes encourages competition rather than cooperation. This tension became apparent during the meeting of the Clients' Panel at the seminar, with blacks expressing resentment at what they considered the favored treatment received by the elderly in the area of subsidized housing.

In summary, divisions within and among minority communities reduce the chances for effective political action on behalf of pressing housing needs. If blacks and the elderly are to improve substantially their housing opportunities in older urban areas, they first must deal with problems of internal fragmentation and then explore the possibilities of coalition to a greater extent than has been apparent to date.

Significant improvement in the performance of urban minorities in the larger competition for scarce housing resources will not come about in the absence of increased efforts to deal with these basic problems of political action.

8

BLACKS IN THE HOUSING MARKET:
THE POLITICS OF EXCLUSION
Phillip Thigpen

Older cities and urban problems are an integral part of the black experience. Today, three-fifths of the 24 million black Americans live in the central cities of our metropolitan areas; 26 of these core cities had black communities in excess of 100,000 people in 1970.[1]

Of course, it is foolish to talk about blacks as a single, monolithic community. Our origins, incomes, and education differ in much the same way as those of every ethnic group that has appeared on the urban scene during the past 150 years. There is one thing, however, that does unite all blacks, men, women, and children alike—a common racial identity and the response that this heritage has evoked from the white mainstream. While we surely differ as individuals, racial discrimination has produced a rather unique experience that is common to all black people in America.

In the matter of housing, blacks have suffered incredibly poor conditions throughout our urban history. Traditionally, we have been isolated in the dark ghettos described by Kenneth Clark,[2] where poverty, substandard and overcrowded housing, high unemployment, and other social ills are widespread. In 1970, some 653,000 or 14 percent of all dwelling units occupied by blacks in metropolitan areas were classified substandard, while only 5 percent of all units occupied by whites were in this condition.[3] Limited numbers of black people have been able to escape only recently from the worst neighborhoods in America.

Despite reports that conditions are improving for blacks, many of whom are now moving up to middle-class status,[4] we still lag behind whites in almost every area of opportunity. Nearly one-third continue to live below the poverty level and the average black

family still earns just three-fifths of the income received by the white
family. The list of inequities has been well documented and need not
be recited here.

However, let me recommend to those who believe that blacks
and whites are not far from living together in harmony and equality
that they read the Detroit newspapers in late May 1974 and the St.
Louis papers a few weeks later. In both cities crosses were burned,
cars destroyed, and homes damaged when black families moved into
previously all-white neighborhoods. This is not the 1930s, but seven
years after the passage of federal fair housing legislation and the
Supreme Court decision in Jones v. Mayer, which upheld the right
to purchase or rent housing anywhere without regard to the color of
a man's skin.

Although the legislative and judicial events of 1968 have
made it somewhat easier for blacks with money to buy housing on
the open market, blatant hostility and subtle real estate practices such
as the "steering" of prospective buyers into racially homogeneous
areas, maintain patterns of residential discrimination. Middle-income
blacks must continue to struggle for the right to buy housing suited
to their tastes and pocketbooks. For most, the American Dream remains unfulfilled.

Historically, the effects of racial discrimination in housing
have affected all blacks. Yet, those with limited incomes unquestion-
ably have suffered the most. Accordingly, in this presentation we
shall be concerned primarily with the living conditions of blacks in
low- and moderate-income categories[5]—the potential clients of public
housing and other federally assisted programs. By presenting some
reflections on my experience in housing as a manager at the Pruitt-
Igoe public housing project in St. Louis, then as urban renewal participant and housing developer in various cities, I will attempt to show
how the political system has functioned to the detriment of these
groups.

Poor Blacks and Private Housing

Before relating my experiences with publically assisted
housing programs, a few words about blacks and the private market
for low-income housing are necessary. Much emotion is generated
ordinarily in discussion of the questions that arise in this area. Lack
of income rules out the purchase of a home for most poor people,
thereby restricting the topic to landlord-tenant relations. I do not
wish to engage in a battle of words, nor do I intend to assess blame
for the poor living conditions endured by most low-income blacks

who rent. Instead, I would like to make three points that underscore the nature of the problem while indicating the general direction that any serious improvement strategy will have to take.

First, the vast majority of all black urban dwellers in the low- and moderate-income categories reside in private housing. As new housing is built on the fringes of the urbanized area, older housing becomes available to lower-income families. As housing "filters" or "trickles-down" in this manner, wear and tear and normal maintenance' needs increase. Things brings us to a second important point.

Limited incomes cannot provide for adequate maintenance and repair work. In the case of those who rent, this means that they often cannot afford to pay rents high enough to allow for the maintenance of safe, healthful accommodations. It is this simple economic fact of life, rather than greed or any particularly villanous behavior on the part of the typical landlord, that accounts for the pitiful condition of the housing in most slums. Although there probably are landlords that fit the popular image of the "slumlord," the preponderance of the evidence suggests that low-income rental housing is not very profitable to own and operate. Quite simply, poor people cannot afford standard housing. [6]

My third and final point is that substantial public subsidies are required to put the poor in decent housing. Americans believe that government ought to compensate for inadequacies in the functioning of private market mechanisms. Housing for low- and moderate-income blacks residing in our older urban areas falls clearly within this set of expectations. This is the reason why discussions of housing improvement strategies aimed at these groups almost always concern themselves primarily with public subsidy programs, the topic to which I now turn.

Public Housing Experiences at Pruitt-Igoe

My initial involvement in housing began when I received a Ford Foundation fellowship to attend the Urban Studies Center at Rutgers in the early 1960s. Housing was part of the curriculum, and upon completion I was offered and accepted a job with the Housing Authority in Newark, New Jersey. By the time of my arrival in 1963, public housing there was inhabited largely by blacks. My assignment was in manpower training and job development. Many of the residents were in various stages of hopelessness. Some were illiterate and were given remedial reading; others were made employable through training and placement.

In 1966, I came to St. Louis as manager of Pruitt-Igoe, where I remained for three years. A new executive director, Irvin Dagen, had just been appointed to head the combined housing and renewal agencies. He was vitally interested in improvement of public housing conditions, but that did not bar him from attack by militants in the community.

My first tour of the project at Pruitt-Igoe was very disturbing. Windows were broken and missing in many buildings and the people and structures seemed in a state of disorder. The neighborhood around the project was generally rundown and becoming increasingly abandoned. Private landlords were giving up on the area because the economics of ownership made property a poor investment. In some cases, buildings were being given away.

Pruitt-Igoe had been built on 57 acres. It consisted of 33 identical 11-story buildings. They were without human scale, stark in appearance, and overwhelming in dimension. Open spaces were barren and strewn with litter and broken glass. It seemed like an extension of the junkyards located just south of the project.

Almost three-fourths of the 10,000 residents were under the age of 20 and public assistance was the major source of income for 70 percent of the residents. Many occupants were part of large families headed by females and they were very poor. These were difficult families to house in the private market, even in substandard dwellings. The welfare recipient in Missouri receives very little income. An average family of four at that time received a monthly allotment of $124. In Pruitt-Igoe, they paid as much as $70 a month for rent, leaving only slightly over $50 for food, clothing, and anything else. [7]

It was difficult to mobilize the inner resources of these families to face their seemingly insurmountable problems. By themselves, they could not increase their independence and competence, and the state of Missouri would not offer more assistance or supply incentives helping them to greater stability.

In addition, many of these families had been displaced by urban renewal. Their previous housing, while considered blighted and substandard by public agencies, was located in functioning neighborhoods. Urban renewal, which was designed to provide economic benefits to the city, meant great sacrifice to many families that I found in Pruitt-Igoe. Urban renewal displaced poor blacks from settled neighborhoods and relocated them in high-rise public housing. It left them in a condition of almost forced internment. [8]

Pruitt-Igoe was not an accident. Even disregarding obvious physical inadequacies, such as the high-rise design that prevented a mother on the 10th or 11th floor from properly supervising her children at play down below, there were other factors that had a strong negative impact. The project very quickly becomes a warehouse for the poor and the troubled, who were removed from the rest of society.

The St. Louis Redevelopment Authority was supposed to find relocation housing for low-income families displaced from the Mill Creek urban renewal area, which was a very large project undertaken in the 1950s, in a section adjoining the St. Louis business district. Residences, shops, and small plants were torn down so that new offices, warehouses, university facilities, and moderate to middle-income housing could be built. Because the housing authority was also the land clearance agency at that time, there was no way to keep the poor Mill Creek relocatees from overwhelming Pruitt-Igoe. Whenever there was clearance in the project, the pressure for housing increased and more moved into public housing.

The St. Louis Housing Authority did not set out to shelter the poorest of the poor in Pruitt-Igoe. Admission requirements were relaxed in response to pressure from the Missouri Department of Welfare, and the result was inevitable—the crowding of poor, large families into apartments too small for them. Despite attempts by Irvin Dagen to change conditions when he became director in the mid-1960s, the die had been cast. To evict all the problem tenants from the project would have been impossible, politically and legally. He inherited an impossible situation.

In the five-year period prior to my arrival, conditions were so bad that only those with no alternative would reside there. Despite overcrowding in many units there were more than 800 vacancies out of the total of 2,800 apartments. These were the smaller units which were unsuitable for large families. Few of the elderly, who might have otherwise found the smaller units satisfactory, would move there because they viewed the project as a dangerous place. They thought kids would rob, hurt, or even kill them. Only large welfare families with no income and no alternatives moved into the project in appreciable numbers. By the mid-1960s, public housing in cities in the East and Midwest was almost exclusively inhabited by subpoverty black families.

Dagen was faced with two problems. One was the welfare agency's inadequate payments to the poor and the other was the federal government's pressure on him to cover maintenance and operating costs. The federal government wanted him to throw the bad tenants out and raise the rents of the others. Dagen entreated the state to increase welfare allotments at the same time that he pleaded with the federal government to provide operating subsidies.

On his first trip to Washington, funds were requested to modernize Pruitt-Igoe. The federal government had just developed a plan to spend $12 million on rehabilitating public housing throughout the country. Dagen was able to capture a substantial part of this amount. Although this accomplishment was outstanding, the sum constituted only about 25 percent of what was needed in Pruitt-Igoe alone.

With only limited funds, I would like to believe that our efforts improved conditions at Pruitt. Building committees were organized and neighbors started working together. Parties were held and the men, who were a minority in the project, formed a club. An experiment was attempted in five buildings to convert them to two-thirds elderly and one-third family. Weighting this ratio in favor of elderly units was intended to recruit more aged couples by providing them with a strong voice in their housing conditions, and for a time the experiment proved reasonably successful. Conversion costs were $40,000 per building—far less than our estimates for demolition at the time, which were $300,000 for each structure.

Our long-term goals were reduction in density and removal of some of the problem families. No decision could be more politically unacceptable. What community, whether city or suburb, wants the black poor? If there is any single explanation for Pruitt-Igoe, it is that most urban dwellers will exert their influence to keep families of this type contained and distant.

In retrospect, there were short-run accomplishments. One program utilized the services of females living in the buildings as custodians. These women were paid and did a better job than the male janitors. They would come to tenant association meetings and tell mothers that their children were messing up the building where they had been working. There was a developing sense of community pride. If funds were available, there was plenty of work directly at the project for the many young unemployed residents. Landscaping, decorating, staffing the day care center, and teacher aides were only a few possibilities, but the need for dispersal—for diversification of tenantry—would have existed in any case. Many more employed tenants were needed to stabilize the rent structure and strengthen the neighborhood. The politics of isolation that prevented this from happening undermined efforts to improve conditions at Pruitt. Maybe my greatest achievement was to leave the project in 1969 with all the windows intact.

Whether Pruitt-Igoe has been a learning experience is questionable, as demonstrated by two recent articles appearing in major metropolitan newspapers. In an editorial titled "Lessons of Pruitt-Igoe," the St. Louis Post Dispatch cast the tenants as unfortunate victims of government neglect:

> The problems of public housing . . . continue
> to be perceived in terms of race, as if some-
> how Pruitt-Igoe's failure was the fault of the
> blacks who once lived in the now-vacant build-
> ings. . . . They were the victims of inadequate
> efforts by the Government to provide housing
> for those who could only afford the slums. [9]

At the same time, the Washington Post described an attempt by public housing managers to screen tenants and try to improve conditions in the projects. "Unruly children, irregular rent payments, poor housekeeping by tenants and signs of emotional disorder in families" were being scrutinized. [10] Both articles miss the point by failing to broaden their view of the problem. The reality is that flexible income limits for public housing must be accepted. Even the most competent management and the best designed housing will have trouble if the vast majority of the occupants are poor people dependent on public assistance for survival.

The Need for Diversification

It is a mistake to build a city, neighborhood, or housing project exclusively for poor people. A mixture of social and income groups is needed to avoid the kinds of problems that destroyed Pruitt-Igoe. In the words of John Macey of the Urban Institute, "[i]t is neither good business nor good community policy to develop projects peopled exclusively by people in the lower-income groups, and to force them to leave when their incomes rise."[11]

With few exceptions, publically assisted housing in the United States has ignored this advice. Income restrictions are a universal condition for admission to assisted housing. In Chicago, for example, a family of four was limited to a maximum income of $6,000 to qualify for admission to public housing in the early part of 1972. At the same time, the 235 and 236 programs designed for so-called "moderate-income" persons carried an income ceiling of $8,100 for the same family. [12] Until recently, families already living in public housing and whose incomes rose above established levels had to get out.

Provision was made in the Housing Act of 1961 that under "special circumstances" a family with income over the limit for continued occupancy could remain until it was able to find housing on the private market. Pressuring people to move out as a basic policy was softened somewhat. In many cases, however, this change came too late. In St. Louis, for example, it wasn't until the mid-1960s that the executive director of the local authority insisted on no more than 25 percent welfare tenants in new projects.

The problem of income limits and the need for diversification have also risen in a renewal project presently being undertaken in Camden, New Jersey by our firm, Leon N. Weiner and Associates, in cooperation with Campbell Soup, RCA, and Boise Cascade. Our particular skill in this joint venture is construction knowledge and we are managing partners for the entire redevelopment project.

The vista from the renewal site is a magnificent one extending from the Delaware River to Society Hill in Philadelphia. East St. Louis, Illinois and Jersey City, New Jersey are similarly situated. All function traditionally as working-class ethnic communities with a high degree of industrial land use. Since World War II, however, much of the industry has moved away and blacks have replaced the white ethnics. Riverfront land has become available due to changing technology, but finding a market for reuse activities is difficult, despite the attractiveness of the location.[13]

While the site is only four or five blocks from the downtown area, there are no shops or schools, although some are being planned. As a first step, we are developing 200 units of public housing that will be sold to the local authority under the turnkey program. However, the ultimate success of the entire effort will depend upon diversification of new land uses and achieving a residential mix. Accordingly, a 15-story project for the elderly and moderate-income homeownership units are planned, in addition to the turnkey units. An income mix is essential to support commercial families and bring vitality to the area. A riverfront marina has been discussed, but who will use it if only poor people live nearby?

Redevelopment efforts in Camden are encountering obstacles. For example, there are some local policemen and firemen who would like to live in the new turnkey units, but their incomes are a few thousand dollars too high. While this type of tenant could provide a stable base in public housing, there is no way to circumvent the admission requirements. Our efforts also are constrained by a high degree of dependence on federal programs. As suggested by the moratorium on federally subsidized housing programs, which was lifted only recently, availability of funds is questionable and amounts provided are limited in any case.

Even with a more secure financial picture, creating diversity in housing is far from easy. This point is clearly evident in the experience of the developers of new towns, who have found that the economics of the marketplace make income blending a most difficult goal. In Columbia, Maryland, for example, planners sought to build a community where all income types could live, especially those of moderate means who would be employed at new plants. To the dismay of the developers, it has turned out quite differently. The median annual income for white families is $19,000 and for blacks it is $22,000.[14] Rising construction costs, interest rates, and land prices have placed new housing in Columbia outside the reach of all but the comparatively well-to-do.

In sum, improving conditions in publically assisted housing is dependent upon diversification of land uses and achieving a mixture of social and economic backgrounds. Low-income families should be dispersed and not dominate the community in which they live. The key question that needs to be explored is why it has proven so difficult to break down the barriers that isolate the poor in the least desirable portions of our metropolitan areas.

Politics of Project Site Selection

Although the original public housing legislation never intended dwelling units to be repositories for "no income people" or an exclusive reservation for those receiving public assistance, site selection practices have dictated this outcome. Public housing across the nation has suffered from federal, state, and local policies that have isolated and contained the poor, the black, and the troubled.

Let me describe one of the country's largest and most depressing low-income housing complexes. Located in New Orleans, the project carries the ironic name of Desire. About 12,000 blacks, 10,000 of them under 18 years of age, live in a series of two-story brick buildings on streets named Piety, Humanity, and Pleasure. The project's 1,860 units are situated on one-seventh of a square mile of land in a deteriorated part of the city. It is no accident that Desire was located where the poor were cut off from the major activities of the city. In this case, separation was enforced by a railroad line running between the project's only entrance and the rest of the city. Occasionally, freight trains have blocked the entrance for hours at a time, making it impossible for any vehicles, even fire trucks, to enter the area. As in much public housing, Desire was placed in a location where blight was evident and poverty abundant. Railroads and junkyards are traditional neighbors of public housing, and adequate shopping and schools are usually absent.

Throughout the history of public housing in the United States, there has been a political consensus to isolate those who are low income and dependent, especially blacks. Housing projects in many places were racially segregated by force of law until the mid-1950s, when the Supreme Court prohibition as a matter of right on segregation in education was extended to government housing programs. Still, projects in urban areas became increasingly black, as many poor whites were able to escape to cheap homes and apartments outside of the ghetto.

The decision to build Pruitt-Igoe on the near north side of St. Louis in the most decaying part of the ghetto was made at a time when a black was the chairman of the Housing Authority board. It is not known whether he objected to this decision, but his voice would have meant little in the eventual outcome. Blacks did not make the rules of the game. Our participation at present may be slightly less symbolic, but in the 1940s and 1950s we were purely window dressing. If it had not been for the riots of the past decade, there probably would not have been any discernible improvement in the plight of poor blacks.

Even today, the simple fact of the matter is that few white communities welcome blacks, whether rich or poor. Most equate subsidized housing, whether for moderate- or low-income people, with black housing. The intrusion of assisted projects is stoutly resisted, largely through the use of zoning ordinances and the management of federal subsidies.

Because of the demography of city and suburbs, zoning serves to institutionalize racism. One federal judge noted that "[z]oning ordinances have long been used to contain particular racial groups inside the ghetto—it is critically important to classify these zoning practices for what they are: sophisticated means of invidious racial discrimination. . . . "[15] Instead of using zoning as was intended, to provide for orderly growth and development of land uses, suburban governments have used this power to insure economically and racially homogeneous populations. As a result, blacks are locked in the older cities.

The recent incorporation of the city of Black Jack in St. Louis County provides an extreme and telling case of how this process operates.[16] When a housing developer proposed a subsidized 236 project for an unincorporated place in the northern part of the county, the area's white population petitioned successfully for incorporation. Armed with the zoning power, the new municipality banned all multi-family housing, thereby torpedoing the proposed development. White residents' complaints that the project would have an adverse impact on school costs, traffic congestion, and property values should be viewed for what they are—thinly veiled rationalizations for racial discrimination.

The federal district court upheld the legitimacy of the city's discriminatory use of the zoning power, but the Eighth Circuit Court of Appeals reversed unanimously the ruling of the lower court in a landmark case in late December 1974. Because the Supreme Court has declined to hear Black Jack's appeal for reinstatement of the ban on apartments, the proposed complex may finally be constructed. Unfortunately, the five-year delay and increased building costs may well have destroyed the feasibility of the proposed undertaking. Assuming the developers proceed, the original project will have to be scaled down considerably.

While the overturning of Black Jack's zoning ordinance is a move to be commended, it will not change the exclusionary realities of our metropolitan areas overnight. Legal change proceeds at a snail's pace. Discriminatory ordinances will have to be challenged one by one at great expense of time and money. Meantime, there is no lack of other devices that can be used to keep blacks locked up in older core city areas.

Traditionally, federal housing subsidies were administered in a fashion that encouraged the containment of poor blacks in the center-city ghetto. Charles Abrams describes the early position of the government as follows:

> From 1935 to 1950, the federal government insisted upon discriminatory practices as a prerequisite to Government housing aid. The Federal Housing Administration's official manuals cautioned against "infiltration of inharmonious racial and national groups," "a lower class of inhabitants," or the "presence of incompatible racial elements" in the new [suburban] neighborhoods. [17]

Although these restrictions have been dropped, less obvious measures continue to support racial separation to the present day. A perfect example has been the requirement that municipalities must establish a local authority in order to qualify for public housing funds. Until quite recently, affluent, upper-middle-class suburbs were able to keep out "undesirables" simply by never creating the required administrative apparatus. Another device, recently enacted, that may lend itself to discriminatory use is the federal regulation that requires a housing developer to demonstrate that his project will not cause a negative "environmental impact" in order to qualify for subsidy dollars.

The effect of policies that enforce the containment of poor and moderate-income blacks within the inner city has been disastrous on their chances for upward mobility. Historically, low-income people have lived in the core areas to be near places of employment. Work opportunities were centralized and those engaged in labor-intensive industries could get to work quickly and inexpensively. Today, much of the industrial plant development is in suburban areas. It is still true that low-income people need to be near their places of work and for the same reasons, but with industry in the suburbs, many of the black poor are left behind in the core areas where good jobs and quality education are much more difficult to obtain.

An important point about site selection of federally assisted housing is that until housing authorities are able to build or lease on a metropolitan basis, tax dollars spent on these programs will continue to produce unsatisfactory results. Even under revised Section 23 leased housing and the new Section 8 program that will replace it in 1975, there is a requirement for local government review. [18] The revised section 23 required passage of a formal resolution of approval by the local governing body. The new Section 8 program dropped this requirement but inserted what amounted to the same thing—a provision allowing local chief executives to review all proposals for subsidized housing. How many communities, without a substantial body of low-income residents, or plans to assist in their housing, will welcome assisted units? Probably very few. Of the more than 3,000 local housing authorities in this country, none has adequate authority to function on a metropolitan-wide basis. Whether it is New Castle County in Delaware, Camden County in New Jersey, or St. Louis County in Missouri, no housing authority is able to meet the demand for good low- and moderate-income shelter in the suburbs.[19]

For a while in the early 1970s it appeared that the so-called Fair Share plans designed to disperse federally assisted units throughout suburban municipalities on a voluntary, fair share basis might open up the housing markets of our metropolitan areas, but this simply did not happen. The plan enacted in Washington, D.C. metropolitan area is dead, and opposition to the fair share notion from whites in Westchester County, New York was so strong that in January 1973, plans were withdrawn by then-Governor Nelson Rockefeller. Fair share has enjoyed limited success in just two places, namely Dayton, Ohio and Minneapolis-St. Paul, Minnesota regions. The Miami Valley Regional Planning Commission pioneered with the fair share concept in the Dayton area in 1970. Still, only 7,000 units have been produced to date and resistance is stiffening. In the case of Minneapolis-St. Paul, just 3,000 units have been constructed.[20] It is obvious that the voluntarism that furnishes the basis for the fair share plans is a poor substitute for mandatory controls and national legislation with teeth in it.

Unhappily, the federal government has provided timid leadership in this area. The real dilemma here for blacks is that they are clearly outnumbered in the political process, comprising only about 11 percent of the total population. On most sensitive issues the political process will respond to an aroused majority, and most whites do not want their suburbs opened up for low- and moderate-income housing projects. Thus, the federal government is reluctant to act aggressively to break down the barriers to dispersal that exist in virtually all of our metropolitan areas.

Quite simply, the political constituencies for moves to open up the suburbs are both weak and fragmented. During the 1960s, white liberals were of great help in knocking down the laws that required separation of the races in schools public accommodations, and housing. On the matter of affirmative action in housing, however, their support has been questionable, especially when it reached into their suburban backyards. For many liberals, equality of the races is supportable only as a verbal ideal, not as a reality to be seen over the back fence and barbecue pit.

Some blacks are not enthusiastic about opening up the suburbs. Most established groups like the National Association for the Advancement of Colored People favor equal access to housing opportunities everywhere. Others, such as the Congress of Racial Equality, are opposed to actions that would result in the geographical dispersion of blacks. In this view, dispersion would dissipate the potential power base that blacks may be able to build as a result of their increasing predominance in many central-city areas. For better or worse, too, there are many black politicians, landlords, and antipoverty officials who have a stake in the status quo. In sum, powerful opposition from most whites and internal divisions within the black and white liberal communities make it very unlikely that any substantial number of suburbs will be opened up to residency by low- and moderate-income families in the near future.

Black Developer in a White Game

The segregated residential patterns that face the black buyer in urban housing markets also affect his counterparts in housing production. Opportunities are severely limited for minority craftsmen and entrepreneurs in construction. If you are a skilled black in electrical work or plumbing, you are probably nonunion and working only in ghetto neighborhoods where your income is irregular. As a percentage of the population, blacks have never been adequately represented in the building trades unions. This is particularly the case in those occupations that require training and pay well.

Black builders and developers have not fared appreciably better in their efforts to establish a sound basis for upward economic mobility. They, too, have been restricted to working in black communities, although, in the last decade, their opportunities have been expanded by public construction programs for low- and moderate-income housing, community facilities, and thoroughfares. When these programs are cut back, as occurred during the 1973-74 moratorium on federal housing subsidies, blacks are in much trouble. White developers who experience a cutoff of federal funds can switch to producing housing in the suburbs. But I can't think of an instance where a black-owned construction or development firm has built significant numbers of single-family homes or apartments for a white suburban clientele.

Compated with these realities, I have been quite fortunate in the home construction business. I am a black officer in a predominantly white firm, Leon N. Weiner and Associates, which is located in Wilmington, Delaware. Only about 30 percent of our work has been

in subsidized low- and moderate-income housing under federal programs; the remainder has been in suburban developments available
to people of all colors. Even here, the world I work in is not totally
color-blind.

In some ways I am more sensitive to racial considerations
in business than Leon Weiner, who is the primary owner and director
of our company. Although he, too, is a member of a minority group,
the Jews, he does not have to deal with problems arising from prej-
udices concerning skin color. In my work, I try to evaluate each
situation to determine whether I or someone else from our firm
might establish better rapport. Sometimes I can relate better with
whites, particularly in cases where there may be strong feelings
about other minorities. At other times, my skin color may be a
disability.

In general terms, however, I am in a better position than
most black builders. To a great degree, I can concentrate on accom-
plishing the task at hand—organizing construction, financing the project, marketing the units, and maximizing profits. Unlike officers
in most all-black construction firms, I do not have to waste large
amounts of time and effort countering stereotypes that hold that
blacks are financially unstable and lacking in integrity or competence.
These racist perceptions are sometimes held by local and federal
bureaucrats, especially those who feel uncomfortable in dealing with
a black who is enterprising and intelligent.

Because of narrow opportunities in the private sector, blacks
often have resorted to nonprofit housing corporations and subsidized
projects. In the aggregate, nonprofits have not contributed substantially to the production of housing in America. I have yet to see one
contribute anything of substance. Nonprofits are, in a sense, symbolic
attempts at housing. Much of the nonprofit movement was a reaction
to the riots of the 1960s, where the goal was resident participation
and self-determination as opposed to efficient production. Unfortunately, experience indicates that sympathy for the poor does not build
houses.

As illustrated by my experience in East St. Louis, Illinois,
building subsidized projects also is a difficult task. East St. Louis
is a community of 70,000 people, 75 percent of whom are black.
Historically, it has functioned as a working-class suburb of St. Louis,
Missouri. Much of the industry in the immediate area is located in
tax-sheltered enclaves just outside the municipal boundaries. Today,
there are widespread unemployment, declining population, poor housing
and abandonment, high dependence on welfare, and governmental in-
solvency. It is a miniature version of Newark, New Jersey.

About four years ago, our company submitted a proposal on
a turnkey public housing project to be located on a long-vacant renewal

site adjoining the East St. Louis central business district. The renewal plan originally called for commercial land use, but without commercial demand the site remained undeveloped. Public housing was the only activity for which funds were readily available. Our proposal was chosen from among the four submitted to the renewal agency, the Housing Authority, and their consultant. It was the best design for the best price, but our cost per unit was not the lowest.

This project was initiated when militancy was at its peak. In a town like East St. Louis, this meant that blacks wanted involvement in all phases of construction. This is easier said than done because for years blacks have been excluded from acquiring experience in the trades. As a result, many of the subcontractors were involved in a learning process. Although some proved to be incompetent, others made gigantic strides when provided with opportunities that previously had been unavailable.

A job given to a white contractor by the East St. Louis Urban Renewal Department for streets, sewers, and sidewalks also proved to be a disaster. He employed inexperienced and inept subcontractors and there was no control on performance, from the standpoint of either quality or time. Eventually the contract had to abrogated, with the Department of Housing and Urban Development (HUD) approving a cost overrun so that this aspect of the project could be completed. Another cost overrun for construction is pending. Neither the local housing authority nor our firm had anything to say about this essential feature of the program. As a result, it has taken four years for the first 72 out of the total 247 units to be purchased by the Housing Authority. The remaining 175, which are turnkey homownership units, should be turned over to them shortly.

Black contractors rarely have a large pool of experienced black subcontractors from which to choose for their projects. Consequently, they often are unable to apply the most efficient business techniques. Most black contractors only get public work because of governmental insistence on affirmative action. With poor enforcement, they do not even get their fair share of public works. They work in black neighborhoods or communities because they do not have the opportunity to compete in white areas. Because of historic exclusion, black developers often have to hire inexperienced, less productive workers. From a businessman's perspective, this means that if three people must be hired to do the work of one, there then must be a subsidy. It is nonsense to ask someone to bid for a job, then tell him to use workers who are only half as productive as those that he had in mind when preparing the bid.

On the turnkey project in East St. Louis we acted as the developer and a very competent but small and underfinanced local black builder acted as contractor. Because of his desires and because of affirmative action requirements, he hired black trainees. He requested but did not receive on-the-job training funds from the federal government, only a flat fee from us to supervise construction. Had I directed the East St. Louis project, we would have received more cooperation or closed down. There were delays caused by the Urban Renewal Department, HUD procedures, and the unskilled nature of many of the employees who, deservedly, were receiving their first chance. Without the participation of our firm, the black contractor would not have had sufficient financing to survive in this situation.

A black builder must work under these conditions to gain experience. A white developer can learn by working in an easier atmosphere. Until the affirmative action requirements connected with turnkey public housing, road projects, and public facilities are enforced fairly, black builders will never be able to acquire the organizational and management skills required for larger projects.

Costs mushroomed on the East St. Louis project, but we still managed to keep our contractor from being hurt. Had the contract been a normal one, he would have borne the escalating costs incurred as a result of numerous delays. Probably, he would not have been willing to take on trainees and less productive workers. As it turned out, however, our flat-fee arrangement protected him from loss. Our experience in construction enabled us to foresee some of these problems and to protect against some of the cost overages. In effect, we provided a financial umbrella for the local contractor. Without out support, no black builder in East St. Louis could have participated. Obtaining the bond for a project of this magnitude would have been beyond his capacity. This should have been the federal government's responsibility, not ours.

Bonding is a very serious problem faced by the black contractor. When a construction project is undertaken, the developer ordinarily requires the building contractor to secure a bond, which is a form of insurance to protect the developer from loss should the builder fail to complete the work for which he contracted. Blacks often find it difficult to secure bonding because they usually are short on financial assets and experience with jobs done for the "right" customers. In effect, minority contractors are caught in a vicious circle. You cannot get the "right" jobs and build your assets without bonding, yet bonding presupposes that you already have the requisite assets and experience. To overcome this difficult situation, it is necessary to improve the black contractor's access to credit and, perhpas, to relax the bonding requirements associated with most construction work. Lending and insuring institutions will be very reluctant to undertake either one of these steps without adequate governmental guarantees.

In sum, black developers or builders are limited in various ways. They must work on projects that cannot be financed in the private market, their bonding capacity is limited, and they are shut off from the larger market of middle- and upper-income whites. They also are hampered by inadequate resources and pressured into hiring less experienced workers. With all of these restrictions, it is a miracle that any blacks are able to survive in the housing production business.

Conclusion

Housing quality for blacks falls far below that of whites. As noted earlier, black urban dwellers are about three times as likely as whites to reside in substandard urban dwelling. Clearly, there is a need for better housing and a wider choice of neighborhoods. However, when evaluating these needs it is not useful to consider blacks as a single group. At a very minimum, it is necessary to differentiate by income. At present, approximately one-third of all black families have incomes over $10,000 annually; another third earn between $4,500 and $10,000; and the remainder have incomes below $4,500.[21] Each group has a different capacity for upward mobility and differentiation within the groups is wide except in the category below poverty. This bottom group, while wanting to make it, has few of the necessary skills I can assure you that many of the parents at Pruitt-Igoe had high aspirations for their children, but they had no notion of how the game was played by various segments of the larger society.

Barring economic reversals, middle and upper-income blacks will continue to increase their freedom of movement. Despite continuin hostility and subtle forms of discriminatory real eastate practice, thing are better than in the past when even money could not buy passage for those who wanted to live outside the ghetto.

Moderate-income blacks are being hurt now. They are squeezed by rising costs of new construction, escalating interest rates and taxes on older houses, and, until recently, by the moratorium on federal assistance in the 235 and 236 programs. In all probability, their past housing patterns will continue, with the bulk of their rental and purchase requirements met through the filtering system and the private market. They will push out from the central-city enclaves, staying one step ahead of abandonment and one step behind their white counterparts.

The future of the bottom one-third is bleak. Even assuming favorable congressional action in the near future, the concept of month housing allowances made directly to those in need probably will not help. Let me explain with the following example. Assume that a welfar family was presented with a gift of a $20,000 suburban home—no strings, no repayment. Taxes might cost $800 annually; insurance, another $150; utilities, $600; and maintenance, $300. The family's housing bill would total over $150 per month even without principal or interest payments. To house these families adequately, the size of the monthly allowance would make it politically unacceptable.

Section 23 Leased Housing and the new Section 8 that will replace it in 1975 seem to hold very limited promise. Low-income tenants will be kept out of the more affluent suburbs even though HUD has authority to overrule local government decisions under the new Section 8. In addition, there are insufficient rewards to induce developers to participate in the program and additional responsibilities will be given to them without additional compensation. In particular, the relationship between the landlord and tenant will change. They will have to deal directly with each other rather than exclusively through an intermediary—the local housing authority—as in the past. There will not be as many housing authority guarantees of income, and there will not be the housing authority provision of social services. For all of these reasons, developers will be reluctant to become involved.

The public housing program will probably continue to operate largely within the self-defeating constraints imposed by the politics of disadvantage and exclusion. Conventional projects will remain storage bins for poor blacks whom society does not want and will not accept. Even allowing that some public housing, especially that for the elderly, may be working and that new public structures are probably far superior to those found on the private market in surrounding neighborhoods, the basic rules of the game must be changed to allow for dispersal and an income mix in public housing. Failing this, more Pruitt-Igoes are not only possible, but probable. America simply must come up with a revised public housing program worthy of popular support and consistent with the fundamental concepts of self-respect and human dignity. I sincerely hope that the necessary changes are made, even though I find it difficult to be optimistic.

NOTES

1. U.S. Bureau of the Census, Current Population Reports, Special Studies, Series P-23, No. 48, The Social and Economic Status of the Black Population in the United States, 1973 (Washington, D.C.: Government Printing Office, 1974), pp. 10, 11, 130-134.

2. Kenneth B. Clark, The Dark Ghetto: Dilemmas of Social Power (New York: Harper & Row, 1965).

3. Bureau of the Census, op. cit., p. 109.

4. See the controversial piece by Ben J. Warrenberg and Richard M. Scammon, "Black Progress and Liberal Rhetoric," Commentary 55, no. 4 (April 1973), 35-44.

5. In the sense that we are using the terms, low-income households are those at or below the levels that qualify them for public housing occupancy. This amounted to an annual income of roughly $4,000 or less for a four-person household as of 1972. Moderate-income households are those above the low-income level, but still too poor to permit rental or purchase of decent shelter without direct subsidies. For a moderate-income four-person family in the same year, annual income ranged between approximately $4,000 and $8,000 By these definitions, about 28 percent of all black families would have qualified as low-income, and 32 percent as moderate-income. Our basic concepts are taken from Anthony Downs, Federal Housing Subsidies: How Are They Working? (Chicago: Real Estate Research Corporation, October 1972), p. 22.

6. For evidence on these points, see George Sternlieb, The Tenement Landlord (New Brunswick, N.J.: Urban Studies Center, Rutgers, State University, 1966) and Michael A. Stegman, Housing Investment in the Inner City: The Dynamics of Decline, A Study of Baltimore, Maryland, 1968-1970 (Cambridge, Mass.: MIT Press, 1972).

7. In 1969, tenants in St. Louis public housing conducted a rent strike that resulted in a ceiling on rents amounting to no more than 25 percent of the tenant's income. While this change may have benefited tenants in the short run, it made it more difficult for the authority to meet its operating and maintenance needs.

8. See William L. Yancy, "Institutional Incompetence and Economic Irrelevance," paper prepared for the annual meeting of the Society for the Study of Social Problems, San Francisco, California, August 27-29, 1967, p. 5.

9. St. Louis Post-Dispatch, May 10, 1974, p. 2C.

10. Judy Luce Mann, "District Public Housing to Screen Residents," Washington Post, May 6, 1974, p. 1C.

11. John Macey, Publically Provided and Assisted Housing in the U.S.A. (Washington, D.C.: Urban Institute, 1972), p. 5.

12. Illinois Housing Development Authority and Northeastern Illionois Planning Commission, Housing: A Community Handbook (Chicago, n.d.). p. 21.

13. For an interesting discussion of a related case, see Robert E. Mendelson, East St. Louis, The Riverfront Charade (Edwardsville: Regional and Urban Development Studies and Services Southern Illinois University, 1970).

14. Bill Richards, "Columbia: Too Much Wealth," Washington Post, May 6, 1974, p. 1C.

15. Ranjel v. City of Lansing, 293 F. Supp. 301 (W. D. Mich. 1969), opinion by Judge Noel P. Fox.

16. See "The Justice Department vs. Blackjack, Missouri," in Louis H. Masotti and Jeffrey K. Hadden, eds., Suburbia in Transition (New York: New Viewpoints, 1974), pp. 158-164.

17. Charles Abrams, The City Is the Frontier (New York: Harper & Row, 1965) p. 61.

18. These programs are well described in the essay by Charles Edson in this work. In essence, both programs subsidize the leasing of units on the private market for occupancy by low-income tenants.

19. For a detailed analysis of the problems involved in this area, see Anthony Downs, Opening Up the Suburbs: An Urban Strategy for America (New Haven, Conn.: Yale University Press, 1973).

20. Paul Delaney, "Public Housing Goes Suburban," St. Louis Post-Dispatch, December 5, 1974.

21. "America's Rising Black Middle Class," Time 103, no. 24 (June 17, 1974), p. 26.

9

THE POLITICS OF HOUSING THE ELDERLY
Ira F. Ehrlich

Introduction

Many people tend to believe that senior citizens comprise the "most favored minority" when it comes to having their unmet housing needs satisfied by government action. In this view, the elderly are a potent political force and providing shelter for them is good politics, at least when compared with the relatively intractable problems faced by other minority groups. Like so many attitudes and perceptions surrounding the elderly and their problems, popular wisdom is sadly mistaken on this point.

An effort is made in this presentation to dispel some of the larger myths relating to the aged and their housing needs. We shall begin by developing some basic facts and concepts necessary for comprehending the problems encountered by senior citizens in their search for and utilization of housing in older urban areas. Government performance will then be weighed against needs for shelter and consideration will be given to attempts by the elderly to secure public policy responses to those needs through the political process.

Number One Priority: Good Life Space

Housing the elderly often is seen as a physical problem of bricks and mortar. It should be perceived in relation to a broader psychosocial framework which takes into account the totality of human needs and experience. Physical shelter is merely one component of what we might call good life space, a comprehensive concept that encompasses the physical, psychological, and social prerequisites necessary for the attainment of satisfactory life-styles.

Gerontologists have utilized several indicators to describe life-styles of the elderly. Among these are the concepts of social space, social time, and social network. These relate to the individual's active participation in his environment, the opportunities he uses for exchange or interaction with others, and the ease of access he has to the basic services and people who are important to him. Investigators have focused on the older adult's utilization of these life-style indicators, with special reference to his overall satisfaction and capability for autonomous action. [1]

The conditions subsumed under good life space should allow the elderly person to live according to the life-style that best fits his developmental needs. Recent studies on the relationship between the aged person and his environment indicate that an urban setting should provide the older adult with opportunities for expression of individual differences. [2] Contrary to popular belief, senior citizens are not a homogeneous group, and diversity calls for the provision of housing options.

We should emphasize here that good life space requires congruence between personal needs and environmental resources. If given sufficient choice, elderly people will select environments suitable for them. Often, familiar objects and people are of great importance in this selection process. With the shrinking of life space that frequently accompanies retirement and the onset of old age, people and objects near at hand provide more and more of the person's social and psychological support. The immediate environment assumes increased importance for the aged. [3] Naturally, some less competent, more fearful, more impaired individuals will require skilled help in matching needs and resources. In these instances, housing professionals such as architects, urban planners, and environmental consultants may need to design supportive environmental aids. If these exist, the senior citizen will then be able to develop patterns of privacy and involvement with others as he sees fit. [4]

Basic Options in Elderly Housing

Much of the recent debate surrounding the housing needs of senior citizens has focused on the relative merits of age-integrated as opposed to age-segregated housing. As suggested by the success of the popular TV show, "The Waltons," Americans tend to romanticize the virtues of the extended family setting wherein individuals of all ages live together or close by and older adults retain a valued function as repositories of wisdom and sources of guidance and inspiration for the younger generation. Contrary to popular stereotypes, many senior citizens continue to live in these age-integrated communities. Recently, however, a growing number have come to reside in age-segregated environments such as downtown hotels, high-rise apartments, and mobile home parks. In this context, it may come as a shock that less than 4 percent of the population 65 years of age and over resides in long-term care institutions.[5] A lingering sense of guilt has been compounded by periodic exposes of deplorable conditions in some of these institutions to jaundice public opinion about age-segregated housing in general.

Instead of resolving issues, gerontological research on the matter of age-integrated versus age-segregated housing has brought added heat to public debate in this area. Proponents of age-integrated housing, such as Kleemeier, Mumford, and Vivrett, consider the segregation of the elderly in special retirement communities to be a form of social isolation that further removes the old person from the mainstream of daily life.[6] Paulson, Peck, and Trillin describe this type of living as the gateway to boredom and emptiness.[7]

In contradiction of these views, advocates of age-segregated housing argue that elderly people living in predominantly segregated housing are better off than those living in age-integrated environments. Bultena and others have shown that there are greater opportunities for social interaction in age-segregated communities and that they also provide greater support for the development of life-styles conducive to retirement roles.[9] A recent study of 2,001 elderly living in 104 public housing projects supports this view. Elderly tenants living in the more age-segregated projects were more active socially, enjoyed better health, were more satisfied with their housing, and had greater mobility, higher morale, and more frequent interaction with their families than did those elderly tenants residing in the more age-integrated settings.[10]

Additional study is needed to produce more information on the comparative merits of the two basic options in elderly housing. At this point, we would perhaps do well to reeall that diverse housing patterns fulfill one basic criterion of good life space—the ability to choose the kind of housing that best suits the felt needs of the aged individual. Although the needs of some may be met by age-segregated accommodations, others may prefer to live in age-mixed settings. In this sense, social planners should avoid monolithic solutions that would eliminate options and the healthy exercise of individual choice. Professionals must learn to plan with the elderly, rather than for ther

Poverty, Old Age, and the Search for Decent Housing

Housing markets in the United States function reasonably well for the affluent. Those who must survive on modest incomes, however, face severe problems. It follows that the reduction of income that normally accompanies retirement and the onset of old age is a major constraint on the ability of the elderly to secure and maintain decent living quarters in our older urban areas. The 1970 census showed that the income of the white family headed by a 65er drops to half the national average for all families. The income of the black elderly family falls to approximately one-third the national average.

Of course, not all of the elderly are poor. In 1970, however, fewer than 2 million, 10 percent, had incomes better than $9,000 a year. Considering that there were approximately 20 million Americans 65 and over in 1970, it is somewhat startling to find that only 179,000 families with elderly heads of household had annual incomes of $25,000 or more. Fewer than 23,000 older adults living alone had incomes in this bracket. [11]

In 1970, the federal government set the official poverty level for nonfarm elderly persons at $1,861, a figure that seriously underestimated basic living expenses. Despite this stringent standard, approximately one in every four seniors found himself below the poverty line. In a more realistic assessment, Brotman found that half of the 20 million elderly in America lived on less than $10 a day in 1971. [12]

One of the most pernicious myths concerning the elderly is built into official poverty standards, which specified in 1970 that non-farm individuals under 65 years of age needed $149 more than the 65er to keep above the poverty level. The truth of the matter is not, as this figure implies, that the elderly need less food, shelter, clothing, transportation, health care, education, and recreation than do younger people. Quite simply, many older adults just can't afford these items.

Another myth in this context has it that the aged are adequately provided for by Social Security. It is true that there have been some recent improvements in Social Security benefits. In 1973 Congress approved a two-step increase, revised the cost of living provision, and raised the limit on earned income to $2,400. In July 1974, legislation was passed that raised average retirement benefits to $181 a month for single persons and $310 for couples. However, these increases will not make Social Security more than a shaky floor above want, especially in these times of spiraling inflation.

As a consequence of meager benefits, a substantial number of older adults have taken up living together while remaining unmarried in order to preserve the greater benefits available to single persons. Even worse, half of the elderly are forced to survive below the floor above want established by Social Security and there still are some unskilled and domestic workers who have no social insurance coverage Is it any wonder that many senior citizens must swallow their pride and resort to the generally inadequate payments provided by the welfare system?

These harsh economic realities severely limit the ability of the elderly to exercise meaningful choice in the housing markets of our older urban areas. Data from the Senate Special Committee on Aging show that older people living in urban areas are "house poor" in that they are spending too much of their limited resources for shelter. Although two-thirds of the elderly own their homes and 80 percent of these are free and clear of mortgages, housing continues to absorb 34 percent of the retired couple's budget. [13] Between 1965 and 1970, the cost of buying and maintaining a home increased by 80 percent, while elderly incomes increased only by half that amount during the same period. [14] As a result of these trends, home ownership among the elderly declined from 71 percent in 1967 to 69.5 percent in 1970. [15]

It is interesting to note that the lack of income has not deprived senior citizens of ample physical space. More than half of all elderly persons have three or more rooms available to them, while younger urban families average a room and a half per person. [16] In a sense, then, the urban elderly may be characterized as being "overhoused." Still, the aged often lack the wherewithal to maintain their homes in proper repair, a problem aggravated by generally increasing property taxes, insurance rates, and the fact that many elderly reside in older, center-city and suburban areas where needs for upkeep are great. Unless the elderly individual has maintenance skills of his own, he must purchase these services at high cost or perhaps rely on the good offices of friends and neighbors. Often, maintenance is deferred or put off altogether, with disastrous consequences for public health and living conditions.

Although many elderly homeowners will struggle against hea odds to retain their homes, there are others who would prefer to quit the costly burden imposed by homeownership. Unfortunately, many aged homeowners are trapped in older center-city areas for which there is little or no market. Even if a buyer is found, it may be difficult to arrange financing if the dwelling is located in an "unsound" neighborhood where conventional mortgagors are unwilling to lend. For those who have mortgages on their homes that exceed the curren resale value of the property, there is little choice but to remain whe they are, even if they are unable to afford minimum upkeep on the building. The challenge to public policy in this context is clear. Government should subsidize the maintenance efforts of those who would retain their homes, and underwrite the resale market for those who would rather be free of the responsibilities of homeownership.

Problems of Mobility and Relocation

Lack of income is in large part responsible for the fact that senior citizens move far less frequently than do younger adults. A survey conducted in Los Angeles showed that more than 90 percent of the elderly were dissatisfied with their living arrangements, yet only 13 percent actually moved in a year's time.[17] This and other studies suggest that there may be more unhappiness but less mobility with housing among the aged. Like it or not, a great many of the elderly, perhaps one-half of the total, have very little to say about where or how they will live.

The elderly poor are confined to the bottom end of our metropolitan area housing markets. The 1970 census showed that one-third of the aged were living in the older, central-city portions of the 243 standard metropolitan statistical areas. The neighborhood systems that supported senior citizens in the preautomobile era are gone from large areas of the city. In the past, the elderly could congregate in places such as the ma and pa corner grocery, in parks, pubs, and cafes. Many of these facilities have either vanished from the older core city or can no longer be used without incurring grave risk to life and limb. Moreover, it is not easy for the aged to "go where the action is."

With the accelerated movement of jobs and people to the suburbs, patterns of urban land use have changed markedly. Prior to World War II, housing, commerce, and industry as well as educational and recreational activities were interspersed and could be reached easily by walking or by public transportation. Today, land uses are more distinct and separated by distances that require an automobile if they are to be bridged conveniently. These changes have disadvantaged the urban elderly, many of whom are either unable to drive any longer or find themselves too poor to afford their own cars. Public transport has not fulfilled the need for a cheap, convenient means of movement across the sprawling landscapes of our metropolitan areas. Buses are limited in their routing; taxis and rapid transit are too expensive; the service cars and trolleys of yesteryear have almost entirely disappeared. All of these influences have combined to seriously limit the mobility of the older city resident.

Studies by Newcomer, Niebanck, and Rosow have dealt with this problem of limited mobility, with special attention to the relationship between proximity and use of particular services.[18] Newcomer's examination of group congregate housing for the elderly revealed that 62 percent would utilize on-site outdoor space several times a week, another 25 percent used it at least monthly, while 13 percent never did. This use pattern was quite similar for distances up to three blocks from the housing site. Beyond three blocks, daily utilization dropped to about 25 percent and the "never use" group increased to 50 percent. Mobility for space and service needs was limited to three blocks or less for three out of five elderly. Such considerations are clearly important for housing construction and environmental planning for the urban aged.

The relocation of the elderly poses special problems, especially if undertaken on an involuntary basis. Ample research has been done on the effects of changes in the environment on the health and well-being of the aged. The loss of familiar surroundings as well as of family and friends may produce despair and occasion the onset of physical and psychological disorders.[19] The adverse impact of relocation is probably made more severe when the older adult has no choice in the matter. One study of the institutionalized elderly showed that death rates were higher among those given no choice about being placed in an institution than among those who had alternatives.[20] Another investigation of the relationship between involuntary relocation and the life adjustment and health of older people was undertaken recently in a new housing project for the elderly. Despite the presence of supporting services, relocation was found to be a most stressful experience. In this particular case, new housing failed to produce measurable improvements in the lives of those involuntarily relocated.[21]

The negative effects of forced relocation on senior citizens are also apparent in the findings of a recent survey conducted by students of St. Louis University's Institute of Applied Gerontology.[22] This study focused on the problems of elderly "single room only" occupants of downtown St. Louis hotels that were located in the path of urban redevelopment. Although no social service programs were available to meet their needs, these elderly pensioners generally chose to live in, and had no desire to leave, the downtown area. But when the bulldozer and the "headache balls" come they must go with the old buildings. But where? Because most of the elderly residents of these hotels are poor, they are left without options. They have become living symbols of social priorities that demand newness at the expense of the old.

In summary, lack of income and limited mobility seriously constrain the urban elderly in their pursuit of decent housing and good life space. When aged people choose to move or are forced to relocate by factors beyond their control, they encounter fewer and fewer options. Increased housing costs, our youth-oriented culture, dependence on the automobile when many elderly cannot or will not drive, and the sprawling, compartmentalized land use patterns that have accompanied suburbanization are factors tending to isolate senior citizens from the mainstream of American society.

The Physical Dimension of Elderly Housing: Need versus Reality

Having emphasized the social and economic aspects of housing for senior citizens, we should add that physical quality and design also are important components of good life space. In this context, gerontological research has established several design features that should be made available in any new housing built for the elderly.[23] Most of these features follow directly from the special needs of older adults.

An adequate system of temperature and climate control is needed. Older persons often require more warmth than young people do in order to be comfortable. For this reason, an efficient heating system with thermostat control, a well-insulated unit free from drafts, and a humidity control device is needed. In those parts of the country where summer temperatures and humidity are high, air conditioning is recommended as well.

There should be adequate sun and artificial light. Older people frequently have difficulty seeing and require greater light intensity than do the young.

Sound and noise control would be beneficial. Although noise can be a source of irritation to older people, too much quiet can be equally disturbing. Housing should be designed to keep sound levels within a moderate range. Persons hard of hearing should be provided with amplifying systems for doorbells and telephones.

Efficient housing design for the elderly should minimize the need for lifting, pulling, bending, reaching, and climbing. Although a moderate amount of exercise can be beneficial, excessive exertion should be avoided. Design features that speak to this particular need involve electrical outlets placed a little higher than normal, railings and support bars located in strategic places, as well as access ramps and halls and doorways wide enough for wheelchairs.

Safety features should be built into housing units for the elderly. The old tend to be more prone to accident than younger adults, and most accidents occur in the home. Housing for the aged should be designed to minimize the possibility of falls, fire, and other hazards.

It is perhaps unnecessary to note that few dwellings would meet all of these design requirements. In fact, there is every reason to believe that much of the housing occupied by the urban elderly does not even meet minimal requirements necessary for health and safety. A recent report from the President's Council on Aging based on the 1970 Census of Population and Housing indicated that 30 percent of all elderly household heads live in substandard dwelling units. Data also showed that 26 percent of owner-occupied and 40 percent of all renter-occupied units in the 65 years and over category were dilapidated, deteriorating, or lacking some or all plumbing facilities. [24]

The quality of housing occupied by the elderly poor is even worse. A study of the housing conditions of older adults on public assistance in 17 southern states revealed that two-thirds occupy housing with major defects. This particular survey showed that 15 percent of elderly dwelling units had no running water, 30 percent had no inside flush toilets, and 46 percent had rooms not heated in the winter. [25] These dismal statistics constitute a rough measure of the inadequacy of public policy responses to date in the field of elderly housing. Viewed in a more positive light, they are a rough measure of the gap between the housing needs and aspirations of our senior citizens and the harsh realities of the present moment. Bridging this gap is one of the major challenges facing public policymakers today.

Government Response to Elderly Housing Needs

A variety of public programs designed specifically to meet the housing needs of senior citizens have been enacted in the years since the New Deal. Although they have taken some limited steps to assist the elderly with their housing problems, state and local governments have in general been rather slow to move into this area. As a result, our discussion will focus on federal efforts to assist the aged in their pursuit of decent housing. Before dealing in specifics, however, a few general remarks on federal involvement in housing are in order.

Federal housing programs involve two basic kinds of assistance: direct and indirect, or implicit. [26] Direct subsidies have been approved by Congress to serve explicit goals, and they are duly recorded in the federal budget. On the whole, these subsidies have been designed to benefit low- and moderate-income groups for whom the private market in housing has not worked well. Some examples are cash payments to local authorities for principal and interest on public housing bonds, below-market interest rate assistance to developers of low- and moderate-income housing, direct loans to nonprofit and

limited-profit housing corporations, and rent supplements for low-
income tenants of leased housing.

    Indirect subsidies are much more difficult to pin down be-
cause they do not appear in the federal budget. Federal income tax
savings related to housing as well as mortgage insurance and most
mortgage credit activities of the federal government are the basic
forms of indirect assistance. The Federal Housing Administration
and the Veterans Administration provide mortgage insurance and
loan guarantees, while the Federal National Mortgage Association
(FNMA or Fannie Mae), the Federal Home Loan Banks, and the
recently created Federal Home Loan Mortgage Corporation engage
in secondary market operations designed to increase the flow of credit
to housing.

    Shelter would be more expensive and financing less available
were it not for the actions of these agencies. Clearly, then, their
operations do constitute an important housing subsidy, even though
they do not provide cash assistance and generally have been able to
pay their own way.[27] Although the implicit character of these subsidies makes it difficult to specify precisely the distribution of benefits, it seems clear that, on the whole, the government's indirect
housing assistance programs, especially its tax deduction provisions,
favor middle- and upper-income groups over those in lower brackets.

    Consider the implications of these statements. Direct sub-
sidies are designed primarily to be of benefit to lower-income groups,
while the implicit variety tends to favor the more affluent.[28] At the
same time, whether one chooses to look at dollar value or number of
units produced, the magnitude of indirect subsidies to date has been
far greater than that of direct assistance. Federal housing policy has
favored middle- and upper-income groups over low-income people.
Ironically, those least in need of assistance get the best deal.

    The facts on this point speak for themselves. In 1970, direct
assistance for housing totaled $1.4 billion, while shelter-related tax
deductions alone, not counting several billion in expanded mortgage
insurance, credit operations, and loan guarantees, amounted to $5.7
billion.[29] If one includes the estimated $3 billion represented by the
housing portion of public assistance payments made in that year, the
indirect subsidies still outweight the direct. With regard to the number
of units subsidized, the same pattern is found. Direct assistance
produced only 1.65 million units in the years between 1950 and the
end of 1970. During the same period, some 31 million units were
built, the great bulk of them for middle- and upper-income consumers.
Virtually all of this new construction benefited from the government's
indirect support of housing markets in one way or another.

    Measured against these figures, federal subsidies designed
specifically to meet elderly housing needs have been meager. The

largest single direct subsidy for housing for the elderly has been
made under the auspices of the public housing program. First enacted
in the United States Housing Act of 1937, this program was later amended by Congress to authorize construction of low-rent projects specifically for the elderly. Through 1970, approximately 160,000 public
housing units had been produced for the aged. [30]

Another major subsidized program, Section 202 of the Housing Act of 1959, provided direct loans to nonprofit or limited-profit
sponsors, consumer cooperatives, and public agencies for construction or rehabilitation of rental or cooperative housing for senior
citizens and the handicapped. Before it was phased out temporarily
in 1969 in favor of a program of interest reduction subsidies, Section
236 of the 1968 housing legislation, some 45,000 units had been produced under Section 202. [31] This popular program was recently re-
enacted in revised form in the Housing and Community Development
Act of 1974 as a result of considerable lobbying by senior citizen
groups and Senator Harrison Williams, New Jersey Democrat, of
the Senate Subcommittee on Housing for the Elderly.

The rent supplement program authorized by Section 101 of
the Housing and Urban Development Act of 1965 was not designed
solely for the elderly. It was intended to subsidize rents for a variety
of low-income families occupying substandard housing by providing
for rental payments in excess of 25 percent of the tenant's income.
As of December 1970, only 3,000 aged residents of rental housing
were receiving this form of assistance.

Although hampered by chronic funding problems in its early
years, the rent supplement concept is likely to become a major source
of direct housing subsidy to the elderly in the immediate future. In
this regard, the Section 8 Leased Housing Assistance Plan contained
in the 1974 legislation authorized the leasing of units from private
owners, with rents subsidized down to no more than 25 percent of the
tenant's income. All units built under the revised 202 program will
also be eligible for assistance under Section 8.

In the not too distant future, perhaps within the next decade,
rent supplements may well be supplanted by a program of cash allowances made directly to the tenant, who would then be made fully responsible to the landlord for payment, rather than only partly responsible as is now the case under the new Section 8. If cash allowances
do become a major form of subsidy for senior citizens, [32] Section 8
will have been an important halfway house along the way.

Of the housing measures for the elderly discussed up to this
point, all are primarily direct subsidy programs. [33] There are also
public policy instruments directed specifically at the elderly that rely
on indirect subsidies. The oldest of these was enacted in Section 221
(d) (3) of the National Housing Act of 1954, a program that authorized

the Federal Housing Administration to insure loans made privately
for rental units to be occupied primarily by elderly, handicapped, or
displaced families in low-to-moderate-income brackets. In addition
to the mortgage insurance provision, 221 (d) (3) also entitled private
developers to accelerated depreciation on their investment, thereby
enabling them to defer taxes on current income and, eventually, to
pay reduced taxes on capital gains. These implicit subsidies resulted
in the production of some 70,000 units by the end of 1970.

Other programs relying on indirect subsidies are Sections
207 and 231 of the National Housing Act, provisions that were intended
to encourage production of rental units designed to meet the special
needs of the elderly and the handicapped. Begun in 1956, approximately 44,000 units were produced under these programs through the end
of 1970. Finally, Sections 232 and 241 of the National Housing Act
were enacted to insure loans for nursing homes and intermediate care
facilities. During the 1960s, some 76,000 beds and 1,000 units were
created under the auspices of this legislation.

Altogether, considering the impact of direct and indirect
subsidies designed specifically for the elderly, Leeds estimates that
268,000 units had been built between the inception of federal housing
efforts during the New Deal and the close of 1970, resulting in shelter
for approximately one-half million old people. [34] Given the fact that
there currently are some five million elderly poor and that perhaps
6 million older adults are forced to endure substandard accommodations, it seems clear that federal programs have fallen far short of
the need. This assessment holds despite the fact that elderly programs
constitute about one-fourth of all direct assistance currently provided
by the Department of Housing and Urban Development.

It should be noted here that we have considered only programs
that are more or less directed explicitly toward the housing needs
of the urban aged. The total impact of federal housing policies on all
senior citizens may be somewhat different, although it is difficult to
believe that our final judgment would be altered substantially in any
case. The brightest spot for the elderly who own their homes is undoubtedly the income tax deductions for mortgage interest and local
property tax payments. Other programs, however, have had a very
definite negative effect on housing conditions of the urban aged. Foremost in this category are the federal urban renewal and highway clearance programs. The federal highway program demolished roughly
330,000 units between its enactment in 1956 and 1968. [35] Under the
renewal program initiated by the Housing Act of 1949, some 439,000
dwelling units were demolished through the fiscal year 1968, while
only 124,000 new ones were constructed to replace those destroyed. [36]
Moreover, the rentals on the new units were too high for most of those
displaced to afford. In sum, if elderly homeowners have benefited

from tax deductions, urban land clearance and renewal activities have disrupted the living conditions of many old people to a painful extent. The rhetoric of federal commitment to the housing needs of the urban aged has far outdistanced actual performance.

Public Relations and "Senior Power"

Despite the apparent inadequacy of public response to the housing needs of the elderly, some people continue to believe that the aged are a kind of "most favored minority" with great political clout. Although they have made significant gains during the last decade, senior citizens are still far from fulfilling these expectations. A more balanced view of the potential of the elderly for influencing public policy priorities calls for a brief examination of the rhetoric and the realities of political action by older adults.

First, it is necessary to distinguish public relations, or PR, from actual political influence. PR and effective pressure politics differ in their immediate objectives and style. While the former relies on attention-getting tactics and the manipulation of symbols in an effort to win over public opinion, the latter usually seeks "hard," tangible objectives through the pursuit of conventional strategies such as voter organization and legislative lobbying. Both kinds of activities are essential to any effective political movement, and elderly groups have pursued both.

When a minority group begins to awaken politically, a good deal of propagandizing is necessary to create a semblance of power and "sell" the public on the justice of the group's demands. Flamboyant protest tactics and verbal bombast are staged for the mass media and all the world to see and hear. The immediate objective is PR— a favorable change in public attitudes toward the group in question. In the case of senior citizens, two examples of this sort of consciousness-raising activity come readily to mind: the Townsend Movement and the Gray Panthers.

An important forefunner of attempts to promote "senior power" in the United States was the Townsend Movement, a phenomenon that appeared in California in 1933, grew quickly to the point at which it could claim 1.5 million members, and then died prematurely in 1940.[37] Francis Everett Townsend, the charismatic leader of the movement, advocated a $200 monthly pension for every citizen over 60 that would be financed by a tax on all business transactions. The lack of an effective Washington lobby and internal strife within the movement were largely responsible for its early demose. Nonetheless, The Townsendites did succeed in focusing public attention and gaining legitimacy for some form of old-age insurance.[38]

Another militant elderly group has emerged in the 34 years since the passing of the Townsend Movement. Led by a 68-year old former national official with the United Presbyterian Church and the YWCA, Maggie Kuhn, the "Gray Panthers" were formed in the spring of 1970. In addition to a variety of specific accomplishments, such as liberalized commercial bank policies on check cashing and loans for older people, the Panthers have projected a new, militant image of the elderly. Whether threatening to march on legislatures or stop public transit with their wheelchairs, the Panthers advocate a new independent way of life for the aged. In Maggie Kuhn's words, senior citizens should adopt "a new life-style of outrage against those things that diminish and oppress us."[39] Like the Townsend Movement before it, the Gray Panthers are more likely to be remembered for their consciousness-raising activities than for any substantive accomplishments. Of particular interest in this context is the Panther's claim that our society is "age-ist," that it discriminates agains the old and the infirm, who often are "scrap[ped] just like old automobiles."[40]

Gerontological research by Arnold Rose sees the senior citizen becoming increasingly age-conscious and seeking to live in age-segregated retirement communities congenial to the formation of elderly life-styles.[41] The hostility toward the aged that is implicit in our youth-oriented culture is promoting the formation of a common group identity among the elderly and, according to Rose, this sense of identity may well result in the appearance of a cohesive voting bloc in the foreseeable future.

Rose's conclusion probably exaggerates the group-mindedness of the elderly. For example, Riley and Foner's inventory of research on aging shows that older adults' attentions are by no means confined to their own age group. Research indicates that the aged interact more frequently with younger people, especially their children, than they do with friends and neighbors in their own age group.[42] In addition, Rose has overstated the movement of senior citizens into retirement communities, where group identity and solidarity allegedly are fostered. With the inflationary economics of the present day, the mobility of most elderly people is sharply restricted. In a recent five-year time span, less than one elderly person in 10 moved across county lines and the majority had resided in the same place for an extended period.[43] Finally, the example of the Townsend Movement and other minority causes suggests that enhanced group consciousness and solidarity need not go hand in hand. With increasing political sophistication and awareness, important differences of a tactical and philosophical nature are likely to emerge, thereby making it very difficult for the elderly to act as a unified political bloc. Like it or not, it often happens that the advocates of change never really come to grips with the opposition because they are too busy squabbling among themselves.

In summary, consciousness-raising activities are not sufficient to build a strong political organization. PR is helpful, and indeed, necessary in the early stages of movement formation. However, one must move on to other things once public attention is gained. In addition to PR, the demanding tasks of voter organization and legislative lobbying are necessary to convert good intentions into effective public policy. It is here that the elderly will have to multiply their efforts if they hope to improve the responses of government decision-makers to their housing needs.

Political Participation and the Elderly

On the surface, many of the facts relating to political participation by the aged are encouraging.[44] Researchers have found, for example, that if the effect of education is controlled, older people have both continued interest in politics and are more likely to have political opinions than younger people. One study showed that those with the greatest interest in politics were 60 years of age and over. This interest is manifested by increased attention to political campaigns and keeping up with public affairs through written and visual media. Research also indicates that the frequency of strong identification with a political party and political activities such as petition signing and voter registration work increase with age and that 65ers vote as frequently as the 45 to 64, middle-age group, despite problems of ill-health and lack of transportation that may keep many elderly from the polls. Approximately 15 percent of those who actually vote in presidential elections are 65 years of age and over. Last, it seems clear that older adults have equal if not proportionately greater opportunity for political roles and activity; in fact, senior citizens are overrepresented in numerous elective and appointed offices at all levels of government.

What do these facts mean in terms of political influence or power for the elderly? In two words, very little. The notion of "senior power" is largely PR, more myth than reality. What limited success the elderly have had in the political arena has less to do with the power of older adults in itself than it does with the understandable reticence of most people to oppose causes that would benefit the senior citizen. This judgment is supported by two basic facts. There are no organizations capable of deliverying the elderly vote in return for favorable public policy responses and, even if the aged were able to deliver a bloc vote for selected candidates, serious problems of accountability and influence would still exist.

In all but a few places, the elderly have been unable to put together a coherent force capable of making itself heard at the polls. This is not surprising when one considers that there are numerous factors working to dilute the capacity of the elderly for unified political action. Elderly voters are about evenly divided in their voting preferences between Democrats and Republicans. [45] While this division of forces may be useful for some purposes, it seriously undermines the credibility of those who would use the bloc vote as a threat to gain leverage in the political process. Differences in party identification make it unlikely that the aged will coalesce around any single age-related issue. Then, too, the fact that older adults in urban areas are a relatively dispersed population group, when compared with blacks, for example, makes it difficult to forge a solidary political organization.

Certain physiological and psychological problems related to advanced age compound the task of political organization. The infirmities that accompany old age may absorb very large amounts of the individual's energy, leaving little left for political concerns. In this context, there is research indicating that a significant number of older adults become fatalistic and mistrustful of others, thereby producing a generalized sense of alienation. Although these persons may recognize the need for political action to improve the position of older people, their sense of fatalism makes it unlikely that they will try to do anything about it. [46] Thus, alienation among the elderly reinforces their lack of power. [47] In those instances in which the alienated are mobilized by particular events or personalities, the results may be dysfunctional if activism comes in response to the appeals of demagogues or extremist movements. According to Harold Wilensky, " . . . the aged must be seen as a peculiarly potent pool of extremism; apathy and activism, may in the end, be blood brothers. "[48]

The aging process works to restrict the range of political options open to "senior power" advocates in yet another way. Notwithstanding some of the threats made by the Gray Panthers, the elderly are not well suited to cope with the stress and discomforts associated with direct action methods such as lengthy vigils, sit-ins, and physical confrontations. For the most part, senior citizens are forced to operate in more conventional channels. [49]

There are numerous problems that stand in the way of attempts to create a unified political organization among the aged. It can also be argued that "senior power" would not follow necessarily from election of candidates committed to the cause of the elderly. Persons 65 years and over constitute only about 10 percent of the total population. Even if the elderly were to become an "intense" or unified minority, it still is doubtful that they would have sufficient clout to bring about a drastic reallocation of public resources to meet their demands for shelter and other necessities of life. Beyond this, the elderly would find it difficult to hold elected candidates accountable to their needs.

The problem of accountability is a universal one of representative government, but it appears particularly acute in the case of the aged. As noted, the elderly are overrepresented in public offices at all levels of government. It is common knowledge, for example, that most key congressional committees in Washington are headed by older adults; Congress, it often is charged, is a gerontocracy in which influence generally increases with logevity. It does not follow, however, that elderly representatives automatically will sponsor or even support legislation for the aged. Many older public officials attempt to maintain a youthful image, thereby resisting identification with the elderly. Many of these senior leaders are not affected by such problems as compulsory retirement, inadequate income, and substandard housing. Because these are not their problems, the needs of the aged are not automatically a compelling concern.

In effect, variables other than age influence most of the basic decisions made by the so-called "gerontocrats." When subjected to conflicting pressures, they will provide strong support for programs for the aged only to the extent that their constituencies feel strongly about such programs. The problem of the elderly political leader is part of the more general problem of ambivalent societal attitudes toward the aged. "Sure, I'm for the old folks, just so long as it doesn't call for personal involvement or cost me anything much." This typical, if implicit, view helps to explain the less than adequate response of government to the requirements of the aged for decent housing and other necessities.

Pressure Group Activity

Lest we paint an overly gloomy picture of political prospects for the aged, we should note that there are some bright spots on the contemporary scene. Foremost among these are the lobbying groups that seek public policy changes favorable to the elderly. If they have had only limited success to date, some of these organizations have demonstrated an increasing level of performance of late and may hold considerable promise for the future.

Political support for legislation benefiting the elderly develops from a number of sources and for a variety of reasons. There are numerous non-age-based organizations, such as labor unions and religious groups, which have provided support for elderly needs and causes. Some members of these organizations who have responsibility for aged family have a practical stake in legislation that shifts the burden of support to government bureaucracy in such basic areas as income, health, and housing. Others support legislation for the elderly for altruistic reasons. As a rule, no major organization wants to risk the alienation of potential supporters by overtly opposing legislation for senior citizens. As noted earlier, it is primarily this fact rather than an aggressive, unified "senior power" that accounts for what success the aged have had in the public policy arena to date.

Non-age based organizations generally advocate for the elderly on a noncontinuous, ad hoc basis. For example, in preparation for the 1970 White House Conference on Aging more than 400 organizations were invited to send representatives to help formulate a legislative agenda for the aged in the 1970s.[50] Labor, business, the professions, consumer, religious, and community action groups attended. As a general rule, however, each group had a rather circumscribed interest and limited its activity primarily to those particular areas of concern to it. Vinyard points to a similar case in the behavior of many special interest groups toward the Senate Special Committee on Aging.[51] As a focal point for national legislative activity on behalf of the elderly, many of these groups periodically initiate contacts with the committee to support or oppose particular policies or positions where their own interests are involved. Although the support of these groups often is essential to the passage of legislation for the elderly, one wonders whether the interests of the aged are fully compatible with those of their occasional allies. In cases where interests diverge, the cause of older adults commonly is subordinated to the ally's objectives. From this perspective, senior citizens would do well to develop organizations capable of some degree of autonomous action. Otherwise, the elderly can never be sure that their interests are the ones being served by pressure group activities.

There are now a wide variety of organizations engaged on a continuing basis in national politics directly related to the aged and their problems. Four of these are trade associations that are concerned with long-term care facilities for the aged: the American Association of Homes for the Aging, the American Nursing Home Association, the National Council of Health Care Services, and the National Association of State Units on Aging. The activities of these groups are designed primarily to achieve increased federal funding for their work.

The largest organizations occupied exclusively with national issues relating to the aged are the National Council of Senior Citizens (NCSC), the National Retired Teachers' Association–American Association of Retired Persons (NRTA–AARP), and the National Association of Retired Federal Employees (NARFE).[52] These groups, which function as both service provider and public advocate for senior citizens, are mass organizations with a combined membership exceeding 9 million.[53]

These large associations differ somewhat in the character of their membership and activities. The 3 million-member NCSC recruits primarily from organized labor and senior citizen clubs, and gerontologists perceive the "typical" member as a working-class Democrat from the East. As with the other mass organizations, the NCSC would lose its tax-exempt status with the Internal Revenue Service if it had formal ties to any political party. As a result, it does not officially endorse candidates for public office and its relationship with political parties is an informal one. Still, the organization has become somewhat more politicized in recent years with the establishment of a political action branch called Concerned Seniors for Better Government. One of the NCSC's major victories in the public policy arena came with the passage of the Medicare health insurance program for the elderly in 1965. In addition to its lobbying activities, group insurance plans and discount prescription drugs are provided to members.

The NRTA and the AARP function in national politics as one organization with a combined membership of over 6 million members. In contrast to the workingman-image of the NCSC, the "typical" NRTA-AARP member is perceived by gerontologists as a retired business-man or professional with Republican leanings and not closely identified with any one section of the country. Originally, the organization subordinated political goals to those of individual uplift and social betterment, but it too has become more active in the public policy arena in recent years. As the largest mass organizations, both the NCSC and NRTA-AARP claim to speak for all elderly Americans.

The last of the mass-based groups advocating for the aged is the NARFE, which currently has approximately 250,000 members. It has been active politically only during the last five years, and membership has increased, but modestly compared to the other two big associations, perhaps because it has chosen to concentrate on narrow bread-and-butter questions instead of concerning itself with the larger political and socioeconomic problems of the aged.

Beyond these mass organizations and trade associations, we might mention briefly a few other groups that have been active in national politics on behalf of the elderly.[54] The National Council on Aging serves primarily as a technical resource and consultant on matters pertaining to the elderly for its membership, which encompasses a loose confederation of some 1,400 public and private welfare agencies. The most recent organization currently active on the national scene is the National Caucus of Black Aged, a political action group of 150 professionals that is attempting to highlight the special problems of black senior citizens. Finally, the Gerontological Society with its more than 2,000 professional members has recently become active in national policy issues related to the aged.

Of all the varied groups advocating for the elderly, the three large mass organizations—the NCSC, the NRTA-AARP, and the NARFE—seem to hold the most promise for the future. According to Pratt, these mass-based "aging organizations [already] are having an impact on the national political scene."[55] This increasing strength is due to at least three factors, namely: the establishment of efficient organizations with staying power, success in cultivating sources of funding beyond their membership, and the development of a climate of public opinion favorable to the problems of the aged.

The growing clout of these organizations was recently demonstrated in the passage of the Housing and Community Development Act of 1974. The three associations were asked to testify before the congressional committees charged with putting together this legislation, and it turned out that most of their major demands, especially the one calling for reenactment of the Section 202 program, were incorporated in the final bill. If the elderly lobby is able to resist the ever-present tendencies toward factionalism and petty bureaucratic infighting, it may become even more successful in years to come.

Closing Evaluation and a Look Ahead

Although some signs of improvement are present, the elderly, to date, have had but limited success in their search for decent housing and good life space in the public policy arena. The consciousness-raising activities of groups like Maggie Kuhn's Gray Panthers are complemented by the pragmatic legislative lobbying of various organizations concerned with the needs of senior citizens. Three of the entities in the latter category—the National Council of Senior Citizens, the National Association of Retired Federal Employees, and the National Retired Teachers' Association-American Association of Retired Persons—are mass-based associations with growing national influence. Still, neither public relations nor practical politics have been able to offset the basic constraint inherent in the fact that the elderly by themselves constitute only about 10 percent of the total population. Even if the aged were able to forge a solidary political organization, which they have not done, bloc voting would be effective only in scattered areas where elderly retirees are highly concentrated. No minority can "make it" alone in national politics, and "senior power" today is more mythical than real.

If the elderly are to improve their performance in the politics of housing in the foreseeable future, at least two strategic measures must be adopted.

Greater activity within their own camp is absolutely essential. Senior citizens must somehow be instilled with a greater sense of group identity than they have shown to date. Most importantly, ways must be found to bridge social class and income differences among the elderly. Frequently, those older persons who have adequate income to secure decent shelter do not identify with the problems of the aged poor, and no one has really attempted to articulate programs that would help to create a cohesive political force among the disadvantaged aged. The leadership of national organizations advocating for the elderly has hardly begun to tap this potential source of support. Of course, increased political activism is likely to compound problems of factionalism, but this difficulty is by no means unique to older adults. If intelligent leadership can work out housing programs of common benefit to all groups concerned, sufficient unity of purpose may be achieved or at least there will be a good chance to control the most destructive aspects of internecine conflict.

Another course of action also should be pursued. As "senior power" is at best a minority force, efforts must be made to seek out and extend workable alliances with other groups. Organized labor has long been a supporter of the aged, as have the national religious organizations. However, not enough effort has been spent in exploring alliances with other similarly circumstanced groups, such as the handicapped, racial minorities, and the poor. Given the needs of all these groups for improved housing, grounds for common effort would seem to exist. This strategy of broadening alliances makes especially good sense tas the mass organizations representing the aged become stronger. With autonomous bases of power, it becomes less likely that elderly interests will be subordinated to those of their allies. Alliances can be pursued with less fear of a "sell out."

If the public response to elderly housing needs has fallen short to date, the future is not without hope. The favorable climate of public opinion on questions of aging and the increased lobbying and managerial skills of their mass organizations may augment the political effectiveness of the aged on the national scene. Still, much effort must be made along the lines suggested above if most of the elderly are to have any chance to select life-styles and housing congenial to their needs. Without that additional effort, the status quo will change little, if at all, and many senior citizens, especially those residing in older urban areas, will continue to endure sorry conditions that are inimical to human life and dignity.

NOTES

1. Frances M. Carp, "Life-style and Location within San
Antonio" (paper delivered at the 26th Annual Meeting of the Gerontological Society, Miami Beach, Florida, November 1973.)
2. Eva Kahana and Boaz Kahana, "Strategies of Adaptation
in Institutional Settings" (paper delivered at the 26th Annual Meeting
of the Gerontological Society, Miami Beach, Florida, November 1973.)
3. James E. Birren, "The Aged in the Cities," The Gerontologist 9, no. 3, part I (Autumn 1969), pp. 163-69.
4. Ira F. Ehrlich, "Life-styles Among Persons 70 Years
and Older in Age-Segregated Housing," The Gerontologist, vol. 12,
no. 1, part I (Spring 1972), pp. 127-31.
5. Robert C. Atchley, The Social Forces in Later Life: An
Introduction to Social Gerontology (Belmont, California: Wadsworth
Publishing Co., 1972).
6. Robert W. Kleemeier, "Attitudes toward Special Settings
for the Aged," in Processes of Aging: Social and Psychological Perspectives, eds., Richard H. Williams, Clark Tibbitts, and Wilma
Donahue (New York: Atherton Press, 1963); Lewis Mumford, "For
Older People—Not Segregation but Integration," Architectual Record
119, no. 5 (May 1956), pp. 191-194; and Walter K. Vivrett, "Housing
and Community Settings for Older People," in Handbook of Social
Gerontology, Clark Tibbitts, ed. (Chicago: University of Chicago
Press, 1960), pp. 549-623.
7. M. C. Paulson, "Are All the Days Balmy in Retirement
Communities?" National Observer, October 2, 1967, p. 24; Joseph
H. Peck, Let's Rejoin the Human Race (Englewood Cliffs, N. J.:
Prentice-Hall, 1963); and Calvin Trillin, "Wake Up and Live," New
Yorker, 40 (April 4, 1964), pp. 120-177.
8. See, for example, Gordon L. Bultena and Vivian Wood,
"The American Retirement Community: Bane or Blessing?" Journal
of Gerontology, 24, no. 2 (April 1969), pp. 209-217; Irving Rosow,
Social Integration of the Aged (New York: Free Press, 1967); and
Kermit K. Schooler, "The Relationship between Social Interaction
and Morale of the Elderly People as a Function of Environment
Characteristics," The Gerontologist 9, no. 1 (Spring 1969), pp. 25-
29. In these studies, the elderly age-segregated environment is defined as one in which approximately 50 percent of the people residing
in a given neighborhood are 65 years of age and over.
9. Bultena and Wood, op. cit.
10. J. D. Teaff and others, Impact of Age Integration of
Public Housing Projects upon Elderly Tenant Well-Being" (Paper
presented at 26th Annual Meeting of the Gerontological Society, Miami
Beach, Florida, November 1973.)

11. See Herman B. Brotman, "Income and Poverty in 1970," Advance Reports, in Facts and Figures on Older Americans, no. 3 (Washington, D.C.: Department of Health, Education, and Welfare, 1971).

12. Herman B. Brotman, "Measuring Adequacy of Income," in Facts and Figures on Older Americans, no. 1 (Washington, D.C.: Department of Health, Education and Welfare, 1971).

13. U.S. Senate, Special Committee on Aging, Developments in Aging, 1969 (Washington, D.C.: Government Printing Office, 1970).

14. U.S. Senate, Special Committee on Aging, Developments in Aging, 1970 (Washington, D.C.: Government Printing Office, 1971).

15. Morton H. Leeds, "Housing Directions for the Elderly," in Institute on Housing for the Elderly, R. H. Davis, ed. (Los Angeles: Ethel Percy Andrus Gerontology Center, University of Southern California, 1973), p. 13.

16. Ibid., p. 14.

17. Birren, op. cit., p. 164.

18. R. J. Newcomer, "Housing, Services and Neighborhood Activities: A Preliminary Revision of Service Proximity Criteria," paper presented at the 26th annual meeting of the Gerontological Society, Miami Beach, Florida, November 1973; Paul L. Niebanck, "The Relocation of Elderly Persons: Planning for the Residents of Older Urban Areas" (Ph.D. dissertation, University of Pennsylvania, Philadelphia, 1966); and Rosow, op. cit.

19. See Ruth Bennett, "Social Context: A Neglected Variable in Research on Aging," Aging and Human Development 1, no. 2 (May 1970), pp. 97-116; and George L. Engel, "A Life Setting Conducive to Illness: The Giving Up—Given Up Complex," Annals of Internal Medicine, 69 (August 1968), pp. 293-300.

20. Marcella Farrar and Nelida Ferrari, "Case Work and Group Work in a Home for the Aged," Social Work, 5, no. 2 (April 1960), pp. 58-63.

21. F. N. Brand and R. T. Smith, "Life Adjustment and Relocation of the Elderly," paper presented at the 26th annual meeting of the Gerontological Society, Miami Beach, Florida, November 1973.

22. Phyllis Ehrlich and others, "Needs and Characteristics of Aged Single Room Only Hotel Occupants: A Pilot Study" (Paper delivered at the 27th Annual Meeting of the Gerontological Society, Portland, Oregon, October 1974.)

23. William F. Anderson, "The Spectrum of Housing and Environments Required by Older Adults" (Paper delivered at the International Symposium on Housing and Environmental Design for Older Adults, Washington, D.C., December 1973.)

24. President's Council on Aging, The Older American (Washington, D.C.: Government Printing Office, 1973), pp. 25-26.

25. Leeds, op. cit., p. 14.

26. See Anthony Downs, Federal Housing Subsidies: How Are They Working? (Chicago: Real Estate Research Corporation, October 1972), p. 4. Although our basic definitions follow Downs, the concept of indirect subsidy has been expanded by including the government's mortgage insurance and secondary market operations under this heading.

27. Until 1968, Fannie Mae had a small direct subsidy program that involved the purchase of mortgages above market value. In that year, this function was transferred to the newly created Government National Mortgage Association (Ginnie Mae), while Fannie Mae's remaining, implicit subsidy, programs were converted to private ownership.

28. For supporting evidence, see Henry J. Aaron, Shelter and Subsidies: Who Benefits from Federal Housing Policies? (Washington, D.C.: Brookings Institution, 1972).

29. The data in this paragraph are taken from Downs, op. cit., pp. 12, 15, 95.

30. Unless otherwise noted, figures on production under the various housing programs are taken from Aaron, op. cit., appendix A.

31. Special Committee on Aging, United States Senate, Memorandum 6, no. 5, 23 August 1974, p. 1.

32. See the discussion on cash allowances by James P. Zais in this volume.

33. We have not discussed the various Farmers Home Administration programs designed to meet the housing needs of older adults living in rural areas. Altogether, direct subsidies produced approximately 23,000 units for the rural aged through the end of 1970.

34. Leeds, op. cit., p. 16.

35. National Commission on Urban Problems, Building the American City (Washington, D.C.: Government Printing Office, 1968), pp. 82-83.

36. "Opportunity to Improve Allocation of Program Funds to Meet the National Housing Goals," Report to Congress by the Comptroller General of the United States, October 2, 1970, p. 18.

37. Abraham Holtzman, The Townsend Movement: A Political Study (New York: Basic Books, 1963).

38. Old Age Survivors and Disability Insurance (OASDI) was passed by Congress in 1935, some two years after the appearance of the Townsend Movement.

39. "The Gray Panthers," Parade, January 28, 1973, p. 22.

40. Ibid., p. 20.

41. Arnold M. Rose, "The Subculture of Aging: A Framework for Research in Social Gerontology" and "Group Consciousness among

the Aging," in Older People and Their Social World, eds. Arnold M. Rose and Warren A. Peterson (Philadelphia: F. A. Davis Co., 1965), pp. 3-36.

42. Matilda W. Riley and Anne Foner, Aging and Society (New York: Russell Sage Foundation, 1968).

43. Ibid., pp. 537-560.

44. The information in this paragraph is taken from Norval D. Glenn, "Aging, Disengagement and Opinionation," Public Opinion Quarterly, 33, no. 1 (Spring 1969), pp. 17-33; and Riley and Foner, op. cit., pp. 463-482.

45. Glenn, op. cit., p. 30.

46. Jeremy Tunstall, Old and Alone: A Sociological Study of Old People (London: Routledge and Kegan Paul, 1966).

47. David Blau and Martin A. Berezin, "Some Ethnic and Cultural Considerations in Aging," Journal of Geriatric Psychiatry 2, no. 1 (Fall 1968), pp. 3-5.

48. Harold Wilensky, "Life Cycle, Work Situation and Participation in Formal Associations," in Social and Psychological Aspects of Aging, eds. Clark Tibbitts and Wilma Donahue (New York: Columbia University Press, 1963), p. 924.

49. Robert H. Binstock, "Interest-Group Liberalism and the Politics of Aging," The Gerontologist 12, no. 3, part I (Autumn 1972), pp. 265-280.

50. Ibid.

51. Dale Vinyard, "The Senate Special Committee on the Aging," The Gerontologist 12, no. 3, part I (Autumn 1972), pp. 298-303.

52. Our discussion of these organizations in the next few paragraphs owes much to Henry J. Pratt, "Old Age Associations in National Politics," Annals of the American Academy of Political and Social Science, no. 415 (September 1974), pp. 106-119.

53. It is difficult to say what proportion of the total aged population belongs to these groups since there are no data to indicate how many persons are members of more than one group or to what extent sponsors may be persons under 65 years of age.

54. The Gray Panthers, discussed earlier, might also be mentioned in this context.

55. Pratt, op. cit., p. 119.

PART

V

THE NEW DIRECTIONS

Historically, most federal housing programs designed explicitly to aid low- and moderate-income families have involved so-called "supply-side" subsidies. These are programs that have attempted to help the consumer of housing services indirectly by providing incentives to those engaged in the production and delivery of housing. In recent years, turnkey public housing and the various below-market interest rate programs, such as those provided under Sections 221(d)(3), 235, and 236 of the national housing legislation, have been of this nature.

The commitment to work through the supply-side of the housing market has been criticized as inefficient and unnecessarily rewarding to housing producers and middlemen, who are charged frequently with enriching themselves at the expense of taxpayers and those in need of housing assistance. Largely in response to such complaints, current trends in low-income housing policy have moved in the direction of "demand-side" subsidies designed to assist needy families directly by providing them with dollars that they can use to obtain standard housing in the marketplace. This "new direction" in federal housing policy is described and analyzed in detail in the two main offerings of this concluding section.

In his essay, Charles L. Edson traces the evolution of the leased public housing program from its appearance in 1965 to the present. Originally intended to allow local housing authorities (LHA's) to lease units from private owners, Section 23 leasing has undergone major changes in the past two years. The revised Section 23 and its successor, the Section 8 program enacted in the Housing and Community Development Act of 1974, were consciously intended as a step in the direction of direct cash allowances for housing low-income families. Under the revised leasing concept, public housing tenants have been placed in direct contact with private owners. The LHA no longer serves as a buffer and go-between. Its basic role in the leasing program has been reduced to one of tenant certification, dwelling inspection, and, in the case of existing units under the Section 8 program, serving as conduit for the Housing Assistance Payment subsidy. The Department of Housing and Urban Development (HUD) has interpreted Section 8 to mean that the LHA can serve as manager for the private owner or developer in relatively few cases. This reduced role of the LHA is compatible with the objectives of the cash allowance concept, which is being analyzed now in a wide-ranging set of social experiments in selected cities around the country.

The components of the Experimental Housing Allowance Program (EHAP) are described in the essay by James P. Zais. The basic allowance concept would provide low-income clients with a cash subsidy sufficient to enable them to obtain standard housing in the market. Housing allowances differ from existing public assistance programs, which are intended ostensibly to cover housing needs as well as food, clothing, and other necessities, in that the former are earmarked explicitly for meeting shelter needs. The numerous problems and issues raised by this demand-side program are set forth concisely by the author, who observes that the results of the on-going Experimental Housing Allowance Program studies may be lost in the heated debate that is certain to accompany any legislative initiative towards a full-scale system of cash allowances. According to Zais, the politics of EHAP and the allowance concept are such that any reasoned discussion of the substantive issues involved will be very difficult.

In the final chapter in this section, the editors present a brief discussion concerning the politics of the new directions in housing policy. The advocates and opponents of the demand-side programs are identified and their stakes in the housing game are analyzed. Special attention is directed at the central role of academic researchers and scholars in defining and clarifying the issues that find their way into the public agenda on housing. The authors conclude that the new directions in housing policy will not replace fully the traditional supply-side programs. The politics of urban housing is that of mutual accommodation and trade-offs, and actors with stakes invested in traditional programs must be considered. At best, the new directions in housing policy are likely to produce a gradual, incremental improvement in the position of low-income people, who experience serious difficulties in competition for scarce housing resources.

Several facts support the view that the new policy directions do not represent a sharp break with the past. First, in a strict sense it is incorrect to assert that demand-side subsidies are new in housing policy. The income-tax deductions that are available to homeowners and provide a disproportionate amount of benefits for middle- and upper-income families are really a form of demand-side subsidy that increases consumer purchasing power. Even low-income groups have had a demand-side program of sorts in the housing portion of public assistance payments. According to a piece by William C. Baer in The Public Interest, No. 39, Spring 1975, welfare payments for housing exceeded government programs explicitly designed to meet the shelter needs of low- and moderate-income families by a margin of $2.6 to $2.5 billion in 1972. The question naturally arises, how much difference will a cash allowance specifically earmarked for housing make in the living conditions of the poor? This question is especially salient in view of the Ford administration's intention to hold the line on all new "nonessential" spending in the aftermath of the 1975 tax cut and rebate package.

A couple of cautionary points should be noted in this context. Most important, perhaps, is that badly deteriorated neighborhoods will not be rebuilt by a cash allowance program. Even the most ardent advocates of allowances agree that existing proposals will not result in large-scale rehabilitation in the core areas of older urban regions like St. Louis, Newark, and Philadelphia. Instead, there seems to be an assumption in the housing allowance proposals that most of the substandard housing stock is only modestly substandard and that receipt of the allowance would enable tenants to bargain effectively with the owner and have their units upgraded. One of the major concerns of the EHAP staff now is to find a way to ensure that the additional dollars received from allowances will not merely result in windfall rent increases for the "slumlord" without substantial improvement of existing housing. In the case of seriously substandard units, it should be recognized that there probably is no subsidy large enough to induce a favorable response from the landlord.

Like their predecessors, the new directions in housing policy are likely to be found wanting in another respect as well—they probably will do little to alter residential patterns in U.S. metropolitan areas, which continue to be characterized by a high degree of racial and social class segregation. Neither leased housing nor allowances as such will succeed in "opening up" the suburban frontier to occupancy by the poor and racial minorities. The revised Section 23 program allowed well-to-do municipalities to exclude assisted units by simply failing to pass a resolution approving leased housing projects. The new Section 8 leasing program enacted in the Housing and Community Development Act of 1974 has dropped this exclusionary device and put in its place something far more subtle—the so-called Housing Assistance Plan (HAP).

The location of leased housing units is now dependent upon conformance with a HAP for low- and moderate-income families, a housing plan that every city must have in order to qualify for federal community development funds. The problem with this approach is that affluent suburban municipalities probably will not draft a HAP or else will claim that they have no need for subsidized housing. Even those communities that do have a HAP can disapprove of particular proposals by arguing that they are inconsistent with the plan. HUD has the power to override that decision if it determines that the proposed project is, in fact, consistent with the plan. Nonetheless, the politics of local-federal relationships suggest strongly that HUD will not impose a Section 8 project over the opposition of established local governments.

In theory, a cash allowance program should further the deconcentration of the poor and minorities because it would not require local government approval or review. However, change probably would come about very slowly if at all. Early reports on the Kansas City demonstration found this to be the case, and the difficulties encountered in locating acceptable sites for the EHAP Supply Experiment discussed by Zais point in the same general direction. Segregated residential patterns in this country are, in large part, the product of a deeply ingrained set of social preferences. It follows that the removal of legal impediments will not necessarily result in changed residential patterns.

Finally, Edson's essay makes it clear that the new directions in housing policy will likely encounter substantial difficulty in the attempt to alter the emphasis on new construction that typifies the urban housing game as it is now being played. The original Section 23 leasing program was intended exclusively for existing units, but pressure from the home builders' lobby soon changed this. As of June 1, 1973, the Leased Housing Association reported that nearly one-half of the 162,000 units subsidized under the leasing program were new construction. An attempt will be made under the new Section 8 program to limit assistance for new construction to those places where existing units are not available, but it is questionable whether housing conservationists will be able to do much better under the new program than they did under the original Section 23.

As for the cash allowance concept, most insiders are now betting that it will supplement rather than replace existing supply-side programs. The reason for this moderate view on the part of allowance proponents is rather simple—if reduced to a narrow question of allowances or new construction, it is highly doubtful whether the allowance advocates could generate enough clout to overcome their well-entrenched opponents.

In closing, both the Section 8 leasing program and the cash allowance concept make important assumptions about the response of the marketplace. Both are designed to work through rather than contrary to market forces. As explained in the introduction, this basic commitment to the market acknowledges implicitly the existence of an uneven distribution of costs and benefits in the housing game. For this reason, the "new directions" in federal housing policy do not represent a fundamental break with the past. At best, the demand-side emphasis will result in a gradual, marginal improvement in the living conditions of low- and moderate-income families. At worst, the cash allowance concept may never get past the experimental stage or may simply bid up the price of the stock of existing housing. In either case, the urban housing picture is not likely to change drastically over the next five to ten years.

10

LEASED HOUSING: EVOLUTION
OF A FEDERAL HOUSING PROGRAM
Charles L. Edson

Federal housing programs are neither produced by legislative fiat nor follow directly from the recommendations of "experts." They emerge slowly, with numerous pragmatic adjustments designed to satisfy the needs of diverse and sometimes conflicting interests. Policy-making processes do not stop with the passage of a new piece of legislation. Administrative decisions can, and frequently do, modify or completely transform the original intent of lawmakers. Thus, the development of a new program assumes the character of an ongoing game in which the players are not counted out if they lose the first round. There is always time to fall back, regroup, and return to fight another day. By trying different strategies or new pressure points, participants may get what they want. The disjointed, incremental nature of the housing process necessitates continual accommodation, and policy is modified accordingly.

The evolution of the leased housing program over the past decade provides a fascinating illustration of this general pattern. The program, which was begun in 1965 as federal legislation designed to allow local housing authorities to lease privately owned existing structures for occupancy by low-income families, was quickly altered to encourage new construction. During the past year, it has gone through two major legislative revisions. The original Section 23 Leased Housing was replaced in April 1974, by a short-lived revised Section 23, which gave way to the Section 8 program enacted in the Housing and Community Development Act passed by Congress in August of that

The author would like to acknowledge the editors' assistance in the preparation of this paper.

year. These recent changes in the leased housing legislation are seen
by many as an important step in the direction of yet another experimental program based on the concept of providing low-income families
with direct cash allowances for housing. As the government's main
housing subsidy program for low-income persons at the present time,
the prospects of Section 8 can be better assessed after reviewing the
experience of the Section 23 programs that preceded it.

Development of the Section 23 Programs

In 1965, leased housing provisions were written into Section
23 of the national housing legislation under the sponsorship of Con-
gressman William B. Widnall of New Jersey—then the ranking Republican on the House Banking and Currency Committee—as an alternative
to the Johnson administration's Rent Supplement Program. Congress-
man Widnall intended his program to be utilized for leasing existing
housing, while rent supplements were to subsidize the construction
of new units. Accordingly, the Section 23 legislation permitted the
Department of Housing and Urban Development (HUD) to make annual
contributions only for the leasing of "existing units." Congressional
intent notwithstanding, HUD placed a liberal interpretation on the
statutory wording by ruling that newly constructed, once built, units
were "existing," and thus eligible for the Section 23 subsidy.

This ruling is interesting for what it suggests about the
character of federal housing policy formation. From the legislative
point of view, the emphasis on existing housing was intended to correct some of the major deficiencies of the conventional public housing
program. By leasing existing units from private owners, people could
be put in occupancy quickly, making the government appear highly
responsive in the face of the ghetto riots that began in the summer of
1964. Unlike conventional projects, the emphasis on existing, privately owned units also promised to lower the visibility of public
housing clients, while keeping property on the local tax rolls. Finally,
the existing units' provision represented a bow in the direction of
housing conservation as a long overdue alternative to the traditional
stress on new construction. With the passage of the Section 23 legislation, however, it soon became apparent that construction interests
could not be kept out of the promising new program.

HUD also exercised administrative discretion in another
aspect of the leased housing program. Original legislation limited
Section 23 leases between private landlords and local housing authorities to three years, which was subsequently lengthened to five years
in 1966. Although reasonable for leases involving already existing

structures, this restriction was not appropriate for a program designed
to encourage new construction because lending institutions do not loan
without assurances of an income stream stretching over an extended
period of time. To get around this problem, HUD pointed out that the
Section 23 statute specifically permitted lease renewals and it ruled
that there was no reason why these renewals could not be made at the
beginning as well as at the end of the leasing term. Thus, with an
original five-year lease and seven automatic renewals there could be
a 40-year commitment that would enhance the financial feasibility of
projects proposed under HUD's new Construction for Leasing
Program.[1]

In 1970, Congress ratified HUD's modifications of the leased
housing program by removing the word "existing" from Section 23 and
allowing leasing terms up to 20 years for new construction and 15 for
existing units. With this change in the statute, construction began to
dominate the program. In 1972, for example, Section 23 subsidized
over 25,000 newly constructed units, 3,100 rehabilitation units, and
19,500 existing ones.[2] Overall, from the program's inception in 1965
through June 30, 1973, there was almost an even split between existing
units and new ones, with 86,759 compared to 75,244 subsidized units,
respectively.[3]

During its nine-year history, Section 23 generally proved to
be a popular program. In 1970, Congress demonstrated its approval
by requiring that at least 30 percent of all public housing units be
placed under Section 23. After "Black Monday" in January 1973, when
President Nixon declared a moratorium on federal housing subsidies,
a six-month study was conducted that concluded that Section 23 should
be the government's primary subsidy vehicle for low-income families.
On September 19, 1973, the president issued an important policy
statement that read in part as follows:

> I am advised by the secretary for housing and urban
> development that one of the existing construction pro-
> grams—the Section 23 program under which new and
> existing housing is leased for low-income families—
> can be administered in a way which carries out some
> of the principles of direct cash assistance. If admin-
> istered in this way, this program could also provide
> valuable information for us to use in developing this
> new approach. Accordingly, I am lifting the suspension
> of January 5 with respect to these Section 23 Programs.[4]

This indication of the administration's desire to pattern the
leased housing program along the lines of direct cash assistance is
essential in understanding the framework of the revised Section 23,

which was worked out in the six months following the president's statement. On September 19, Nixon also announced that he was making available 100,000 units of Section 23 to be put under contract during fiscal 1974, with half of those for new construction and half for existing units. House Joint Resolution 719, passed October 2, 1973, authorized $140 million in public housing contract authority, an amount sufficient to provide adequate funding for a good portion of the 100,000 units. However, because HUD did not issue its final program handbooks for the new construction aspects of the program until April 22, 1974, there was little chance that the fiscal 1974 goal would be met. Although the moratorium was lifted on September 19, 1973, not one Section 23 unit was under construction as of June 1974.

HUD's April 22 handbook for new construction and the subsequent counterparts for existing and rehabilitated units and state agencies enjoyed no easy birth. They were preceded by two Federal Register publications—a "Policy Statement" containing the essence of the program published in November 1973, and proposed regulations published in the Federal Register in January and February 1974. More than 170 comments suggesting changes were filed concerning the proposed regulations. The final handbooks differed in some significant respects from those published in the earlier versions, but the basic housing assistance payment concept remained unchanged.

By April 1974, the final regulations in the Federal Register had transformed the old 23 program into one resembling direct cash assistance. Before the issuance of HUD's new handbooks, a local housing authority (LHA) would lease units from an owner of private accommodations and then, with the assistance of a HUD subsidy, the LHA proceeded to sublease the units to low-income families. This relationship can be diagramed as follows:

Owner ◄── Lease ──► LHA ◄── Sublease ──► Tenant

In the old 23 program, there was a straight-line relationship between the owner, the local housing authority, and the tenant. This relationship allowed the local housing authority to lease all of the units in a building or project from the owner. The housing authority, in turn, would lease the units to 100 different tenants, but the owner dealt with only one entity. Under the lease arrangements, management of the units usually was given to the local authority, which also agreed to pay for all the units, occupied or vacant, whether or not the tenant paid his rent. As a result, the lease with the housing authority guaranteed the owner a fixed income stream that could be pledged to a lender. HUD stood behind the lease by entering into an Annual Contributions Contract with the local authority. The amount of the HUD subsidy provided under the contract generally was equal to the

difference between the market rent charged by the private landlord
and the reduced amount collected from tenants by the LHA.

This straight-line relationship was abandoned with the initiation of the "new" Section 23 program in April 1974. Under this
revised program, the relationship among the main actors assumed
the shape of a triangle:

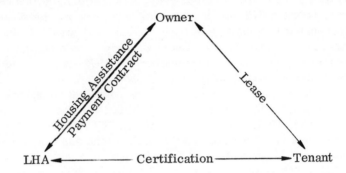

Under this arrangement, the owner was placed in direct contact with
the tenant through a standard landlord-tenant lease. Another contract
called the Housing Assistance Payment Contract, was negotiated between the owner and the local housing authority to cover the difference
between the HUD-established Fair Market Rent[5] and the lesser amount
collected directly from low-income tenants. The only relationship
between the local authority and the tenant was that the LHA had to
certify tenant eligibility by attesting to low-income status. This minimal relationship between LHA and the tenant lies at the base of the
Direct Cash Assistance Program, which some hope may one day become the government's basic form of housing subsidy for low-income
families.[6]

Essentially, under the revised Section 23, the owner entered
into two agreements. One was the Housing Assistance Payment Contract with the housing authority and the other was the lease with the
tenant. A landlord-tenant arrangement was established, with the
tenant paying a portion of the rent, usually about 25 percent of his
adjusted income. The difference between that and the Fair Market
Rent came from the Housing Assistance Payment Contract with the
local authority. Therefore, the owner had to look to two sources for
payment. If there was no tenant in the unit, the owner received nothing
for that particular unit. Thus, vacancies would affect the income
stream dramatically, making it much harder for an owner to go to a
banker and finance his project.

BASIC ELEMENTS OF THE REVISED SECTION 23

Although now primarily of historical interest, the basic requirements and guidelines of the revised Section 23 program which went into effect in April 1974, differ little from those that govern the Section 8 program that replaced it on January 1, 1975. A review of the main provisions of the short-lived "new" 23 program provides a benchmark against which the prospects of the current leased housing program can be measured.

Eligibility Requirements

The first eligibility rule represented an attempt to reinstate an element of the "existing units only" provision of the original Section 23 legislation passed in 1965. In the absence of a special HUD waiver, newly constructed units could be used only if no existing ones were available. Although the revised Section 23 was not around long enough to provide a serious test of this effort to emphasize conservation over the production of new units, the basic requirement has been carried over into the Section 8 program.

The second eligibility requirement of the revised 23 program—the so-called 20 percent priority—provoked a good deal of controversy. In fall 1973, when HUD made its initial announcement about the revised Section 23, the indication was that only 20 percent of the units in any project could receive assistance. There were to be no more Pruitt-Igoes, no more projects inhabited almost completely by the dependent poor. Although the infamous St. Louis project rates as an exception to what has generally been a successful program, HUD has, in recent years, viewed all public housing as one big Pruitt-Igoe, requiring the kind of stern medicine exemplified by the 20 percent rule.

This limitation was opposed strongly by developers. It was fine in theory, but in practice no owner who could see an unassisted market for 80 percent of his units would plod through HUD to lease the remaining 20 percent. HUD backed off from the requirement by stating that priority for leased housing funds would go to those projects seeking a 20 percent subsidy. Even this change seemed insufficient, and in the final regulations, exemptions from the priority were granted to elderly projects and to those with 25 units or less. Additionally, if there were no applicants for the units on a 20 percent basis within 60 days, then HUD would make funds available to housing authorities seeking support for projects with 100 percent assisted units. A major issue ceased to be a real problem.

Of greater importance was the restriction in Section 23 (a) (2) limiting leased housing to areas where local governing bodies passed a resolution approving the program. Once a resolution was enacted, the approval requirement was satisfied for all subsequent Section 23 projects, unless the terms of the resolution were more restrictive. For example, if the resolution limited the number of units or restricted them to certain neighborhoods, then a new resolution might be required for future projects.

Many liberal and civil rights groups complained with cause that these provisions would have the effect of keeping Section 23 housing out of many affluent municipalities, which would simply not pass an enabling resolution. In effect, this eligibility requirement made it very difficult to get any Section 23 units outside of those communities that were already experiencing substantial problems with poverty and blighted housing. Thus, Section 23 was weakened seriously as a vehicle for breaking down the residential segregation of the nonelderly poor.

With regard to the kinds of housing that qualified for assistance under the "new" 23 program, single-family detached, row houses, and multi-family structures were eligible. Congregate housing for the elderly or handicapped was also permitted, as well as single-room-occupancy units planned as a relocation resource for single persons. High-rise elevator projects for families were not permitted unless HUD determined there was no practical alternative, and mobile homes were not eligible under the new construction program.

Under the revised Section 23 for existing structures, units could be leased in dwellings that had been constructed with the aid of certain other federal subsidy programs. Units were eligible in Section 202, elderly, Section 221 (d) (3) or Section 236 multi-family projects provided that the total amount of Section 23 and rent supplement-assisted families in any such project did not exceed 40 percent, without special HUD approval. In those projects already subsidized, housing assistance payments covered only the difference between the rent paid by the family and the basic rent in a 236 project or the fully subsidized rent in the case of a 202 or 221 (d) (3) project.

Administration and Financing

The revised Section 23 legislation specified that the leased housing program was to be administered by a "public housing agency." Of course, this included the local housing authority, the traditional administrator of the program, but HUD regulations, pursuant to the broad statutory definition, stated further that the administering agency

might include any state, county, municipality, or other governmental
entity or public body that is authorized by state law to engage in the
development or administration of low-income housing or slum clearance. In the past, cities, economic development agencies, and even
public power districts have assumed the role of a "public housing
agency." Indeed, there was nothing in the law to prevent a general
purpose city government from running a leased housing program in
competition with the local housing authority.

Under the revised Section 23, HUD envisioned that new
entities would be involved significantly in the program in conjunction
with local housing authorities. These were the state housing finance
agencies that HUD expected to perform two important functions. They
would use their ability to raise money at a tax-exempt rate to make
below-market loans to project developers and they could also act as
housing authorities by handling such functions as processing leases
and certifying eligible tenants.

Large amounts of Section 23 funds were set aside by HUD for
state housing authorities, and application procedures were simplified
for them. The Illinois Housing Development Authority received 700
units of new construction, the largest allocation for any state. Missouri received permission for 200 units of existing housing. In general,
state agencies have grown in importance as the leased housing program
has evolved. There are 36 such agencies at present; at least six
states, including California, established them in 1975. In all probability there will soon be 50.

Beyond the state housing finance agencies, HUD also allowed
Section 23 financing under the 207, 221 (d) (4), and 231 multi-family
insurance programs, as well as under the 221 (d) (3) market-rate
program for nonprofit sponsors. At first glance, FHA insurance
seemed a distinct possibility for lenders and developers of Section 23
housing, but a problem was encountered on this point that was not
described in the program handbook. HUD instructed the field offices
that FHA insurance for Section 23 projects would only be made available if the units could be built or rehabilitated and rented at market
prices without considering Section 23. This meant that HUD wanted
FHA insurance to be available only in middle- and upper-income
neighborhoods where projects were already economically feasible
without subsidy. This was an incredible ruling, because no one would
build under Section 23 if there was a demand for rentals at levels
sufficient to amortize conventional-rate financing and yield a profit
to the owner. With this rule in effect, there was to be very little FHA
financing under Section 23.

Fair Market Rents

One of the new concepts of the revised Section 23 program
was Fair Market Rent. If the owner was leasing new or existing units,
he would be able to charge a "Fair Market Rent" established by HUD
for his particular area. HUD determined the Fair Market Rent by
making a survey of the rental market for particular geographic areas.
The figures were published and made readily available through the
area HUD offices. Two sets of rents were devised, one for new
housing, which included substantially rehabilitated units, and one for
existing housing.

By and large, the Fair Market Rents for new construction
seemed fair, although there were complaints. It was not universally
understood that the published rents were trended two years in advance
for use in 1976—"bicentennial rents" as one critic dubbed them—when
buildings in the planning stages would be ready for occupancy. Because
inflation has resulted in rapid rises in construction costs, the early
euphoria about the adequacy of the established rent levels soon faded.

Fair Market Rent was defined as the gross rent for a dwelling
unit, including utilities, stove and refrigerator, and all management
services, to be determined at least once a year by HUD. In theory,
Fair Market Rent was the figure necessary to obtain privately owned
and developed rental housing of a modest nature that met minimum
property standards. For purposes of determining gross rent, all
utilities, except telephone, were included whether or not paid directly
to the utility company by the tenant.

An owner was to obtain his rent payments in two ways. Part
was to be collected from the tenant, and the remainder from the local
housing authority through the Housing Assistance Payments. Two
monthly checks were to be received rather than one. The Brooke
Amendment to the national housing legislation, enacted by Congress
in 1969, limited the tenant's share of the rent to no more than 25 percent of his adjusted family income. For example, if the Fair Market
Rent for new construction was $300 per month and the tenant could
pay only $50, the subsidy would be $250 x 12 or $3,000 per year.

It was the landlord's duty and responsibility to collect this
rent from the tenant. If the tenant failed to pay the rent, the owner
could not look for help to the LHA or HUD. This was the key difference
from the straight-line arrangement in which the owner had a lease
with the LHA, which in turn subleased the units and bore any collection
losses.

Housing Assistance Payments constituted the difference
between the HUD-established Fair Market Rent and the tenant's share.
Local authorities entered into Housing Assistance Payment Contracts

with owners and the LHA's were financed in this arrangement by HUD's Annual Contributions Contracts. The term of the Housing Assistance Payment Contract for new construction was five years, with three renewals. An owner knew, then, in advance of construction that he had a 20-year Housing Assistance Payment Contract. Assuming a reasonably low rate of vacancies and rent arrears, it was hoped that this period of time would be long enough so that the developer could obtain at least a 25-year mortgage to build the project.

Except for the 20 percent priority, none of HUD's original proposals for the revised Section 23 provoked as much controversy as the rule prohibiting subsidy payment for unoccupied units. Under the old Section 23 program, the local housing authority usually leased 100 percent of the units and bore the risk of occupancy loss. As a result, the owner had an assured income stream that could be pledged to the lender. In addition, the owner generally would accept a reduced rent for his units because of this favorable provision. In an early policy statement, HUD allowed Housing Assistance Payments only when the unit was occupied by a tenant. This stringent rule was modified in the January 22, 1974 regulations to provide for payment when a tenant violated a lease during the lease term. In such event, if the owner was making reasonable efforts to find a tenant, payments would continue until the expiration of the lease. The final handbook continued this provision and also provided that payments would continue if the LHA delayed in certifying tenants supplied by the owner.

Although HUD expected leases generally to be for one year only, the handbook permitted leases up to a five-year term for newly constructed units or a three-year term for existing ones. Owners undoubtedly would try to obtain the longest lease possible to protect their Housing Assistance Payments. However, even if the owner received these payments when the tenant moved out, he still lost the tenant's portion of the rent. Thus, there was incentive to obtain a substitute tenant as quickly as possible. Obviously, the owner bore the risk of loss if he could not find any tenants.

One of the pluses of the revised 23 program was that it allowed for adjustments in the Fair Market Rent. Rigidity of rental schedules had been harmful under both the 236 multi-family program and the old Section 23. In the "new" 23, the Fair Market Rent could be adjusted annually according to an index of rents for the area in question. In addition, HUD might approve adjustments for substantial changes in property taxes and utilities when leases came up for renewal. There was one catch in these provisions for rent increases. They were allowable only to the extent that HUD had Annual Contributions Contracts available, and that was a difficult problem because HUD cannot commit future congresses. Reserve funds, hopefully adequate, were created to take care of rent increases in such cases.

Project Management

The changeover to the revised Section 23 in April 1974, brough
about an important modification in the management of leased housing
projects. All too often, management of low-income housing had been
treated as a low priority item, and HUD set out to alter this pattern
in the "new" 23 program. Potential owners under the revised program
had to demonstrate management capability to receive an allocation of
Section 23 units because the owner could no longer delegate management functions automatically to the local housing authority.

Under the "new" Section 23, HUD's approval was necessary
for the LHA to become project manager and HUD would only grant
approval if there was no other management agent in town. In other
words, the LHA became the "manager of last resort." Local housing
authorities were understandably upset over this provision. Unless
the owner contracted the managerial duties, the LHA's had relatively
few responsibilities. Authority personnel felt ignored by the program.
Basically, their job was to certify tenants sent to them by the owner,
determine income eligibility, inspect units to insure standard conditions, and make Housing Assistance Payments.

Assessment of the Revised Section 23 Program

The revised Section 23 program was barely underway when
it was replaced on January 1, 1975 by Section 8, which had been
enacted in the Housing and Community Development Act of August
1974. Nonetheless, analysis of the "new" 23 is useful because many
of its basic features were carried over into the Section 8 program.
In addition, discussion of the major issues and problems surrounding
the leased housing program is particularly relevant if viewed as a
step in the direction of cash allowances for housing. While there is
insufficient evidence to evaluate fully the effectiveness of the revised
23, there are questions of law, public policy, and economics worth
raising about the program.

Passage of the 1974 legislation eliminated questions concerning the legality of the revised Section 23 program. Although the "new"
23 outlawed the straight-line relationship in favor of the triangular
arrangement described earlier, there was doubt whether HUD had the
power to prescribe either way of operating the program. When Section 23 was passed by Congress in 1965, the straight-line relationship
was defined as the normal arrangement, but the triangular relationship was considered an alternative. Indeed, Congress intended to

allow sufficient flexibility for local authorities and owners to implement
the program in ways they found most suitable. That is not what HUD
did. Instead, it mandated one particular way of proceeding. If the
Section 8 legislation, which legitimized what HUD was doing, had not
passed, there probably would have been litigation challenging the
legality of the revised Section 23 program.

Passage of Section 8 did not resolve another major doubt
concerning the leased housing program. Could it work financially and
would lenders make money available to leased housing developers?
As emphasized earlier, the "new" 23 program provided no assured
income stream to the project owner upon which the lender could rely.
Basically, Housing Assistance Payments were made only when units
were occupied. Even with enough demand to guarantee reasonable
occupancy rates in the case of the elderly and some family projects,
this limitation on Housing Assistance Payments could prove too slender
a reed for financing.

The revised Section 23 also encountered some tough political
going. Civil rights groups were particularly upset over certain provisions in its regulations. They complained that the local housing
authority had traditionally served as an important intermediary between the private owner and the low-income family and that the low-
income tenant would be placed at a disadvantage in dealing directly
with private owners. This was a problem that was aggravated further
when minority families sought to move out of areas of racial concentration and were forced to negotiate with unsympathetic landlords.
Although the revised Section 23 regulations required the LHA to assist
families under such circumstances, this was hardly the same as the
LHA being the direct bargaining agent.

Another civil rights issue was whether the revised Section 23
would insure dispersal of low-income families, particularly blacks,
in metropolitan areas. The answer was a qualified "no." To participate in the Section 23 program required a simple resolution from the
local governing body, but suburban areas such as the city of Black
Jack in St. Louis County, Missouri, were not about to pass one. In
the mid-1960s, when Section 23 was a program for existing housing,
many jurisdictions approved resolutions with little thought that new
construction would eventually be emphasized. Section 23 units paid
full taxes, were originally dispersed and almost invisible. With the
shift of emphasis, however, it was doubtful that many suburban jurisdictions would pass the same resolutions.

These problems did not mean that the "new" Section 23 was
a failure; there were important pluses in the program that should not
be ignored. For the first time, the housing assistance subsidy was
figured on a realistic basis—the amount needed to rent decent, safe,
and sanitary units. Under the old Section 23, the HUD subsidy was

calculated on the basis of a complex "flexible formula" that bore little relationship to actual project needs. As a result, new construction under the old Section 23 was unworkable in many sections of the country. The HUD subsidy, based on Fair Market Rent, is far more realistic.

A second improvement was the escalation clause that permitted taking into account increased operating expenses. This was a problem plaguing owners under the old Section 23 program. Realistic increase provisions were included in the regulations of the revised 23 program, even though some doubt remained whether HUD would have enough funds available to pay for increased costs of utilities, taxes, and maintenance.

Third, a subsidy mechanism allowed the very poor to be served. Unlike Section 236, a tenant did not have to pay a basic rent that could be as high as 30 or 40 percent of his adjusted income. Under the revised Section 23, he paid no more than 25 percent of his income and the housing assistance payment was designed to cover the difference. If 25 percent of his income meant that he paid no rent, then that was what he paid. Theoretically, then, the "new" 23 program could reach to the very poor. In fact, however, it is unlikely that the landlord would go out of his way to take the dependent, problem family or the poorest of the poor when he could serve the working poor. That is why the LHA is needed as middleman and one of the reasons why civil rights groups voiced such strenuous objections to the program.

Congressional Action on Section 8

By the time the revised Section 23 program got under way in April 1974, Congress had already taken major steps toward the passage of a piece of legislation designed to replace it. In March, a 380-page bill was passed by the Senate that basically retained the existing policies in housing by continuing the 235 and 236 subsidy programs, conventional public housing, and a revised leased housing program that had been renumbered Section 8. The House took a different legislative approach, from the beginning working closely with the administration. Senior House Democrats, many of them old-line liberals, and Republicans joined with the administration to fashion a bill with which HUD could live.

At the time the bill came out of the House Banking and Currency Committee onto the floor, housing drew only minor attention in Washington. Congress was anxious to get housing legislation out of the way because it anticipated that impeachment proceedings against Richard Nixon would begin in mid-July. It was a race against time,

with impeachment on everybody's mind. This was readily apparent to
anyone who bothered to attend the deliberations of the House Banking
and Currency Committee, which conducted its sessions in a room
adjoining that used by the Judiciary Committee for its impeachment
hearings. In comparison with the overflowing chambers of the Judiciary
Committee, the housing deliberations attracted a scant handful of people.

Differences between the Senate and House versions of leased
housing needed resolution. The Senate bill placed greater emphasis
on local housing authorities running the program, choosing the developers, and managing the units while the administration-House bill
specified that HUD would select the developer and control the choice
of managing agent. It was ironic that the liberal Democrats in the
Senate, or at least some of them, wanted more local control than did
the administration, for all its talk about returning power to the grass-
roots with revenue-sharing and the New Federalism. This curious
reversal of positions also appeared in contrasting approaches to the
setting of Fair Market Rents, with the Senate bill allowing the LHAs
to establish rents and the House assigning this prerogative to HUD.

House and Senate versions also differed substantially on the
matter of income eligibility limits. In general terms, the Senate
version was far more liberal toward tenants than was the House bill.
If the Senate version had passed, the income limit would have been
four times the Fair Market Rent. Assuming fair market rental of
$300 per month, a tenant with income of $1,200 a month or $14,400 a
year could qualify. In New York, with a maximum Fair Market Rent
of $700 per month, the income limit would be over $33,000 per year.
The limit was much lower in the House bill—80 percent of the area's
median income, which was slightly above the 236 levels. Overall, the
Senate bill would have cost the leased housing tenant a good deal less
than the House version, 25 percent of adjusted income with deductions
for dependents, as opposed to a maximum of 25 percent of gross income
in the House bill.

Several parts of both bills differed from what the administration wanted. Originally, HUD said that no Housing Assistance Payments were to be made for unoccupied units. After some strong
lobbying by groups like the National Leased Housing Association, it
was decided to allow payments for up to 60 days for unoccupied units.
There were marked changes on HUD's initial request that assistance
be restricted to 20 percent of the units in any project. Full assistance,
100 percent of the units, was approved, but the House retained a
provision that priority would be given to those developers requesting
20 percent or less for their projects.

When legislation was finally enacted and signed into law on
August 22, 1974, it was clearly an administration and House victory.
Efforts by the Senate to revitalize the 235 and 236 interest subsidy

programs failed, despite support from many powerful groups who felt
that the act deemphasized production. Republicans in the House and
in the Nixon administration wanted to direct federal efforts toward
housing allowances. They felt that the past attempts to provide housing
were costly, inefficient, and conducive to fraud. Disillusioned senior
Democrats, many of whom had championed the housing cause for
years, shared that opinion. Section 8 was perceived as a transition
to allowances and was selected as the federal subsidy program for
housing low-income families, with funds authorized for 400,000 units
for the next fiscal years.

BASIC ELEMENTS OF THE SECTION 8 PROGRAM

Section 8 was completely phased in as a replacement for the
short-lived "new" Section 23 program by January 1, 1975, and key
Section 8 regulations were issued by that date. In its general outline,
Section 8 was very much like the program that had preceded it. Most
importantly, the basic triangular relationship among owners, tenants,
and local housing authorities was retained. Other similarities will be
apparent in comparing the major provisions of Section 8 under the
final regulations with the earlier discussion of the revised 23 program.

Fair Market Rents

The maximum rent allowed under the Section 8 program is
the Fair Market Rent established by HUD for particular geographic
areas. As with the revised Section 23, it is designed to cover all
utilities (except telephone), including ranges, refrigerators, parking,
and all management, maintenance, and other services required to
obtain privately owned and developed new rental housing of a modest,
nonluxury nature. The owner receives a basic "contract rent" for
leasing the unit to a tenant; contract rent plus any allowance for utilities and other services is the "gross rent." As a general rule, gross
rent cannot exceed the established Fair Market Rent. Exceptions are
allowed only with approval from the HUD area office, when gross rent
may exceed the Fair Market Rent by 10 percent if warranted because
of the location, quality, or amenities of the project in question, and
in unusual cases, when HUD's assistant secretary for housing production and mortgage credit may allow gross rents that exceed Fair
Market Rent by 20 percent.

Contract rents will be adjusted automatically every year with interim revisions as market conditions warrant. HUD will publish the adjustments annually in the Federal Register. In addition, there may be HUD-approved special annual adjustments to reflect increases in the actual and necessary expenses of owning and maintaining the units that have resulted from substantial general increases in real estate taxes, utility rates, or similar costs, [7] if the owner can clearly demonstrate that such general increases have caused increases in his operating cost not compensated for by the automatic annual adjustments. However, such adjustments cannot produce a contract rent materially different for assisted units from the rent charged in the area for unassisted units.

Rental Payments

The owner receives the contract rent through two separate payments—one from the tenant and one from the governmental body that administers the program. Tenants must pay between 15 and 25 percent of their annual income in rent. Very large and very poor families, or families with exceptional medical or other expenses will pay the 15 percent figure. All other families pay at the 25 percent rate.

The difference between the tenant rent and the contract rent is paid by the government through Housing Assistance Payments. These payments can escalate to meet the increase in Fair Market Rents discussed above. The regulations permit a project account to be established as a reserve to meet these future increases. As the maximum total Housing Assistance Payments that may be committed under a contract equal the total gross rents for the project, and because the tenant will be paying some portion of that gross rent, there should be sufficient funds available in the reserve to take care of the cost increases.

Two key points must be understood about the Housing Assistance Payments. First, these payments are available for 100 percent of the units in a project. The 20 percent assistance rule is a preference applicable only to family projects of more than 50 units. The statute is quite specific that HUD cannot delay applications for more than 60 days to await a 20 percent application. Second, Housing Assistance Payments generally can be made when there are vacancies, during the inceptive period for a particular project or during the term of the Housing Assistance Payment Contract. The regulations limit these vacancy payments to 80 percent of the "contract rent" although, in practice, a Housing Assistance Payment might exceed that figure when a tenant is in occupancy. To obtain such payments, the owner must be making efforts in good faith to rent the units.

The Housing Assistance Payment Contract is for an initial term of not more than five years, subject to renewal at the owner's option for up to 20 years. If the mortgage loan is from a state or local agency, the term can be extended up to 40 years at HUD's discretion. In no event can the term exceed 20 years for mobile homes.

Eligibility Requirements and Project Management

The types of housing eligible for assistance under the Section 8 program are nearly identical to those allowed under the revised Section 23. All Section 8 housing must meet HUD-FHA minimum property standards, and mobile homes must conform to specifications set down by the American National Standards Institute.[8] Without special approval, new construction is limited to areas where HUD determines that there is not an adequate supply of existing housing.

With respect to tenant eligibility, the Section 8 program is designed to serve families with "lower" and "very low" incomes. The "low"-income family is defined in both Section 8 and HUD regulations as a family whose income does not exceed 80 percent of the median income for the area, allowing adjustments for family size. However, HUD may change this 80 percent figure upward or downward in order to meet existing market conditions. Limits for the "very low"-income family are set at no more than 50 percent of the area median and they, too, may be adjusted by HUD to suit local circumstances.

Regulations concerning the eligibility of communities for leased housing funds under Section 8 are somewhat different from what they were under the revised 23 program. The change in question represents a compromise between critics of site location provisions under the Section 23 programs and supporters of the status quo, who argued for retention of the traditional exclusionary prerogatives exercised by local communities in matters relating to federally assisted housing development. Instead of the old requirement calling for a formal resolution of approval from the local governing body, Section 8 regulations made the location of leased housing units dependent upon conformance with a Housing Assistance Plan (HAP) for low- and moderate-income housing that every city must have in order to qualify for federal community development funds. HUD is implementing this plan for leased housing by requiring that every project proposal submitted to a field office be forwarded to the chief executive officer of the unit of general local government in which the proposed housing

would be located. This official has 30 days to evaluate the location
and other aspects of the proposal in terms of the HAP. If the local
unit disapproves the proposal as being inconsistent with the HAP,
HUD can override that decision only if it determines that the location
is in fact consistent with the plan. If the local government does not
have a HAP, either because it has not sought community development
funds or has not chosen voluntarily to submit a plan, it still has 30
days in which to comment on the project.

The role of the local housing authority in shaping the HAP
has yet to be determined. Undoubtedly, this question will turn on the
relationship between the LHA and City Hall, but the HAP mechanism
does appear to provide a potential opportunity for the LHA to exert
its influence in the site selection process.

With respect to project management, the Section 8 legislation
provides the chance for LHAs to become more involved than they were
under the revised 23 program under which they could function only as
a "manager of last resort." Subject to HUD approval, a private owner
may now contract with any private or public entity, including an LHA,
to provide management services for a prescribed fee. The only
restriction here is that the LHA cannot manage those privately owned
projects where it was involved in the application process. The LHA
management opportunity is limited to those project proposals that were
filed directly with the HUD area offices. This administrative restriction, imposed without apparent basis in the Section 8 legislation, suggests that HUD remains strongly committed to the move toward cash
allowances, in which LHAs would have minimum responsibilities to
landlords and tenants.

Can Leased Housing Work?

Final Section 8 regulations reflected many comments from
the field concerning HUD's original proposals. Numerous specific
problems remain, however, and they may harm the program's chances
for success. Most complaints concerning the program and its regulations have been forthcoming from project owners and developers.
There is a feeling that an administrative fee should have been included
for the owner, who has had to assume many management duties usually
assigned to a local housing authority. In the case of vacant units,
owners also have argued that they should receive 100 percent of the
contract rent rather than the 80 percent that is allowed at present.
Further, they believe that HUD should broaden its interpretation of
"similar costs" for rent adjustment purposes to allow for increases
in all management and maintenance expenses. Finally, developers

have expressed fears that the usual 20-year lease may not provide an income stream sufficient to permit conventional financing. Overall, no single one of these complaints is likely to destroy participation in the program. Collectively, however, they may have an undesirable effect that HUD and Congress should consider seriously.

The leased housing program also has defects from the point of view of tenants and local housing authorities. Tenant advocates argue that renters will be at a marked disadvantage in direct dealings with landlords now that the local housing authorities are playing a reduced role compared to the situation under the original Section 23. For their part, LHAs remain disenchanted with this reduced role. Even though the Section 8 legislation allowed for the possibility that they might play a project management role under the leased housing program, HUD has qualified this possibility by restricting LHA management opportunities to those cases in which private owners file their project proposals directly with the area HUD offices. In addition, LHAs have argued that the administrative power to increase gross rents by 10 percent over the Fair Market Rent should rest with the local or state agency that administers the program, not with the HUD field offices.

Despite these criticisms, there are indications that the leased housing program can achieve reasonable success in providing units for low-income families and individuals. The willingness of developers to participate in the Section 8 program is suggested by applications made under the revised Section 23, which preceded it and was very similar to the current program. By the end of December 1974, "new" Section 23 leased housing requests totaled 70,482 units, with 77 percent of these for the elderly. As of the same date, 7,493 units had been approved.[9]

The single most important question still plaguing the program is securing mortgage financing in view of the lack of an assured income stream. Several ways have been suggested to provide a security mechanism that might reassure potential lenders. In addition to the normal vacancy reserve, it may be possible to create an additional reserve out of the contract rent received by the owner. In cases where the owner has the benefit of tax-exempt financing from state or local agencies, there should be enough dollar leeway to create this additional reserve. The reserve would not have to be built up in perpetuity. One year's debt service would probably suffice. Of course, the availability of funds for this reserve would depend on HUD's allowing reasonable fair market and contract rents that it did not then lower merely because tax-exempt financing was used.

Also, there undoubtedly will be a great deal of syndication of the tax shelter produced by Section 8 projects, just as was the case in Section 236. In regard to Section 236 equity syndications, some state agencies require that part of the proceeds be used as a project reserve to cover increases in operating expenses. Because the Section 8 has an escalation clause to cover increased operating expenses, this project reserve might be used to secure financing of the project.

As another possible approach, some observers have suggested that private mortgage insurance be utilized. This could be done by having a project receive private mortgage insurance, or through bonds backed by a private mortgage insurance guarantee. At least one company is now in the business of guaranteeing tax-exempt bonds, and this may prove a useful device for Section 8.

Finally, some state legislatures are considering a state loan insurance fund in support of Section 8 financing. Maryland, for example, already has a Housing Fund that insures loans made by that state's housing finance agency, the Maryland Community Development Administration (CDA). For every dollar in the insurance fund, at least 10 times that amount in loans can be insured. Thus, Maryland has appropriated $20 million for the fund to underwrite $200 million worth of loans. As of now, the Maryland CDA has not made any Section 8 loans, but with the Housing Fund insurance, it should be able to do so. This fund could also underwrite loans made by private lenders or LHAs acting as lenders. If this knotty problem of financing can be solved in some way, then the Section 8 program may live up to the hopes of its sponsors.

Closing Comments

Since its appearance in 1965, the leased housing program has developed to the point where it is presently the government's principal subsidy vehicle for aiding low-income families. During the time it has been in existence, the program has undergone a series of changes in response to pressures generated in the marketplace and in the political arena. Especially noteworthy from the tenant's point of view are the efforts designed to encourage smaller projects and the mixing of assisted and unassisted units.

If any set of interests has been diminished as the leased housing program has unfolded over the last 10 years, it has been that of the local housing authorities. With the move in the direction of cash allowances under the revised Section 23 and its successor, Section 8, the LHA no longer serves as intermediary between the tenant and the owner. However, LHA's may assume a new role as lender to developers of low- and moderate-income housing. They may also serve as managers of leased housing projects, although with less frequency than in the past.

LHAs are not likely to disappear, even if cash allowances are adopted as a replacement for leased housing. LHA personnel are a skilled administrative resource familiar with the housing needs of low-income families. As the ongoing cash allowance experiments indicate a continuing need for administrative supervision, the LHA may well creep back into housing allowance schemes. We probably are not going to get a pure housing allowance—an income maintenance plan that puts money directly into low-income people's pockets and lets them fend for themselves in the marketplace. We are a long way from that, and supply-side subsidies for low-income families are likely to continue in one form or another. The odds are that local housing authorities will continue to perform a useful role, whether under leased housing arrangements, cash allowances, or some of the more conventional public housing programs.

NOTES

1. This 40-year limitation was not imposed on HUD by any requirement related to Section 23. Rather, 40 years is defined by statute as the maximum period of time during which HUD can make annual contributions to subsidize any particular project or dwelling.

2. Charles L. Edson, ed., A Section 23 Primer (Washington, D.C.: Section 23 Leased Housing Association, 1973), p. 1.

3. Charles L. Edison, ed., A Leased Housing Primer (Washington, D.C.: Leased Housing Association, August 1974), p. 5.

4. Ibid., p. 2.

5. The concept of Fair Market Rent is dealt with at length below.

6. Although the "new" Section 23 was similar to the cash allowance concept in the sense specified, there also were important differences. Most notably, the proposed cash allowance would go directly from the federal government into the tenant's pocket, and thence to the landlord, while the subsidy in the revised Section 23 leased housing program was funneled to the landlord through the local housing authority.

7. Although the Section 8 legislation does not define the term, HUD has construed "similar costs" in a narrow sense to include only those tax assessments and utilities not covered explicitly by the law. As discussed later, this narrow construction of the statute has been a source of some controversy in the Section 8 program.

8. Mobile home eligibility was expanded somewhat under Section 8. Under the revised Section 23, mobile homes did not qualify

for the new construction program, just for the existing unit option. With the Section 8 program, mobile homes may qualify in either case.

9. <u>Leased Housing Bulletin</u> (February 1975), p. 10.

11

HOUSING ALLOWANCES: ONGOING EXPERIMENTS AND POLICY OPTIONS

James P. Zais

Housing allowances have received considerable attention recently as a policy alternative for providing housing assistance to low-income families. The concept of housing allowances is not entirely new, but the seriousness of the idea of national legislation on the subject is novel. One important indication of this new emphasis was contined in former President Nixon's message on housing, dated September 19, 1973. By its own account, the White House saw this message as an important stage in the policy debate on housing. It identified ". . . direct cash assistance as the most promising approach to help [low-income] families."[1]

Since this presidential message, the debate has accelerated.[2] Indeed, it is the basic premise of this essay that public debate over housing allowances may have already reached a momentum that threatens any reasoned analysis of the policy alternative. The repetition of a legislative history similar to Nixon's Family Assistance Plan—a history that featured, at least by one account, a "curious alliance of left and right" joining to defeat the bill[3]—seems a real possibility if, and when, a housing allowance proposal is drafted.

The author is a Research Associate with the Housing Allowance Project staff of The Urban Institute. The research forming the basis for this paper was funded by the U.S. Department of Housing and Urban Development. Opinions expressed are those of the author and do not necessarily express the views of HUD, The Urban Institute, or the Housing Allowance Project staff.

It is most assuredly not argued here that the politics of housing
allowances, or the politics of the experiments currently being conducted
on housing allowances, is not important. Indeed, the politics of
housing policy may overwhelm the evaluation of housing policy itself,
assuming they can be reasonably separated, to the detriment of a real
public debate on the issues involved. This essay will attempt to compensate for the unfortunate tendency by exploring the major substantive
issues involved in the housing allowance approach and by presenting
some ideas about how the debate might proceed on a reasoned basis.
In doing so, the history of the housing allowance idea will be described
briefly, followed by an analysis of the current Experimental Housing
Allowance Program. Finally, the major substantive issues relating
to the possible enactment of housing allowances as a national policy
alternative will be considered.

History of Housing Allowances

Housing allowances were called "rent certificates" in the period
of the earliest debates on the concept during the 1930s and 1940s.[4]
These debates included those that took place prior to the passage of
the Housing Act of 1937, the hearings before the Taft Subcommittee
in 1944, and those that led to the landmark Housing Act of 1949. In
1953, the President's Advisory Committee on Government Housing
Policies and Programs took up the idea at some length and rejected it
in favor of continuing the public housing program. The committee
objected to the concept on various grounds, suggesting that rent certificates would "create a 'dole' for housing," would "cause a vast number
of families to go on relief," would not add to the housing supply, would
be too complex to administer, and would allow no reasonable way to
limit application of the plan.[5]

Two programs added by the Housing and Urban Development
Act of 1965 indicated a shift towards the housing allowance approach.
They were the rent supplement program and the Section 23 leasing
program. The importance of the rent supplement program is that it
established the concept of income-testing by allocating subsidy amounts
according to need. These subsidies went to residents of privately
owned buildings rather than to public housing, although they were
limited to newly constructed or substantially rehabilitated units. However, the basic point that distinguishes allowances from rent supplements is that the latter were tied to particular housing units.

The original Section 23 leased public housing program enacted
in 1965 moved a step closer to the housing allowance approach. The
Section 23 legislation empowered local housing authorities to lease

"modest but adequate," privately owned dwellings and then sublease them to low-income families, with the government paying the difference between what the family could afford and the full cost of leasing the unit.

This Section 23 legislation differed from a housing allowance in several key respects. First, the local housing authority, rather than the household, was to locate the unit. Second, a household was eligible only if it resided in a jurisdiction that had approved the Section 23 program. Additionally, households did not receive payments directly and could not take the subsidy with them automatically when they moved.

In December 1968, the President's Committee on Urban Housing, known as the Kaiser Committee after Edgar F. Kaiser, issued its final report. In it, the strongest support to date for the housing allowance concept was given in the form of a recommendation to initiate an experiment testing the approach. The Committee noted the arguments concerning the approach and said, "[d]espite its possible shortcomings, the potential merits of the housing allowance approach are such that it should be tried promptly."[6]

Between 1969 and 1972, several events followed the Kaiser Committee recommendations. The Department of Housing and Urban Development (HUD) supported research by the Urban Institute on housing allowances. This work dealt primarily with alternative program designs, the costs of a national program, and the likely response to market rents created by the increase in demand that a housing allowance program would create.[7] Also, two demonstrations of the housing allowance idea were begun in late 1970 under HUD's Model Cities program. Through their Model City agencies, Kansas City and Wilmington, Delaware funded relatively small-scale housing allowance demonstrations. These efforts need to be distinguished from full-fledged experiments, however, in that their design did not include systematic variation of program elements. All participating households received the same treatment, since the major purpose of the demonstrations was to assess the feasibility of implementing a housing allowance, not to measure the impact of shifts in program parameters. In 1970, the culmination of the Kaiser recommendations was enacted in the Housing and Urban Development Act. Congress provided for the initiation of a true experiment in housing allowances.

The Experimental Housing Allowance Program (EHAP)

Although EHAP received its official designation in March 1972, the mandate of the 1970 Act was implemented immediately by HUD.

The Urban Institute developed for HUD a program of experimentation focused on the key issues surrounding housing allowances. This was followed by a detailed conceptual design that would later be called the "Demand Experiment."

Clearly, the most important methodological decision of the period was to distinguish the types of questions that would be addressed in the various segments of EHAP. Eventually, EHAP came to include three separate experiments. The Administrative Agency Experiment (AAE) was designed to evaluate the effectiveness of the methods used by a number of agencies in carrying out an allowance program. The Demand Experiment was designed to test how different forms of a housing allowance would be used by household participants. The Supply Experiment was designed to analyze the housing market effects of a full-scale housing allowance program.

The following table gives a breakdown of the basic information for all three experiments. It indicates the sites selected for each experiment, the administering mechanism used, and the scale of the program in each experiment. The major within-experiment variation is then indicated, an element that corresponds to the basic purpose of each experiment. For the AAE, the major variation is the type of agency. Two each of four types of agencies administer the program at eight different sites. For the Demand Experiment, variation in the payment formula and payment levels constitutes the major feature of the design. This variation makes the Demand Experiment the most complex, since many different "treatment groups" are included in the design. The major variation in the Supply Experiment—again, corresponding to its purpose in the analysis of price and market effects—is according to market characteristics. Both sites will be market-saturated in the Supply Experiment, since participation is open to all households in the eligible low-income population who decide to enroll.

Rather than discuss the detailed analysis plans for EHAP—both those to be done within each experiment and the integrated analysis dealing with cross-experimental analyses and national projections[9]—it would be more useful at this point to take up some of the major substantive questions raised by EHAP. Of course, no one knows how much influence EHAP will have on how these questions ultimately will be answered; for that matter, it is difficult to predict what role the conduct and results of EHAP will play in the entire national debate surrounding housing allowances.

The most that can be said is that EHAP is part of a relatively new way of going about public policy analysis—the use of social experimentation. The state of the art of social experimentation is such that one cannot have total confidence that the results will serve as an infallible guide for future policy. However, this writer believes that the knowledge to be gained from EHAP will be invaluable when judged

TABLE 2

The Experimental Housing Allowance Program

Experiment	Number of Sites	Locations	Administering Mechanism	Number of Participating Households	Major Variations within Experiment
Administrative Agency Experiment	8	Salem, Ore. Tulsa, Okla. Jacksonville, Fla. San Bernardino, Calif. Springfield, Mass. Peoria, Ill. Bismarck, N.D. Durham, N.C.	Eight agencies, 2 each of 4 types; local housing authorities, state agencies, welfare agencies, county metropolitan governments	500–900 per site	Agency types
Demand Experiment	2	Pittsburgh, Pa. Phoenix, Ariz.	Research contractor	ca. 1,000 at each site	Payment formula and levels
Supply Experiment	2	Green Bay, Wisc. South Bend, Ind.	Housing Allowance Office established initially by research contractor	ca. 6,000 at each site	Market characteristics

Source: The Urban Institute.

in the light of current knowledge about housing allowances. Indeed, a great deal has been learned in simply getting the large-scale experimental effort under way. Whether this information will be received wisely and critically by those engaged in the housing policy debate is an open question at this point.

Major Issues and Policy Questions

Housing allowances raise two important kinds of questions. First, should a national housing allowance program be enacted? Second, if so, how should the program be designed? It should be clear that these questions overlap to a considerable degree. At issue in EHAP is whether a housing allowance program can be designed to meet its stated objectives without unacceptable costs. In the broader, political context, of course, the ultimate fate of housing allowances will depend on much more than the answers to the technical questions being explored in EHAP. Whether housing allowances will be enacted or fail may be determined less on the merits of the program than on the relative strength of its political supporters and opponents.

Price and Market Effects. Clearly one of the primary concerns is the effect a housing allowance program will have on the market, because subsidies that encourage the demand side of any market are likely to have price repercussions. Some observers point to the federal government's experience in the area of medical services in the last few years as an example of the adverse price effects accompanying such subsidies. Housing, like medical services, is not immune to these effects.

This concern over prices can be stated simply: in a market saturated with housing allowances, will the supply of housing adequately match the increased demand in order not to unduly inflate prices? Some critics of housing allowances say that it will not, and see the subsidy as an indirect aid to landlords and owners. Because the housing market traditionally has been "sluggish" in the speed with which supply follows demand, few would argue that the short-term response to housing allowances, in the absence of price controls, will not be inflationary. Where observers disagree, and where it is virtually impossible to venture more than an educated guess, is in estimating the long-term price effects of a national housing allowance policy.

Investigation of this price effect furnishes the strongest rationale for a social experiment with housing allowances. Direct evidence will serve as the best indicator of the price response by the market. The design of EHAP's Supply Experiment comes closest to replicating a full-scale, open enrollment program. The short-term and long-term impact on prices will be measured carefully and exhaustively in this experiment. [10]

Price effects are likely to vary considerably by market area. The vacancy rates within a housing market will probably be closely correlated with the price response. A market with a high vacancy rate is likely to have a lesser price impact than one with a lower vacancy rate, all other things being equal. Since housing allowance recipients will be required to live in "standard" housing, the quality of housing in a market area is also expected to be related to the price response. A market with a larger proportion of standard dwelling units probably will experience a lesser price effect than one with more substandard housing. The validity of these expectations is now under investigation in the two Supply Experiment cities of Green Bay and South Bend.

If price effects cannot be predicted with certainty at this time, the same must be said of the general question concerning increased supply. Will the housing allowance program stimulate construction? Will it encourage rehabilitation? If so, how fast will these activities follow the payment of subsidies to recipients? At present, we lack conclusive evidence on all of these points.

Although many object to the effect housing allowances allegedly will have on prices and the market, there are policy alternatives that may be used to alleviate or reduce these effects, if only the will to use them can be found. Several options come readily to mind. Since the supply side of the housing market responds slowly to changes in demand, one part of the solution may be to phase in housing allowances gradually to reduce their inflationary effects. This could be accomplished by steadily increasing the eligible population over a number of years. The elderly often are considered a likely choice for the first phase of such a plan. Poor families with children might also be early eligibles. Such a plan might be designed to steadily approach universal entitlement, where low household income alone would serve as the criterion for eligibility.

Another part of the solution may be to vary housing allowances by market area in terms of eligibility. Such a plan would be based on some notion of "impacted" areas, where the severity of the market response, or lack of it, can be controlled to some extent by the size of the eligible population for a given year after initiation of the program. Although such a plan clearly would be filled with political and other practical pitfalls, it is possible to design implementation plans to meet many of the inadequacies in terms of market-related responses.

A further possibility relates to a creative integration of housing allowances with supply-side programs. A mixture of such programs—for example, construction subsidies—may go a long way in reducing adverse price effects in market areas with low vacancy rates. Other programs that encourage the increase of housing supply will need to be analyzed for their interface with a housing allowance approach. Where the goals of these programs and those of a housing allowance interrelate, the design of a new national policy ought to include the proper restructuring of such programs.

The fear about adverse price effects stems largely from a conceptualization of housing allowances as the single avenue of national policy. It is fruitless to argue the issue as "Housing Allowance versus Construction Subsidies." Instead, it is necessary to analyze what beneficial impact a housing allowance might have and then determine how it might best fit into our national housing policies. Needless to say, agreement on this point is far from universal.

Costs of a National Program. Price increases will be only one of the costs of a national housing allowance program. They represent direct costs to consumers and indirect costs for the government. If the housing allowance is paid for by general treasury funds, there will be direct costs to government and the taxpayer in both the transfer payments themselves and in the costs of administering the program.

While EHAP has allocated a sizable portion of research time for estimating these costs under alternative program specifications, several, less detailed estimates using simplified assumptions have already been made.[11] The most comprehensive of these efforts estimated the transfer costs of national program to be $5-7 billion a year in 1969, depending on the coverage of the plan. Under this estimate, there would be anywhere from 13 to 17 million units receiving assistance at an average cost per household of between $400 and $450.[12] No detailed effort has been made to estimate administrative costs, although considerable information should be gained in the Administrative Agency Experiment (AAE). Any economies of scale will likely be measurable in the Supply Experiment where open enrollment takes place.

The actual cost of any allowance program will vary depending on a number of administrative options. Most notably, cost will be affected by the level of support services beyond the basic allowances that are made available to recipients. These kinds of costs will be observed in the AAE. Transfer costs, on the other hand, will generally be sensitive to two factors, namely, the scope of coverage provided by the program, and the payment formula and payment levels adopted.

It is probably true that decisions on coverage will be the most critical in determining the ultimate level of transfer payments to be made. It will, in fact, be one of the aims of the integrated analysis of EHAP to determine how sensitive cost estimates are to these factors. Should a national program be restricted to the elderly in the beginning, its initial costs will be considerably lower than under a program of universal entitlement including all low-income people. Indeed, the household unit definition determining eligibility could be set in a very narrow fashion—say, families with children—or in a broad manner, perhaps paralleling the household definition of the food stamp program. Costs of the program could be increased over a number of years using a phase-in plan like those discussed previously. In any case, coverage, whether it be universal or limited, will be a major political decision likely to have a crucial impact on the legislative history of housing allowances.

As for the payment formula, the way in which subsidies to households are calculated will affect the total amount of transfer payments for a national program. The most likely candidate equation for calculating a household's subsidy is the "housing gap formula":

$$P = C^* - bY, \text{ where } \begin{aligned} P &= \text{Payment to household,} \\ &\quad \text{adjusted for household size} \\ C^* &= \text{Cost of standard housing} \\ b &= \text{Some percentage, for} \\ &\quad \text{example, 25 percent} \\ Y &= \text{Household's income} \end{aligned}$$

In other words, the payment level will depend on the difference between what it would cost the household for modest, standard housing, and a certain percentage of its income. Clearly, decisions relating to how "C^*" is measured, the level at which "b" is set, and the income definition for program purposes will have an important impact on total transfer costs. It is not difficult to predict that if a national housing allowance proposal finally reaches the Congress, the debate will center about the total cost of the program and what values should be assigned to the various parameters. The ultimate impact of the payments themselves, however, will depend on whether an adequate level of subsidy can be agreed upon.

Who Will Benefit? It often happens, in housing and elsewhere that those who are supposed to be the recipients of assistance from a particular policy are not those who benefit most in fact. The objection that housing allowances will not aid low-income recipients as much a landlords and owners is an obvious example. Some people fear that any cash allowance program is likely to be subverted in its goals.

Nearly everyone agrees that the housing allowance should address primarily the needs of low-income households, and it is believed that the way to do this is to establish an income eligibility test for the allowance. At the same time, it is recognized that scaling subsidy levels to household income is likely to result in more pressure on those just above the eligibility line who will be competing with housing allowance recipients for the available housing stock. This

probable effect will require some rethinking of the ways in which
housing allowances relate to other housing policies that cover these
groups.

Many factors can subvert the goal of housing allowances. The
goal is that they should benefit the poor. Adverse price effects have
been discussed already. The program could also be defeated by the
actions of landlords, market intermediaries, administrators, and the
allowance recipients themselves. The challenge for program design
will be to minimize any adverse actions, and the experiences and
analyses of various segments of EHAP are likely to contribute significantly to solving these design problems.

One important factor relevant to the question of whether low-
income households will actually benefit from a national program is,
obviously, whether these households will participate at all. The level
of expected participation is by no means clear and this uncertainty,
reminiscent of the difficulties encountered in anticipating participation
in the food stamp and aid to families with dependent children programs,
presents considerable hazards in forecasting the impact of a national
program. Little is known about participation rates in advance of the
experimental evidence. Much will depend on how those who are
eligible view the program, on their willingness to find standard
housing, and on their expectations concerning such things as the
availability of housing and the likelihood of discrimination. Just the
investigation of these issues will make the EHAP effort worthwhile.

Ultimately, the true test of housing allowances requires an
assessment of the vertical and horizontal equity inherent in the
approach. The more closely aligned subsidy levels are with actual
needs, the more vertically equitable the program will be. The degree
to which households with similar needs are treated alike in the program, the more equitable the program in horizontal terms. With
analysis and some luck, many inequities may be reduced through
program design decisions.

Improving Housing Quality. In passing the National Housing
Act of 1949, the Eighty-first Congress called for "the realization as
soon as feasible of the goal of a decent home and a suitable living
environment for every American family." It is no secret that this
goal has largely escaped low-income Americans. How much can
housing allowances contribute?

A housing allowance is distinguished from direct cash assistance programs by the requirement that a recipient-household use its
allowance to meet its housing expenses. Thus, housing allowances
are said to be "earmarked." Two methods of earmarking are being
analyzed in EHAP: minimum standards and minimum rent. The
relative effectiveness of the two is unknown and requires investigation.

Should a national program operate with minimum standards earmarking, a participating household would be required to live in a unit meeting minimum housing standards. This requirement might be fulfilled in a number of ways—through certification by the allowance recipient or the landlord, through inspection by an authorized agency, or through reliance on findings of an effective housing code enforcement program in the community. Should minimum rent be enacted as an earmarking policy, it would be based on the assumption that there is a close correspondence between rent and housing quality. Under the classical or "pure" minimum rent formula, recipients would be expected to pay a high proportion of the Fair Market Rent established for a particular unit. More realistically, however, the low-income family probably would be asked to contribute no more than 25 percent of its adjusted income for rent, and the housing allowance would then have to cover a large portion of the fair market value in the case of many poor families. Overall, it can be safely asserted that the minimum standards option is considered by most observers to be preferable to a minimum rent option.

The exact specifications for earmarking are a matter of considerable importance. Administrative costs of a program will be affected greatly by choices in this area. What's more, as Herbert Gans points out, ". . . too much concern with the physical standardness of eligible units will reduce the freedom of choice of poor people who would prefer a not-so-standard dwelling in a safe neighborhood to a standard unit in an unsafe area."[13] Strict enforcement should be weighed against the needs of recipients in any given community.

Changing Residential Patterns. The politics of housing, like the politics of education, has long had heavy racial overtones. Many who analyze housing policies for their likely impact on residential patterns by race argue that housing allowances are likely to suffer the same fate.

One of the distinguishing features of the housing allowance approach, the "freedom of choice" afforded the recipient in choosing a place to live, raises the possibility of increased racial integration of neighborhoods. What may be true in theory, however, may not turn out in fact. The Kansas City demonstration project offers some evidence that a housing allowance may not alter residential patterns significantly. Although black families in that city moved typically to census tracts where the percentage of blacks was less than the tract of origin, the tracts to which they moved tended to be those where the percentage of blacks increased most rapidly from 1960 to 1970. White families tended to move to white areas.[14]

While this evidence is far from conclusive, it does suggest that the likelihood of housing allowances altering existing residential

patterns is not as great as some might expect. The results from the
12 EHAP sites dispersed geographically should further illuminate
this issue.

Conclusion

These, then, are the major policy questions concerning housing
allowances. The answers found for them will determine, in part, the
fate of the housing allowance approach. It is naive, however, to believe
that what is found in EHAP alone will determine the outcome of the
debate. The strength of various interest groups, the threat perceived
by various groups in this new approach to governmental policy in
housing, the ideological repugnance or attraction direct assistance has
for various individuals, and the uncertain politics of the present
period will all have an influence on the outcome. In closing, several
suggestions can be made that, if followed, would facilitate intelligent
discussion of the numerous issues involved.

1) Housing allowances should not be considered as the sole
national housing policy. It would be expecting too much of housing
allowances to consider them an end-all in housing policy. Supply-side
problems cannot be ignored and are not likely to go away once housing
allowances give recipients greater buying power. The best possible
combination of housing programs, however, is a problem of considerable proportions and needs thorough investigation. It should not be
ignored in a hasty endorsement of allowances as the sole approach to
housing.

2) Housing allowances must be set at adequate levels in order
to work. Since allowances are a basic departure from traditional HUD
programs, they are likely to be judged critically in terms of their
short-run results. In order for allowances to have a chance to work,
they must provide more than a token increase in recipients' income.
What that level should be will be an important piece of information
stemming from EHAP.

3) Housing allowances should be consistent with an overall
strategy of welfare reform. Whether a general income maintenance
program is enacted, or whether we continue to operate with a con-
gomerate of programs affecting various segments of the low-income
population, a housing allowance proposal should be consistent, in
general, with the goals of welfare reform—goals of equity, efficiency,
and responsiveness. Any debate on housing allowances should include
consideration of how this program generally would fit into income
transfer programs.

4) Housing allowances as a policy alternative should be debated first for their impact on low-income housing and only second-arily for their effect on the political fortunes of their sponsors. The present political environment makes policy debate exceedingly diffi-cult. With a Democratic Congress and a Republican president, the prevailing atmosphere in Washington is not conducive to reasoned discussion and joint efforts toward compromise. Perhaps a basic restructuring of U.S. housing policies will have to be deferred until more pressing political problems are resolved. Whatever the case, it is hoped that consideration of housing allowances will be made on something other than narrow political grounds.

NOTES

1. White House Press Release, September 19, 1973.

2. See, for example, Herbert J. Gans, "A Poor Man's Home Is His Poorhouse," New York Times Magazine, March 31, 1974; and Malcolm E. Peabody, Jr., "Housing Allowances: A New Way to House the Poor," New Republic, 170 (March 9, 1974), pp. 20-23.

3. Daniel P. Moynihan, The Politics of Guaranteed Income (New York: Random House, 1973), p. 16.

4. Several short histories of the housing allowance concept have been relied on here, especially U.S. Department of Housing and Urban Development, Office of Policy Development and Research, First Annual Report of the Experimental Housing Allowance Program (Washington, D.C., May 1973), pp. 4-8; and Robert Beckman, "The Experimental Housing Allowance Program: An Old Idea with a New Kind of Test in 1973," Journal of Housing 30, no. 1 (January 1973), pp. 12-17.

5. President's Advisory Committee on Government Housing Policies and Programs, Recommendations on Government Housing Policies and Programs (Washington, D.C.: Government Printing Office, December 1953), p. 263.

6. A Decent Home: The Report of the President's Committee on Urban Housing (Washington, D.C.: Government Printing Office, 1969), p. 72.

7. Papers reporting work done during this period include the following by Frank de Leeuw: Time Lags in the Rental Housing Market paper 112-19 (Washington, D.C.: Urban Institute, June 1970); "The Demand for Housing: A Review of Cross-Section Evidence," The Review of Economics and Statistics 53, no. 1 (February 1971), pp. 1-10; and "The Housing Allowance Approach," Papers submitted to Subcommittee on Housing Panels, Committee on Banking and Currenc

House of Representatives (June 1971), part 2, pp. 541-553. Other relevant papers are by Frank de Leeuw and Nkanta F. Ekanem, "The Supply of Rental Housing," American Economic Review 61, no. 5 (December 1971), pp. 806-817; Frank de Leeuw, Sam H. Leaman, and Helen Blank, The Design of a Housing Allowance, paper 112-25 (Washington, D.C.: Urban Institute, October 1970); John D. Heinberg, The Transfer Cost of a Housing Allowance: Conceptual Issues and Benefit Patterns, paper 112-18 (Washington, D.C.: Urban Institute, May 1971); and Sam H. Leaman, Estimated Administrative Cost of a National Housing Allowance, paper 112-17 (Washington, D.C.: Urban Institute, May 1970).

8. See Arthur P. Solomon and Chester G. Fenton, "The Nation's First Experience with Housing Allowances: The Kansas City Demonstration," Urban and Social Change Review 8, no. 1 (Winter 1975), pp. 3-8.

9. The Integrated Analysis is being conduted by the Urban Institute. Analysis of Demand and AAE results is being conducted by Abt Associates, Inc., and the Supply Experiment is being analyzed by the RAND Corp.

10. In addition to the Supply Experiment, EHAP will attempt to predict price effects by modeling with the use of computer simulation techniques.

11. Principal published sources are: Heinberg, op. cit.; two papers by Barbara M. Woodfill and Tiina Repnau, "Estimates of Eligibility and Allowance Entitlement under Alternative Housing Allowance Programs," WN-7974-HUD (Santa Monica, Calif.: RAND Corp., September 1972) and "Additional Estimates of Enrollment and Allowance Payments under a National Housing Allowance Program," WN-8167-HUD (Santa Monica, Calif.: RAND Corporation, March 1973); and Henry J. Aaron, Shelter and Subsidies: Who Benefits from Federal Housing Policy? (Washington, D.C.: Brookings Institution, 1972).

12. See Heinberg, op. cit.
13. Gans, op. cit., pp. 50-51.
14. See Solomon and Fenton, op. cit., pp. 28-31.

"Chinatown," a 1974 motion picture, described how a former
Los Angeles policeman, after working many years in that community
became embittered and disturbed because he had been unable to understand the rules of the game operating there. Behavioral nuances and
subtleties, along with the symbolic use of rhetoric, had escaped him.
Things were never what they seemed to be.

Housing politics is a Chinatown of sorts where bureaucratic
decisions and policy outcomes often are unrelated to legislative goals.
The rationale behind the formulation of housing programs is murky,
because the participants in the process typically attempt to mask their
self-interest. As a result, stated purposes and "real" objectives are
often at variance, and the ability to implement stated goals is serious
limited by the disjointed character of the political and administrative
processes that shape developing programs. Even if these difficulties
did not exist, it is still questionable whether government policy could
produce the desired impact on housing markets, where trends emerge
from the private choices made by thousands of individual producers,
middlemen, and consumers. It is little wonder, then, that observers
and participants in the urban housing game often become frustrated
and bewildered.

This confusion is apparent in the current debate over housing
policy, even among federal legislators who have long been advocates
of subsidies for low- and moderate-income housing. Former Congres
man William Widnall, who devised the original Section 23 Leased
Housing program, summed up much of the disenchantment with existi
approaches to housing in hearings held in October 1973, before the
Housing Subcommittee of the House Banking and Currency Committee

Well, we have had some very bad experiences. I am just
very disheartened as I go around through the country,
and I do not have to move out of Washington to see it, to
see some reasonably new units in low-income housing
that are just going to rack and ruin right now. There is
one over by the Naval Gun Factory that was a very fine
building, and now it looks like it has been in the middle
of the Mideast war. Everything is out, the windows are
broken, and it is very disheartening for those of us that
have tried to help, and tried to provide units of housing
for lower-income families.[1]

Support for the idea of cash allowances as the primary federal
thrust in housing has grown out of this disillusionment. On the surface,
allowances seem uncomplicated. Decisionmaking is taken away from
the bureaucrats and given back to the people who are direct recipients
of the money. It is enticing to conservatives who favor a minimum role
for government as well as for those liberals who believe in government intervention, but have become dismayed because inner-city
neighborhoods have not been improved by supply-side programs.

Although a strong desire for simplicity in housing programs
may be evident, single-faceted or one-dimensional solutions rarely
emerge from the housing policy game. Too many interests are present
in our political system and they compete for benefits. Negotiation and
compromise are essential parts of the process; seldom does one group
get everything it wants, although some habitually get far more than
others. The result is a complexity of programs and policies that go
in different directions because they are trying to please many groups
with conflicting interests. Whenever housing legislation is considered,
pressure groups representing builders, realtors, financial interests,
mayors, citizen organizations, academic researchers, and bureaucrats present their views to Congress and lobby for a share of the
benefits. By examining the current controversy over cash allowances
in the next few pages, it should be apparent that attempts to satisfy a
large number of diverse interests promote confusion and conflict
rather than clarity of purpose in housing policy.

Cash Allowances—Partisans Pro and Con

According to James T. Lynn, secretary of the Department of
Housing and Urban Development from 1972 to 1975, "[t]he principal
root cause of families living in substandard housing is, plainly and
simply, lack of income to afford decent shelter."[2] Based on this

reasoning, market forces will respond to improved incomes. Neighborhoods will be stabilized by providing incentives for owners, through increased rentals, to upgrade their properties. In addition, production subsidies will not be needed because effective demand for new construction will be generated in the marketplace.

Two university researchers and civil rights activists, Chester Hartman and Dennis Keating, disagree with this view and maintain that there are essential flaws in the housing market that make Lynn's belief in allowances a delusion. Those flaws are "[an] inadequate total number of housing units at prices or rents the poor can afford and located where they want to live; the substandard conditions prevalent in the low-income housing sector, urban and rural; widespread discrimination against many classes of housing consumers; rising and uncontrolled rents; and the pattern of legal relationships between landlords and tenants."[3] Allowances may simply enhance the profits of landlords and not help the tenants at all.[4] Hartman and Keating argue, in effect, that freedom of choice for low- and moderate-income people requires more, not less, government intervention in housing because a free market is nonexistent.[5]

Civil rights supporters do not believe that discrimination will be reduced through allowances. Anthony R. Henry, executive director of the National Tenants Organization, stated that even if blacks were able to afford higher quality housing, they would not be welcome in most neighborhoods. Low-income people would stay in their traditional home, the slums.[6] In advocating continued new construction as opposed to allowances, the director of housing programs for the National Association for the Advancement of Colored People contended that ". . . the 'trickle-down' process relegates the poor to not only projects, but to entire neighborhoods beset with blight and undesirable environments."[7] Henry Aaron of the Brookings Institution goes one step further. He believes that Richard Nixon declared the moratorium in January 1973, because some of the subsidized housing was finding its way into the suburbs and economic groups were being dispersed.[8] In this view, there is a suspicion that the debate over allowances is a substitute for the gut issues of race, income, and social class segregation in housing.

The Nixon and Ford administrations have maintained that the housing production programs of the past have been costly, inefficient, and ineffective. They have served only a small proportion of those whose income would permit eligibility and have had an adverse effect on people and neighborhoods. Republicans have been shocked by the scandals that accompanied these programs despite the irony of the fact that they were responsible for their administration. Liberal Democrats, too, are upset over the large profits for middlemen and the accompanying abandonment in areas where subsidies were employe

Their memories are as short as those of the Republicans, for many liberals pushed very hard for enactment of the legislation in question.

In a classic political situation where no one is responsible for the unfortunate outcomes, allowances are a convenient way to get the government out of housing, which is what it wants to do anyway. In his essay, Charles Edson said that conventional public housing has been tainted by the "Pruitt-Igoe syndrome." There also is support for allowances from those who believe that new construction over-houses the poor—that new housing costing upwards of $25,000 per unit is better housing than the poor would purchase or lease on the open market if they had the money.

Although there is validity to the contention of many Republicans and some Democrats that housing quality is less important to low- and moderate-income families than safe neighborhoods and quality schools, many doubt that allowances will accomplish either goal. A recent article by Arthur P. Solomon and Chester G. Fenton concluded that there is little likelihood of changing residential patterns.

> There is no reason to expect that the degree of racial discrimination and prejudice will be lessened or that households' locational preferences will be altered because a widespread direct housing allowance program has been implemented, unless a major effort is made to enforce open housing legislation or devise other types of market intervention. [9]

Sociologist Herbert Gans also believes that the impact of allowances will be limited. It may allow a few poor families to improve their housing, but it will not appreciably relieve poverty. Further, the ultimate result, especially in a tight market, will be increased housing costs without materially improved living conditions. [10]

Arguments over allowances versus new production are only partially ideological. As evidenced by the positions of various trade groups, material benefits are also at stake. Favoring allowances, the National Apartment Association and the National Association of Realtors want to divert subsidies from new construction. [11] By decreasing the number of units produced, demand will be increased for older units and there will be higher rents and greater property turnover. Cash allowances will provide more income for tenants and prospective owners to compete in the market. [12]

On the other hand, the National Association of Home Builders (NAHB) pushes for continued production, and its stake in doing so is obvious. Builders are joined, among others, by the AFL-CIO and the National Association of Housing and Redevelopment Officials, an organization of public housing, urban renewal, and community development specialists whose jobs are dependent on federal funding for construction programs. For these groups, housing allowances would mean increased unemployment.

Traditionally, the NAHB has been extremely successful in its efforts. According to one HUD official and supporter of cash allowances, "[t]he home builders' most significant accomplishment was the establishment of national housing goals, including numerical targets for each year and a requirement that the president make annual reports on federal performance in meeting the goals."[13] Inclusion of these requirements in the Housing and Urban Development Act of 1968 tied the housing system to a construction emphasis, making it difficult for Congress to alter that position or cut funding levels.[14]

Production advocates related their lobbying to the goal of 2.6 million additional units, mostly new, that were to be created between 1968 and 1978. In any year that the rate fell below 2.6 million, there were cries that annual production should be raised to compensate for the deficiency so that the 1978 figure could be reached.[15]

Home builder groups have clung tenaciously to the established targets and fought those who oppose them.[16] Construction beneficiaries want government subsidies to achieve the 2.6 million annual rate although, at times, it is difficult to justify philosophically. In 1973 congressional testimony, the president of the NAHB found himself in a dilemma. "I am a private enterprise builder. I represent a private enterprise sector and I know its value to our society, but left completely to itself, private enterprise cannot solve our nation's housing problem. We need a national policy in housing, one that keeps government control to a minimum."[17] Help us, but don't restrict our freedom.

Cool Heads?

Out of this heated debate comes a cry for reason by Arthur P. Solomon in a recent book: "[w]hile political considerations will always influence, if not dominate . . . [housing programs], a more systematic evaluation of policy alternatives can clarify the options and reduce our singular reliance upon ideological assertions, political horse-trading and undocumented rhetoric."[18] In this view, the academics, the researchers, and the planners are presumed to possess a special quality that distinguishes them from political actors. They have "cool heads" that enable them to remain above the hand-to-hand combat of the political arena and to function as reasonably impartial observers.

The style of the expert requires that he couch his findings and recommendations in language that is appropriately scientific. At best, the views presented will manifest a balance and caution lacking in those put forward by overtly partisan interests. Their public postures usually will appear more conciliatory. In the debate over cash allowances, for example, Richard P. Nathan of the Brookings Institution calls for an income approach to housing in addition to ". . . production stimulation devices such as Section 23 housing grants in those markets where housing is in short supply and vacancy rates are low."[19] Nathan's colleague, Henry Aaron, also took a moderate position when he testified before Congress ". . . that a mixed strategy, which uses both supply and demand subsidies, has very great advantages over either, because each element tends to relieve inadequacies or weaknesses in the other."[20] In his essay, James Zais of the Urban Institute also affirmed the middle ground when he said that it is fruitless to argue the issue as being housing allowances versus construction subsidies.

Occasionally, the outward appearances of scientific neutrality are stripped away and the experts appear for what they really are—political actors with a stake in the action just like everybody else.[21] It is especially difficult to accept their claims to impartiality and special status in the housing game when expert consultants produce diametrically opposite findings and recommendations on particular projects or legislative proposals. With increasing frequency, the mystique of the expert is being challenged. A case in point was acted out recently before a home builders' meeting in St. Louis. Urban economist Anthony Downs of the Real Estate Research Corporation described himself as an objective housing analyst. Following Downs' presentation, Leon Weiner, former president of the NAHB and, like Downs, an advocate of new construction, remarked that he was not objective about his viewpoints and that he did not think his good friend, Anthony Downs, was, either.

Academics, researchers, and planners supposedly deal in facts, but in the politics of housing, facts are what you can persuade people to accept. At best, these groups devise reasoned and reflective methods to substantiate their perceptions of how the world should be ordered. At worst, they hide their advocacy by emphasizing analytic techniques.

In general terms, the experts perform three important functions in the urban housing game. They play a central role in defining the terms of the debate, they help devise ways to distribute benefits to the players, and they monitor and evaluate the results. At each step in the process, the experts are performing a critical political function; that is, their actions effect directly who gets what, when, and how in the competition for scarce housing resources.

Examples of these three roles are readily apparent in the politics of housing allowances. By describing urban housing ills

primarily as a problem of inadequate consumer demand rather than
one of short supply, the experts who espouse cash allowances have
defined the situation in a way that threatens those players who benefit
from the continuation of the supply-side programs, including experts
like Downs. A new distribution of public resources for housing is
implicit in the demand-related definition given to the housing program
by cash allowance advocates. Through the careful use of data and
quantitative techniques, experts on both sides justify their recommendations by showing that their particular approach will lead to a desired
result, while their opponents' strategies will not. These are the
rationalists who tone down the passions of those who are more zealous
by analyzing problems with page after page of supporting data and
charts.

Though measured and logical in their treatment of the problem,
the experts are nonetheless self-interested players in the housing
game. Placing the politics of housing in the context of scientific discussion has its own rewards. The experts receive employment, prestige, and lucrative grants and contracts to analyze existing conditions,
propose solutions, and monitor the results. In recent years, univer-
sities and research corporations have received federal funds to study
housing abandonment and neighborhood decay. In the case of cash
allowances, the Urban Institute, the RAND Corporation, and Abt
Associates, Inc., have contracted to participate in the Experimental
Housing Allowance Program. Without intending to diminish the intellectual or moral stature of those who play this role, it should be clear
that the experts receive rewards and have definite stakes in the recommendations that they espouse. In conclusion, then, the experts in the
urban housing game are political in two senses of the word. They gain
payoffs for themselves and they influence the distribution of benefits
received by the other players.

Games Without End

Because there are so many players with stakes in the outcomes,
the urban housing game lacks neatness. For those who crave clarity
and finality, the game is both disturbing and frustrating. The housing
policy arena encompasses a tugging and pulling process that never
stops. Diverse groups negotiate continually for benefits, with the end
result being a tentative compromise instead of a clear-cut or conclusive victory. Winners and losers emerge along the way, but as
Charles Edson's discussion of leased housing shows, the losers may
regroup and return to fight once again.

From the viewpoints of those supporting the new directions in federal housing policy, the tentative, negotiated character of the game cannot help but be frustrating. In all probability, cash allowances will do not better than come to occupy a limited place alongside established supply-side programs emphasizing new construction. The recent discontinuation of the Section 235 and 236 programs thus represents only a partial victory for allowance proponents; other supply-side programs, such as turnkey public housing, remain. Still others, such as the Section 202 program for elderly housing, were discontinued and then resurrected. In short, the housing legislation currently on the books contains enough variety to provide some satisfaction for many diverse interests. At the same time, nobody is ever quite happy with the status quo, and so the game goes on.

For those low- and moderate-income families who seem forever cast in the loser's role, there is a strong desire for change. They do not want to inherit dwellings unfit for human occupancy or neighborhoods that are a few years away from abandonment, and they presumably would welcome a fundamental shift in the operations of the housing delivery system. Because competing in the marketplace has been a disaster for them, some might welcome establishment of a centralized formal authority with ample power to respond to their needs. In this view, the difficulty has not been so much the lack of legislative will to assist the poor, the blacks, and the elderly, although this remains a problem. Rather, the main issue lies in making the law truly authoritative, in getting the disjointed, fragmented system to respond to changes in formal law.[22] For example, if increasing reliance were placed on cash allowances to spur the demand of the low-income consumer, it is questionable whether the regulations and incentives provided would be sufficient to evoke the desired response from the market.

Alternatives to the present system are not very feasible and this cannot help but intensify the sense of frustration experienced by those who have not done well at the urban housing game. Ironically, those who have the greatest need for housing improvement have few political resources with which they can bargain effectively for an increased share of the available payoffs. As reported earlier, most Americans are adequately housed, at least in physical terms, so the ill-housed minority and their allies have been unable to muster sufficient clout to alter the basic character of the housing game.

While it is unrealistic to expect that the system will be changed dramatically, it also is questionable whether the proposed cures would be much better than the maladies they are intended to treat. To alter the current situation by installing a centralized public decision-making agency to allocate housing resources in urban areas would likely result in a bureaucratic monster with reduced sensitivity to local needs and variations. Even if such an agency were to prove extraordinarily responsive, most Americans probably would find that they missed the individualized treatment and maneuverability presently available to those with resources. If the fate of recent proposals for metropolitan area government is any indication, many disadvantaged clients of the housing system, especially blacks, also would oppose any effort to revamp the status quo on the grounds that it is a ploy designed to dilute their growing political strength in some of the older central cities. For most people the tradeoffs required by alternative arrangements in housing delivery might well exceed the benefits.

From the vantage point of those who are poorly housed, these reflections will seem abstract and perhaps even meaningless. However, solutions for their housing problems probably will have to worked out largely within the system as it now exists. A national cash allowance program, even if enacted tomorrow, would not revolutionize the urban housing game. In the future, as in the past, change will probably continue to take place at the margins.

NOTES

1. U. S. Congress, House Committee on Banking and Currency, Subcommittee on Housing, 93d Cong., 1st Session, Hearings, Housing and Community Development Legislation, part 1 (Washington, D.C.: Government Printing Office, 1973), p. 471.

2. Ibid., p. 303.

3. Chester Hartman and Dennis Keating, "The Housing Allowance Delusion," Social Policy 4, no. 5 (January-February 1974), p. 33.

4. Ibid., p. 37.

5. Ibid.

6. Linda E. Demkovich, "Housing Report/Administration Weighing Plans for Low Income Allowances," National Journal Reports 7, no. 7 (February 15, 1975), p. 248.

7. U.S. Congress, House, op. cit., p. 518.

8. Ibid., p. 794.

9. Arthur P. Solomon and Chester G. Fenton, "The Nation's First Experience with Housing Allowances: The Kansas City Demonstration," Urban and Social Change Review, 8, no. 1 (Winter 1975), p.

10. Herbert J. Gans, "A Poor Man's Home Is His Poorhouse," New York Times Magazine, March 31, 1974, pp. 49, 58.

11. See U.S. Congress, Senate, Committee on Banking, Housing and Urban Affairs, 93d Cong., 1st Session, Hearings, Administration's 1973 Housing Proposals (Washington, D.C.: Government

Printing Office, 1973), p. 373; and Subcommittee on Housing, Hearings, part 2, p. 1001.

12. In this sense, see "Housing Allowances: Cash Payments to Poor Weighed," Congressional Quarterly Weekly Report 32, no. 18 (May 4, 1974), p. 1111.

13. See William Lilley 3d, "The Homebuilders' Lobby," in Jon Pynoos, Robert Schafer, and Chester W. Hartman, eds., Housing Urban America (Chicago: Aldine Publishing Company, 1974), p. 37.

14. Ibid.

15. For an example, see Anthony Downs, Summary Report, Federal Housing Subsidies: Their Nature and Effectiveness and What We Should Do About Them, a study prepared by the Real Estate Research Corporation for the National Association of Home Builders, the National Association of Mutual Savings Banks, and the United States Savings and Loan League, NAHB Library No. 70-19, reprint (Washington, D. C.: National Association of Home Builders, October 1972), p. 15.

16. See U.S. Congress, Senate, op. cit., p. 243.

17. Ibid., p. 251.

18. Arthur P. Solomon, Housing the Urban Poor: A Critical Evaluation of Federal Housing Policy (Cambridge, Mass.: MIT Press, 1974), p. xiii.

19. U.S. Congress, House, op. cit., part 2, p. 1322.

20. Ibid., part 1, p. 786.

21. This viewpoint is argued specifically with regard to the urban planning profession in Dennis R. Judd and Robert E. Mendelson, The Politics of Urban Planning: The East St. Louis Experience (Urbana: University of Illinois Press, 1973).

22. The outline of this argument has been presented forcefully in general terms in the work of Theodore J. Lowi. See, especially, his The End of Liberalism: Ideology, Policy and the Crisis of Public Authority (New York: W. W. Norton & Co., 1969); and its sequel, The Politics of Disorder (New York: Basic Books, 1971).

[housing allowances] recommen-
dations on, 239-40
Housing Assistance Plan (HAP):
in 1974 housing legislation,
203-04, 222-23
Housing and Community Development Act of 1974: omnibus
housing legislation, 29, 184,
201, 203, 206
Housing and Home Finance
Agency: HUD predecessor, 123
Housing and Urban Development
Act of 1965: rent supplements
and Section 23 leasing, 229
Housing and Urban Development
Act of 1970: housing allowance experiments authorized,
230
How the Other Half Lives: muckraking expose, 62; see also
Riis.
HUD: see Department of Housing
and Urban Development
Huxtable, Ada Louise: extolls
city virtues, 69; for sense of
community, xiii

Institute of Applied Gerontology -
St. Louis University: studied
elderly in hotels, 180-81

Jacobs, Jane: extolls city virtues,
69; for sense of community,
xiii
Jefferson, Thomas: antiurban
sentiment, 69
Jersey City, New Jersey: water-
front vista, 161
Johnson, Lyndon: budget surplus,
124; rent supplement program,
207; wants housing production,
105-06
Joint Economic Committee of
U.S. Congress: reports housing
costs, xiii

Jones v. Mayer: decision on
segregated housing, 155

Kaiser Committee: recommended
housing allowances, 230
Kansas City: early cash allowance
demonstration, 204, 230,
238
Keating, Dennis: against housing
allowances, 244
Kleemeier, Robert W.: favors
age-integrated housing, 176
Klein, Woody: East Harlem
tenement study, 61-62, 63
Kosciusko area: St. Louis
renewal project, 106
Kuhn, Maggie: Gray Panther
leader, 187

labor unions: make construction
difficult, 117-18, 166
LaSalle Park: St. Louis renewal
project, 106, 110-11
Lasswell, Harold: defines
politics, 3
Las Vegas: land trading, 103-04
lead-paint poisoning: controversial
housing issue, 60, 67
Leased Housing Association:
reports on subsidized units,
204
Leven, Charles: studied St. Louis
blight, 14
Lewis, Oscar: culture of poverty,
68
Liebert, Charles: conflict of
interest, 111; see also Reno
and St. Louis
Long, Norton: defines civic
leadership, 71; ecology of
games, xvii-xix
Los Angeles: postwar growth, 16;
racial disturbances, xvii
Lynn, James T.: for cash allowances, 244

ROBERT E. MENDELSON is a researcher and associate professor of urban planning at Southern Illinois University at Edwardsville. During the late 1960s he was engaged in varied planning and urban renewal activities in East St. Louis, Illinois, serving as chief planner for the Model Cities Program. From 1953 to 1964, he was self-employed in housing investment and rehabilitation. He is coauthor of The Politics of Urban Planning: The East St. Louis Experience (1973).

MICHAEL A. QUINN is a research associate and assistant professor of government and public affairs at Southern Illinois University at Edwardsville. Since receiving his doctorate in political science from the University of Illinois in 1972, he has been involved in housing research. He is currently project director for a study on housing profitability in St. Louis between 1959 and 1974. His previous writings include a coauthored book, Sinners and Heretics: The Politics of Military Intervention in Latin America (1973).

BRIAN D. BOYER is a journalist who, while working as night city editor of the Detroit Free Press, uncovered major problems in federally assisted housing programs. Following this investigation, he wrote Cities Destroyed for Cash: The FHA Scandal at HUD, which was published in 1973. His book makes the point that abandonment of central cities has been caused by those who profited most from the 1968 Housing Act—bankers, realtors, and public servants.

CHARLES L. EDSON is a graduate of the Harvard Law School, a Washington attorney with Lane and Edson, P. C. , and a national authority on housing. He is author of A Practical Guide to Low and Moderate Income Housing and editor of the biweekly Housing and Development Reporter. An advocate of public housing, and leased housing in particular, he also has published a Leased Housing Primer, which is used as a working document for developers and housing authorities.

IRA F. EHRLICH is associate professor of social work and director of the Institute of Applied Gerontology, St. Louis University. He had more than 20 years of experience in social work activities prior to receiving his D. S. W. from Washington University in 1970. His numerous publications include "Toward a Social Profile of the Aged Black Population in the United States: An Exploratory Study" (Aging and Human Development, Fall 1973); "Life-Styles Among Persons 70 Years and Older in Age-Segregated Housing" (The Gerontologist, Spring 1972); "A Service Delivery Model for the Aged at the Communal Level," coauthored with Phyllis D. Ehrlich (The Gerontologist, Summer 1974); and "The Aged Black in America—The Forgotten Person" (Journal of Negro Education, Winter 1975).

CHARLES B. LIEBERT is a developer of luxury homes in St. Louis County with the firm of Manlin and Liebert, Inc. Between 1948 and 1960, he brokered and purchased real estate for rehabilitation and investment. In 1960, and for seven years thereafter, he speculated in land in Nevada and in Missouri. He then went to work for the St. Louis Redevelopment Authority where he was director of urban renewal between 1968 and 1970.

JAMES E. MURRAY is senior vice president and general counsel for the Federal National Mortgage Association, assuming that position in July 1972. For ten years prior he was a member and partner of Hogan and Hartson, a Washington, D.C. law firm. His publications include "The Developing National Mortgage Market" (Real Property Probate and Trust Journal, Fall 1972); "Fannie Mae Goes Shopping for Conventional Mortgages" (Real Estate Review, Fall 1971); and "The Secondary Mortgage Market: Its Challenges and Opportunities" (Title News, April 1973).

S. JEROME PRATTER is a principal of Team Four, Inc., a St. Louis-based consulting firm. He is an attorney who received a master's degree in urban law from Washington University in 1968 under a HUD fellowship. The firm has been engaged in major urban redevelopment and transit efforts not only in the St. Louis area, but throughout the nation. Mr. Pratter has published articles on housing in the Urban Lawyer and the Journal of Housing and is a citizen member of the Federal Savings and Loan Advisory Council.

PHILLIP THIGPEN is vice president and director of urban housing for Leon N. Weiner and Associates, Inc., a large development firm with headquarters in Wilmington, Delaware. He holds a master's degree in urban affairs and a doctorate in business administration, in addition to extensive experience in housing and renewal. In 1966 and for several years thereafter he was manager of the Pruitt-Igoe public housing project in St. Louis. Subsequently, he was an executive of the combined housing and urban renewal agencies in that city.

JAMES P. ZAIS is a research associate with the Housing Allowance Project staff of the Urban Institute in Washington, D.C. He received a doctorate in political science from the University of Illinois and has taught at the State University of New York at Buffalo. Currently, he is involved in work on the Integrated Analysis of the Experimental Housing Allowance Program, funded by the Department of Housing and Urban Development.

HOUSING COSTS AND HOUSING NEEDS
Alexander Greendale
Stanley F. Knock, Jr.

HOUSING MARKET PERFORMANCE IN THE
UNITED STATES
Charles J. Stokes
Ernest M. Fisher

HOUSING MARKETS AND CONGRESSIONAL GOALS
Ernest M. Fisher

MANDATORY HOUSING FINANCE PROGRAMS: A
Comparative International Analysis
Morris L. Sweet
S. George Walters

PUBLIC HOUSING AND URBAN RENEWAL: An
Analysis of Federal-Local Relations
Richard D. Bingham